A-level Study Guide

Psychology

Revised and updated

Mike Cardwell

Alison Wadeley

Marian Murphy

Revision Express

Series Consultants: Geoff Black and Stuart Wall
Project Manager: Julia Morris

Pearson Education Limited
Edinburgh Gate
Harlow
Essex CM20 2JE, England
and Associated Companies throughout the world

© Pearson Education Limited 2000, 2004

First published 2000
Reprinted 2001
Updated 2004
10 9 8 7 6 5 4 3 2 1
09 08 07 06 05

British Library Cataloguing-in-Publication Data
A catalogue record for this title is available from the British Library.

ISBN 1-405-82122-1

Set by 35 in Univers, Cheltenham
Printed in the UK by Ashford Colour Press

Cognitive and developmental psychology

This section focuses on memory and attachment. Explanations and research into memory can be broadly divided into short-term and long-term memory processes. Both are explored here, together with explanations of forgetting from both short-term and long-term memory. A critical issue in the application of memory is eyewitness testimony, with Elizabeth Loftus's work being the best known.

For developmental psychology, attachment between primary caregiver and child is seen as one of the most significant events in the development of a young child. When this is broken, children may be affected emotionally. The merits of day care are still disputed, but it has been shown to have beneficial effects on the social and cognitive development of children.

Exam themes

→ Models of memory

→ Explanations of forgetting

→ Eyewitness testimony

→ Attachment

→ Deprivation and privation

→ The effects of day care

Topic checklist

O AS ● A2	AQA/A	AQA/B	OCR	EDEXCEL
Models of memory 1	O	O	O	O
Models of memory 2	O	O	O	O
Forgetting	O	O	O	O
Emotional factors in forgetting	O	O	O	O
Eyewitness testimony 1	O	O	O	O
Eyewitness testimony 2	O	O	O	O
The development of attachments	O	●	O	●
Explanations of attachment	O	●	O	●
Deprivation and privation 1	O	●	O	●
Deprivation and privation 2	O	●	O	●
Day care 1	O		O	●
Day care 2	O		O	●

Models of memory 1

Watch out!

Memory is an umbrella term for a number of cognitive processes.

Take note

Brain scanning studies have shown that the majority of brain locations activated during encoding are in the left hemisphere, while retrieval locations are generally activated in the right hemisphere.

Checkpoint 1

Why is this model sometimes called the two-process model of memory?

Example

Sensory traces for touch, taste, smell and sound can also be held in the SIS.

The jargon

Consonant trigrams are strings of three consonants. They should be equally unfamiliar to all participants, thus controlling for the interfering effect of familiarity or prior knowledge.

Memory is a system which is vital to our survival. For psychologists, memory covers processes called:

→ **encoding**, whereby incoming information is changed into a form that the system can cope with
→ **storage** for a particular length of time, in a particular form, in a store with a certain capacity
→ **retrieval**, i.e. getting information out of a memory store.

Atkinson and Shiffrin's multistore model of memory

Atkinson and Shiffrin (1968) suggest that memory is made up of a series of stores as shown in the diagram below. The stores differ in their encoding, storage and retrieval characteristics.

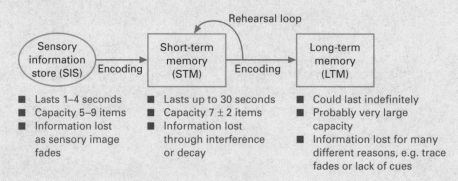

The sensory information store (SIS)

Sperling (1960) believed that information in the SIS is held as a sensation, e.g. a visual stimulus is held as a visual image. To demonstrate this he showed participants three rows of four mixed numbers and consonants for a very brief time, then played them a tone (high, medium or low) to prompt them to recall the top, middle or bottom line. Participants could do this easily if they recalled immediately but the image faded rapidly, lasting for no more than one-quarter of a second. In this way, Sperling was also able to show that SIS holds 5–9 items.

The short-term memory (STM)

Information selected for further processing passes from the SIS into the STM. It is thought that STM holds information in the form of images, sounds or meanings. Information in STM is kept 'alive' by rehearsing (repeating) it.

Two key pieces of evidence about life span and capacity of STM:

→ Peterson and Peterson (1959) gave participants a **consonant trigram** to remember (e.g. KDL) and then a large number. To prevent rehearsal, they counted backwards in threes from the number and then recalled the trigram. Participants were unable to recall the trigram at all after 18–30 seconds indicating that this is the life span of items in STM.

→ Miller (1956) asked participants to listen to strings of numbers or consonants of varying length and recall them in order. The average recall was 7 ± 2 items (Miller's **magical number seven**). Our STM is, therefore, capable of holding between 5 and 9 items or chunks.

The long-term memory (LTM)

Information which is rehearsed enough will transfer into LTM. Such information is encoded in many forms, e.g. LTM contains knowledge, facts, beliefs, pictures, skills, language, and musical knowledge. LTM seems to have unlimited capacity and an indefinite life span.

Further evidence for the multistore model

→ Murdock (1962) asked participants to learn a list of words and free-recall them. Words presented either early in the list or at the end were more often recalled than the ones in the middle. Murdock suggested that words early in the list were put into LTM (**primacy effect**) and words from the end went into STM (**recency effect**). Words in the middle of the list had been there too long to be held in STM but not long enough to be put into LTM.

→ Milner (1967) quoted physiological evidence from studies of brain-damaged, amnesic or alcoholic people who have a good LTM but very poor STM. Some stroke victims and elderly people also have STM problems. People suffering from alcohol-related **Korsakoff's syndrome** may have problems with LTM but not with STM, although the pattern is not always clear.

Evaluation of Atkinson and Shiffrin's model of memory

The model suggests rehearsal helps to transfer information into LTM but some studies show it is not essential. We may, for example, remember certain things because they are funny or interesting or relevant to us in some way (Eysenck and Keane 1990).

Atkinson and Shiffrin thought everything was held in the same LTM but others have argued we have more than one kind of LTM:

→ Paivio (1971) argued that some of our LTM consists of **mental images** from all our senses.

→ Tulving (1972) distinguished **episodic memory** for personal events and **semantic memory** for knowledge about the world.

→ Cohen and Squire (1980) suggest we have **declarative memory** for storing things that we know and **procedural memory** for storing knowledge about how to do things.

Checkpoint 2

How might you apply the chunking principle to help yourself to remember a 12-digit telephone number?

Checkpoint 3

Milner (1966) made a case study of HM whose STM no longer seemed to link with his LTM as a result of damage suffered during brain surgery. What are some of the likely outcomes of this for HM?

Example

We would use *declarative memory* to answer questions in a quiz or to tell a friend about things that have happened to us. *Procedural memory* might include how to ride a bike, do a jigsaw puzzle or hit a tennis ball.

Exam questions   answers: page 28

1 Outline two differences between short-term and long-term memory. (6 min)

2 Outline the multistore model of memory. (6 min)

Models of memory 2

Checkpoint 1

Which of these two theories elaborates on, and which challenges the essence of, the two-process theory?

Take note

Hebb (1949) proposed that until physiological evidence for cognitive processes (such as memory) was available, hypothetical models could be used. Such models could be empirically tested and have provided a valuable method of gaining information in cognitive research.

Action point

Make sure you can define the emboldened terms in this section.

Watch out!

Theories are built on our most accurate knowledge to date and are constantly changed in the light of new developments.

Atkinson and Shiffrin's two-process model is one of the most well-known, information-processing explanations of memory. Some of the models that have followed have extended and elaborated on it, while others have offered alternatives.

Baddeley and Hitch's working memory model

Baddeley and Hitch (1974) elaborated on the idea of STM. They proposed that it was not just for brief storage of information. They thought it also actively processed the information and decided what to do with it – hence the term 'working memory'. The working memory consists of three parts as shown in the diagram below.

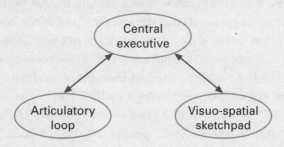

→ The **central executive** decides how to share out the limited resources of STM. It decides what is and is not to be attended to. It is also 'modality free' which means that it deals with both auditory and visual stimuli. The central executive has a limited capacity and deals with tasks that are cognitively demanding.

→ An **articulatory loop** deals with verbal information and is essentially a rehearsal system. It is likely that the capacity of this system is limited to that which can be read aloud in approximately two seconds (Baddeley et al 1975).

→ A **visuo-spatial sketchpad** that can hold and rehearse visual and spatial information. Baddeley and Lieberman (1980) suggested that the visuo-spatial sketchpad relies more on spatial coding than visual coding.

Evaluation of the working memory model

The important difference between the two-process model and the working memory model appears to be in the role of verbal rehearsal. In line with research findings that have cast doubt over the importance of verbal rehearsal, its role in memory is reduced to the articulatory loop only.

The working memory model can explain how, in brain-damaged patients, selective deficits may occur in short-term memory. An updated version of the model has been proposed by Baddeley (1986). This sees the articulatory loop as comprising a passive phonological store (concerned with speech perception) and an articulatory control process (concerned with speech production). The revised model was better able to explain some of the neurophysiological evidence that did not fit the original model.

Craik and Lockhart's levels of processing theory

Craik and Lockhart (1972) disagreed with Atkinson and Shiffrin's idea that memory consisted of separate stores. Instead, they suggested that memory depends on how we process information when it comes in.

→ *Shallow processing* takes two forms. Structural (or iconic) processing is when we encode only the physical qualities (appearance) of something. Phonemic (or acoustic) processing is when we encode its sound. Shallow processing only involves maintenance rehearsal and leads to fairly short-term retention of information.

→ *Deep processing* involves semantic processing which happens when we encode the meaning of a word and relate it to similar words with similar meaning. Such elaborative rehearsal leads to longer-term retention.

Evaluation of the levels of processing approach

The levels model seems to describe what is happening rather than explaining why deeper processing leads to longer lasting memories (Eysenck and Keane 1990), e.g. deep processing may lead to enduring memories simply because it takes more time and effort than shallow processing. It is also difficult to test the model by controlling what kind of processing people use. Various modifications have been suggested:

→ *Elaboration* – Craik and Tulving (1975) found that it was not just depth of processing that affected retention but also the degree of elaboration a person carried out, e.g. elaborating 'table' by thinking of tables of different sizes, made of different materials, for different uses makes it more likely that we will remember 'table'.

→ *Distinctiveness* – Eysenck (1979) suggested that if a memory trace is made distinct from other similar ones, it will not get confused with them. We remember some events, such as personal successes or disasters, because they stand out as being unusual or distinctive.

→ *Context* – Tulving (1979) suggested that the setting (context) in which something is learned is encoded along with the material to be remembered. If we learn something in a particular context we are more likely to recall it in that context than in a different one regardless of how deeply we processed it.

→ *Personal relevance* – Rogers et al (1977) found that participants who processed words in terms of whether they applied to them in some way (e.g. Do you own one of these? PARROT) remembered them even more than semantically processed words.

Checkpoint 2

How would you process the word 'dog' on each of these three levels?

Example

Try to apply this deep processing when you revise, e.g. if you 'go blank' in the examination hall, imagine yourself back in the setting where you first learned about or revised the material you need to recall.

Links

See flashbulb memories in Emotional factors in forgetting (pages 10–11).

Exam questions answers: page 28

1 Outline the levels of processing model of memory.

2 Give two criticisms of this model. (12 min)

Forgetting

For memory to work well, we need to encode, store and retrieve information effectively. Memory failure (forgetting) may result from not doing any one of these properly.

Forgetting from SIS and STM

SIS forgetting

SIS has a life span of only about one-quarter of second and a capacity of 5–9 items (Sperling 1960). Inability to recall items is due to the sensation in the sensory system rapidly fading away.

STM forgetting

Two theories about how information in STM is forgotten:

→ **Trace decay theory** says we lose items because they fade away. As Peterson and Peterson (1959) showed, STM traces have a maximum life span of 18–30 seconds if unrehearsed.

→ **Displacement (interference) theory** says items are lost because when we exceed STM's capacity, something has to go to make room. This is in line with Miller's (1956) magical number seven.

Forgetting from LTM

There are many reasons why LTM information is forgotten. Possibilities include **trace-dependent forgetting** where the memory trace is physically lost from the system and **cue dependent forgetting** where the material we need cannot be retrieved because we have no cue or 'key' to unlock the store. Some of the explanations of forgetting are as follows:

→ **Interference** means that an existing memory is distorted by something already learned (**proactive interference**) or by input of new material (**retroactive interference**). Interference is greatest when two different responses to the same stimulus have been learned. It is this fact that is one of the main criticisms of interference theory. Having to learn two different responses to the same stimulus seems rather rare and, therefore, would only account for forgetting in those kinds of circumstances in real life.

→ **Retrieval failures** may be more likely when there is a mismatch between the retrieval cue and the initial encoding of the stimulus. Tulving and Thomson (1973) formalized this with the **encoding specificity principle** – the value of a retrieval cue depends on how well it corresponds to the memory code. Another explanation for retrieval failure is when the fit between the processing during encoding and retrieval is dissimilar. **Transfer-appropriate processing** occurs when the initial type of processing is similar to the type of processing required by the subsequent measure of retention (Morris et al 1977). Thus, semantic processing during encoding is no use if the subsequent retrieval task requires acoustic processing.

Links

See Models of memory 1 (page 4).

Watch out!

Make sure you are able to expand on these researchers' work in order to explain where these ideas about SIS and STM forgetting originate.

Checkpoint 1

How might these two types of interference operate in learning two foreign languages?

Take note

Childhood amnesia occurs because a structure of the brain called the hippocampus, which is important in consolidating memories, does not fully develop until the age of two to three years.

Prevention of forgetting

Recommendations for preventing forgetting can be derived from all the theories of memory proposed by psychologists.

Recommendations from the multistore model

→ **Rehearsal** (repetition) keeps sensations alive in the SIS making transfer to STM more likely. Rehearsal in STM makes transfer to LTM more likely.

→ **Chunking**   If STM holds 7 ± 2 items we should not overload it. Chunking reduces the number of items to be stored so they are less likely to be lost.

→ **Cues**   We need cues to 'hook' information out of LTM so we should build them into our attempts to memorize things.

Recommendations from the levels of processing model

→ Deep processing is important. When revising for an exam it is not enough to scan a piece of text. This is only structural processing. It would be better to read it aloud (phonemic processing) but better still to put it in your own words or teach it to a friend (semantic processing).

→ Find ways to make material to be remembered more elaborate or distinctive.

→ Try to learn and recall in a similar setting (context). You cannot take your study into the exam room but you can take reminders to trigger memory such as the same pens and pencils, desk layout and sweets you had when revising.

→ Try to make material personally relevant whenever you can.

Recommendations from other sources

→ Many studies have shown the power of *imagery* as an aid to recall (e.g. Paivio 1971). We should use this whenever we can to mentally picture things to be remembered.

→ Much of what we learn for exams involves *declarative* memory but, if we have to learn a skill, we should learn by *doing*, not by watching, i.e. use *procedural* memory.

→ Memories appear to be spontaneously organized (Bower et al 1969, Collins and Quillian 1972). We can capitalize on this by *organizing* material before learning it so that retrieving one thing leads to retrieval of another.

Links

See Models of memory 1 and 2 (pages 4–7).

Watch out!

Eysenck and Keane (1990) commented that rehearsal is not always necessary for material to pass into LTM.

Example

Put revision notes into a number of different forms. Use colour.

Take note

Procedural memory (such as remembering how to ride a bike) is very resistant to forgetting.

Checkpoint 2

How might you rearrange the material from Models of memory 1 and 2 and Forgetting to help yourself remember it all?

Exam question   answer: page 28

Outline two explanations of why we forget. (12 min)

Emotional factors in forgetting

It seems intuitively correct that our emotional state and cognitive processing abilities are interrelated. Emotions can affect our attentional capacity and how we perceive things. They are also implicated in memory.

Repression

Sometimes called **motivated forgetting**, repression is the purposeful suppression of memories. Freud (1901) suggested that memories that are too threatening or laden with anxiety are hidden in the unconscious mind and that it is necessary to expend psychic energy to keep them there. The implication of this is that such memories could be retrieved accidentally because of a precipitating event or deliberately through psychoanalysis.

→ Clinical evidence for repression exists in conditions such as fugue states where, following a stressful event, an individual loses personal identity and is often found wandering miles from home. The amnesia associated with this appears to be psychogenic.

→ It has been difficult to demonstrate repression unambiguously in the laboratory not least because of ethical problems in deliberately attempting to induce it. However, it does seem that participants are less able to remember information when they are made anxious by being given false feedback of failure. Unfortunately, the same effect occurs after feedback of success! Eysenck (1993) suggests that feedback is merely distracting.

Flashbulb memories

Flashbulb memories are of events that were outstanding in some way. People in their forties and older often recall where they were when they heard of J. F. Kennedy's assassination. Younger people are likely to carry a similar memory of when they heard of Princess Diana's death in 1997. Brown and Kulik (1977) analyzed people's recall of similar national events and found recall of:

→ where they were on hearing the news
→ the event interrupted by the news
→ the person who announced the event
→ their own and others' feelings
→ what happened afterwards.

Brown and Kulik also found that such memories carried a high element of surprise, emotional arousal and a sense of the event's importance. Pillemer (1984) added that the degree of emotion aroused by the event was related to the vividness, detail and consistency of recall over time. Interestingly, in free-recall of flashbulb memories, Rubin and Kozin (1984) found that, amongst a variety of topics:

→ 18% of memories concerned accidents or injuries to self or friends
→ only 3% of memories were of national events.

From an evolutionary point of view, it would seem to make sense to encode rapidly any event that threatened well-being or survival.

Example

Freud's explanation of childhood amnesia was that it was caused by the repression of sexual and aggressive feelings towards parents. But virtually all early childhood experiences are forgotten – see Take note on page 8.

Example

A precipitating event could be a trauma, which acts as a reminder of the original threat.

The jargon

Psychogenic amnesia is forgetting brought about by psychological processes.

Links

Flashbulb memory is a special kind of episodic memory. See Models of memory 1 (page 4).

Checkpoint 1

Flashbulb memories are not always of disturbing events. What kinds of pleasant events might lead to such memories?

Bower's network theory of affect ●●●

Bower (1981) and Bower and Gilligan (1984) proposed a theory which links mood and memory. Emotions are seen as nodes in a complex semantic network. Connections run through the network between these nodes and ideas, events, physiological systems and the behaviour patterns by which we express emotions. A node can be activated by an internal or external stimulus. When this happens, activation spreads around the network in a selective rather than general manner. This leads to at least four testable hypotheses:

→ **Mood state dependent recall** – recall is best if mood at recall matches mood when learning.
→ **Thought congruity** – if a person is asked to free-associate, they tend to make statements that fit their mood state.
→ **Mood congruity** – material with an emotional content is learned best if it matches the learner's mood state.
→ **Mood intensity** – as mood intensity increases, so does activation of nodes linked together in the network.

Evidence for the network theory of affect

Experimental tests of the four hypotheses above typically involve attempting to induce an emotional state in participants, for example:

→ Bower et al (1978) tested mood state dependent recall. Participants learned two lists of words in a happy or sad mood and recalled them in the same or opposite mood. Recall was better when mood at learning and recall matched.
→ Bower et al (1981) tested the mood congruity hypothesis by inducing happy or sad mood in participants by hypnosis. Participants then read a story about Jack, who was depressed, and André, who was happy. Later, they were able to recall more about the character who matched their mood state.

Evaluation of the network theory of affect

There is good support for the four proposed hypotheses. However, it is technically difficult to induce mood states in participants and, sometimes, ethically problematic. A possible solution to this is to study mood-disordered individuals but these people may differ in other important ways from 'normal' controls. In addition, emotions and moods vary in intensity and duration whereas semantic information does not. This makes the link between them difficult to understand.

The jargon

Affect is a broad term encompassing emotions, moods and preferences.

Links

A similar idea is expressed in Tulving and Thompson's encoding specificity principle; see Forgetting (pages 8–9).

Checkpoint 2

Identify two ethical issues that might be raised by such research.

Exam question answer: pages 28–9

Explain what is meant by the terms 'flashbulb memory' and 'repression' as they apply to memory. (6 min)

Eyewitness testimony 1

Eyewitness memory researchers are interested in the processes of encoding, storing and retrieving memories of real-life events and how accurate these may be. In courts of law, eyewitness testimony (EWT) is often used as evidence, so an understanding of how it might be biased has important practical consequences.

The constructivist approach to memory ●●●

Bartlett (1932) took a different approach to the study of memory than the two-process or levels models described earlier. Bartlett's approach has particular relevance for memory of real-life events. He suggested that:

→ memory is seen as an active process. We do not simply store a copy of something that we want to remember. We construct memories by combining existing knowledge with the new material.
→ retrieval involves reconstructing the resulting memories. People may remember quite different things about the same event because they have constructed their memories in their own way.
→ we will learn more about real-life memory if we give people meaningful things to memorize rather than lists of words. Bartlett used stories, faces and pictures in his tests of memory.

Evidence for constructivist theory

In one study, Bartlett used a story called 'The War of the Ghosts' which is about 300 words long. Participants were asked to read it and, fifteen minutes later, to recall everything they could about it. At varying intervals thereafter, Bartlett retested some of the participants' recall. (One person was tested ten years later!) Their accounts of the story changed in predictable ways. These changes seemed to make the story neater, so that it fitted with the participant's personal interpretation of events. Changes included:

→ omissions – certain details were left out
→ rationalizations – details were sometimes added if the participant had made additions and needed to justify them
→ alterations in importance – aspects of the story might be played up or down
→ changed order – this might make the participant's version of the story 'flow' better
→ added affect – if participants reacted emotionally to the story (e.g. disgusted or amused) this often affected the way they recalled it.

Bartlett also tested recall of line drawings, as shown below. Participants studied these and then drew them from memory, talking about them as they did so. They tended to interpret and recall each drawing in a way that fitted with their own knowledge and the descriptive words that they used.

Bartlett used the term 'effort after meaning' to explain these effects.

Example

Witnesses to crimes may be honest and well intentioned when recalling what they saw, but psychological research shows that their recall can be biased in many ways.

Checkpoint 1

What real world examples of this process are there?

Speed learning

Remember these five ways of distorting an account by using the acronym 'ORACA'.

The jargon

'*Effort after meaning*'. When people memorize something, they work on it and change it until they understand it in their own way. Forgetting results from the distortions, omissions and additions and makes the remembered version different from the original.

Comments on Bartlett's theory

→ Compared with some other types of memory research, Bartlett's approach can be seen as more relevant to the memory processes we use in everyday life.

→ The approach can be difficult to test because people's responses to the materials used are not easy to score.

→ The approach causes us to consider how and why individuals differ in their recall of the same event, which is especially important in eyewitness testimony.

→ Bartlett's ideas have been developed into a cognitive approach to memory. This approach asks what memory is for and how it interacts with other cognitive systems such as language and perception. (Other approaches have focused more on the structure of memory.) It is especially relevant to explaining eyewitness accounts, which involve a number of interacting psychological processes and characteristics.

Checkpoint 2

How might this kind of research be ecologically invalid?

Further sources of bias in EWT ●●●

Constructivist theories such as Bartlett's are useful for explaining the nature of distortions in people's accounts of events but, as cognitive theory suggests, other factors can also distort memories.

→ Violence – EWT seems to be more accurate for non-violent crimes than for violent ones, possibly because heightened emotion affects encoding.

→ Time – EWT often contains over-estimates of how long a crime lasted. Again, this could be the result of heightened emotion.

→ Confidence – EWT given by witnesses who feel confident tends to be believed more but there is no evidence that it is more accurate.

→ Age – Older witnesses tend to be less efficient at face recognition perhaps because their stereotypes and expectations are stronger (O'Rourke 1989). Children tend to be less accurate than young adults (Eysenck 1994).

→ Interest – We tend to remember more accurately events that are of personal interest to us (Eysenck 1994).

→ Ethnic group – EWT is less accurate if the witness is a different ethnic group to the person observed, say, committing a crime.

→ Knowing the suspect – Stephenson (1992) showed how experimenters could unknowingly communicate correct answers to participants in experiments. It is possible, therefore, that police officers who strongly suspect someone could communicate that to a witness looking at an identity parade or photos of suspects.

Watch out!

Beware of sweeping statements! This research only shows *tendencies* in EWT. Distortions such as these are not inevitable.

Checkpoint 3

Think of an example that supports the idea that events of personal interest are more easily remembered.

Exam question   answer: page 29

'The testimony of an eyewitness is so flawed that it can never be trusted.' To what extent is eyewitness testimony as flawed as the quotation suggests? (12 min)

Eyewitness testimony 2

Links

Memories for events such as crimes are open to all the distortions suggested by Bartlett in his constructivist theory of memory (page 12).

Checkpoint 1

What ethical issues are raised here?

Watch out!

Such findings suggest that leading questions not only distort recall but also affect longer-term memory of an event.

Eyewitness testimony (EWT) research is of particular interest in the investigation of crime. It is important to understand people's memories for events as well as their memory for the individuals involved.

Studies of EWT

Staged crimes

Buckhout (1979) staged a 'shooting' of a professor in front of 141 eyewitnesses (students and others). The eyewitnesses:

→ over-estimated the time the crime lasted for
→ over-estimated the weight of the gunman
→ under-estimated the age of the gunman.

Seven weeks later, only 40% of the witnesses could identify the gunman from photographs. Even the 'shot' professor could not identify him, so victims are not necessarily better witnesses than bystanders. In similar research, Buckhout (1980) used a line-up of suspects and found only 14% of witnesses could pick out the right 'criminal'.

Leading the witness

→ Loftus and Palmer (1974) showed participants in a study a film of a car crash. Later they were asked questions about the film. The wording of the questions was changed in certain ways. People who were asked 'How fast were the cars going when they *smashed into* each other?' estimated faster speeds than participants whose question included the word 'hit' instead. A week later, participants were asked if there had been any broken glass. The film showed none but 32% of the 'smashed into' group said yes compared to 14% of the 'hit' group.
→ In 1975, Loftus and Zanni showed participants a short film of a car accident. Later some participants were asked if they had seen *a* broken headlight and others whether they had seen *the* broken headlight. There was no broken headlight at all, but 15% of the '*the*' group said there was one, compared with 7% of the '*a*' group.
→ In line-ups where a person is led to believe the suspect is present or feels that they must choose someone, wrong guesses are more common (Malpass and Devine 1981).

More recent research on EWT

→ Bekerian and Bowers (1983) showed that the effect of leading questions could be reduced if questions followed the order of events witnessed in an incident. Baddeley (1995) suggests that this is because leading questions distort retrieval rather than the memory trace itself.
→ Yuille and Cutshall (1986) studied witnesses who had seen a real violent crime. They were impressively accurate in recalling main events but could be misled by questions about peripheral incidents.

Face recognition ●●●

This is called for when witnesses try to recall faces using identikit pictures, artist's impressions, albums of 'mugshots' or identity parades.

Bahrick et al (1975) found that face recognition was accurate 90% of the time, if the test picture of a face was the same as the one the participant saw originally. Face recognition is not as good if:

→ the face is seen from a different angle
→ the context the face is seen in is new
→ changes are made, e.g. moustache added.

Such studies suggest efficient face recognition under laboratory conditions where participants may be aware that they will be tested. In real-life situations, witnesses do not observe static faces and may not expect to recall them. Nevertheless, in stress-free, naturalistic situations, females are superior to males in identifying faces after interactions, but males' recognition is superior in stressful situations (Bahrick et al 1975).

Reconstruction of faces from memory is less efficient than recognition. People find constructing photofits, even of familiar individuals, very difficult to do well (Davies et al 1981). However, Bahrick et al (1975) tested people's memories for the faces of schoolmates over periods of time ranging up to 50 years and found high recognition rates in all conditions.

In identity parades it is thought that the right person is picked 45% of the time but witnesses are easily confused by changes in appearance, even in clothing (Baddeley 1991). Accuracy of identification in a line-up can also be improved if suspects appear in different line-ups from each other rather than all together.

Comments on EWT research ●●●

People are very ready to believe EWT but it can be very inaccurate. What lessons can we learn from this?

→ We should ask witnesses to recall in order of events whenever possible and avoid leading questions about peripheral events.
→ People often remember more details of the crime than of the criminal but reconstructing the crime can often jog their memories of the criminal.
→ Evidence from an eyewitness should be corroborated by others. It should also be backed up with other kinds of evidence such as forensic evidence or medical information.
→ People in general, but police officers in particular, could benefit from training in EWT and from a knowledge of some of the associated biases.

> *"I never forget a face, but I'll make an exception in your case."*
>
> Groucho Marx (1965)

Watch out!

An obvious point to note is that criminals may go to great lengths to disguise themselves.

Example

An innocent person who happens to be dressed like the criminal was at the time of the crime might be wrongly chosen.

Checkpoint 2

Why is corroborative evidence important?

Exam question   answer: page 29

Describe two studies into eyewitness testimony. (12 min)

The development of attachments

Maccoby (1980) defines attachment as 'a relatively enduring emotional tie to a specific other person'. Human infants seem to be born prepared to make attachments. However, this 'bonding' between an infant and its caregiver is usually a two-way process.

The development of attachments

Some things that make the infant attractive to caregivers are present immediately; others mature in the first months of life. The infant's appearance and proximity promoting and maintaining behaviour help keep caregivers close to them so attachment can happen.

The infant's physical features

Infants of many species, including humans, have physical features that encourage caring behaviour from adults.

→ The human baby's head is large in proportion to its body, its eyes and cheeks are relatively large and its nose and mouth are small.
→ Babies have a range of cries that are hard to ignore. Using sound spectrographs, Wolff (1969) was able to distinguish basic 'mad' (angry) and pain cries in infants as young as four days old.
→ Babies' movements are jerky and uncoordinated (spastic) and their reflexive responses can lead caregivers to believe that the infant enjoys contact with them.

The infant's behaviour (sociability)

Schaffer (1971) calls the ability to engage in social interactions with others 'sociability'. What does it involve?

→ *Face recognition* Infants have an early ability to recognise faces. Infants tested between four days to six months old gazed at face-like patterns more than at patterns of equal complexity (Fantz 1961). By three months, infants can distinguish a photo of their mother's face from strangers' faces (Barrera and Maurer 1981).
→ *Voice recognition* DeCasper and Fifer (1980) showed infants could distinguish their mother's voice from a stranger's after only twelve hours of post-natal contact, and showed more interest in human speech than other sounds of similar pitch.
→ *Social smiles and cries and responsiveness* Infants first smile within a few weeks of birth and caregivers respond positively to these. Infants' cries usually elicit a response from their carers and they stop crying when they hear a human voice. Such social responsiveness creates plenty of opportunities for attachment to occur.
→ *Taking turns* Stern (1977) showed that, as early as three months of age, infants take turns in 'conversations' with the mother. This is known as 'interactional synchrony' and improves with age.

Watch out!

This definition can apply to emotional attachments developed throughout the life span.

Checkpoint 1

What proximity promoting and maintaining behaviours might develop with time?

The jargon

Konrad Lorenz (1943) called the impact of the infant's appearance the *kewpie doll* effect.

Example

The infant's rooting, sucking and grasping reflexes all help to retain proximity to the carer.

Take note

In all societies, wariness of strangers is usually evident in babies from the age of around seven months. Babies are beginning to be mobile at this age (they have begun to crawl), so this stranger anxiety may have an evolutionary survival value.

Variations in attachments

Secure and insecure attachments

Ainsworth (1978) devised a test of attachment strength and security called 'the strange situation'. This is based on the assumption that, once an infant is attached, it will use the mother as a base from which to explore but will also show fear of strangers. In a setting new to the infant, eight three-minute episodes occur in which the mother and a stranger come and go from the room. Sometimes, the infant is with both of them, sometimes with one of them and sometimes alone. After testing a group of one- to two-year-olds in this way, Ainsworth identified three types of attachment:

→ Type A: anxious-avoidant – 20% of the infants tested seemed to be indifferent to the mother and were not obviously affected by her presence or absence. They generally disliked being left alone but could be comforted equally by either the stranger or the mother.

→ Type B: securely attached – 70% of the infants liked to stay close to the mother when playing. They were distressed when she left but were quickly comforted when she returned. The stranger could give some comfort but, generally, infants treated the mother and stranger very differently.

→ Type C: anxious-resistant – 10% of the infants seemed to have mixed (ambivalent) feelings towards the mother. They sought contact with her and then resisted it. They also resisted contact with strangers. They often did not settle happily to play but kept glancing anxiously at the mother.

Cross-cultural variations in attachments

The percentages given above were taken from American studies. In seven other cultures, Van IJzendoorn and Kroonenberg (1988) found Type B attachment was the most common in the strange situation test, however Japanese and Israeli kibbutzim children were much more likely to show Type C than Type A attachment, while West German, British, Dutch, Swedish and Chinese children showed the opposite. Many Japanese and Israeli children spend their infancy in close-knit groups and do not often encounter strangers whereas, in other cultures, independence is encouraged at a younger age. Such findings highlight the importance of cultural differences in child-care practices but do not indicate whether some practices are superior to others.

Checkpoint 2

What form might infants' conversation take?

Links

Other variations in attachment can occur if the process goes wrong. See Deprivation and privation (pages 20–3).

Watch out!

We should take great care in linking these attachment types to other factors, such as maternal employment. Infants differ greatly in temperament and in how used they are to being left alone. These could contribute to the kind of attachment they typically show.

Checkpoint 3

Why should we be wary of making broad generalizations about cultures?

Exam questions   answers: page 29

1 Describe the procedures and findings of one research study that has explored the development of insecure attachments. (6 min)

2 Consider what research has told us about cross-cultural variations in attachments. (12 min)

Explanations of attachment

Generations of psychologists have speculated about why attachments form. Is it simply 'cupboard love' or something more profound? Explanations of attachment have important implications for how we view the child-caregiver relationship.

Psychodynamic explanations of attachment

Psychodynamic theorists think that activities essential to the infant's survival, especially feeding, are at the root of attachment.

→ Freud believed that young infants are in the oral stage of personality development when stimulation to do with the mouth, particularly through feeding, is important. Infants become emotionally attached to the satisfying breast and, eventually, to the mother herself.

→ Erik Erikson (1950, 1968) agreed that feeding is central to attachment but emphasized the importance of the mother's overall social responsiveness to the infant. Good responsiveness leads the infant to develop a sense of 'basic trust' in the caregiver's ability to meet its needs.

Both approaches agree on the importance of early experience in shaping the quality of the emotional relationship between mother and infant. In both cases, how the caregiver handles the infant's feeding needs and the atmosphere of feeding affect the quality of the attachment. Feeding should be a happy experience if secure attachments are to develop.

Learning theory and attachment

Learning theorists (e.g. Sears 1963) agree with psychoanalysts that the feeding situation is important but for different reasons.

→ Feeding is reinforcing because it reduces unpleasant hunger and is associated with other rewarding experiences such as warmth, comfort and social stimulation. Such things are primary reinforcers because they directly satisfy needs. With time, the mother becomes a secondary reinforcer because she is regularly associated with the arrival of primary reinforcers.

→ Reinforcement is a two-way process – the infant becomes attached to the mother because she meets its needs. She becomes attached to the infant because it responds positively to her caregiving.

Research into learning theory and attachment

→ Harlow and Zimmerman's (1959) study of infant rhesus monkeys challenges this theory. Monkeys could feed from two surrogate models, one made of wire and the other of soft cloth. Tests showed that, although both surrogates provided food, the monkeys preferred the soft mother as a secure base and went to her when distressed.

→ Schaffer and Emerson (1964) also showed that, in 39% of cases, the main caregiver was not the primary attachment object.

Checkpoint 1

In attachment formation, how critical do you think it is that the infant is breastfed?

Links

See Personality development (see pages 140–41).

Today, learning theorists tend to play down the emphasis on feeding that they previously shared with psychodynamic theorists. They still maintain that reinforcement is important but think that this mainly comes through the caregiver responding reliably and appropriately to the infant's signals for attention.

Ethological explanations of attachment ●●●

Influenced by ethologists, who study animal behaviour in natural environments, and by psychodynamic theory, Bowlby (1958) proposed that attachment had a biological and evolutionary basis in survival.

→ The infant's appearance and sociable behaviour are biologically designed to encourage closeness and caregiving in the parent.
→ Attachment is a two-way process which is most likely to happen during a sensitive period in the infant's first months. This has some similarities with the imprinting process seen in some other animals.
→ The feeding situation is one of many opportunities for attachment to take place but is not necessarily the most important one.

Attachment is not inevitable. A distressed or depressed mother may be unresponsive to her infant or the infant may be temperamentally difficult to handle or otherwise 'hard to love'. Bowlby thought that we have a biological preparedness to bond but that babies and caregivers have to learn how to respond appropriately to each other.

Research into ethological explanations of attachment

Ethological theorists hypothesize that close physical contact between infant and caregiver leads to a closer and more secure bond.

→ Klaus and Kennel (1979) studied fourteen mothers who had the (then standard) experience of holding the baby immediately after birth and then not seeing it for six to twelve hours. They then saw their babies four-hourly for feeds. These mothers were compared with fourteen others who saw their babies for about an hour after the birth and then had an extra five hours of contact with the infant each day. The latter group behaved differently from the former: they soothed their babies more and had more physical contact with them.
→ Anisfield et al (1990) encouraged some mothers to carry their infants closely in soft baby pouches and others to use the harder, generally available baby seats. At three months, close contact mothers were more responsive to their infants' signals for attention and by thirteen months the close contact infants were more likely to be securely attached to their mothers.

However, other research shows little or no effect and all studies show small or non-existent long-term effects.

> **Checkpoint 2**
>
> How might two caregivers be equally reliable in meeting an infant's needs but differ in appropriateness?

> **Links**
>
> See The development of attachments (pages 16–17).

> **Example**
>
> Babies may be naturally irritable or have a condition that makes them unresponsive so that the caregiver's attempts to bond may fail.

Exam question   answer: page 29

Describe two explanations of attachment. (12 min)

19

Deprivation and privation 1

When we bond with another person, we can usually form an attachment to them that endures through periods of time apart, but attachments are said to be only 'relatively enduring' because they can be damaged or destroyed. Attachments are emotional bonds so we may be affected emotionally if they are broken.

Maternal absence

It is important to clarify what sort of maternal absence is likely to have adverse effects:

→ *Separation* is the physical parting of the infant and mother or caregiver. It does not always lead to deprivation if it is handled in the right way.
→ *Maternal deprivation* occurs when an existing attachment or bond formation is disrupted and is potentially damaging.
→ *Maternal privation* occurs when the infant has never had the chance to form an attachment and is also potentially damaging.

John Bowlby's 'maternal deprivation' hypothesis

Bowlby (1953) claimed that '. . . a warm, intimate, continuous relationship with the mother . . . or permanent mother substitute . . .' was essential. Through this, attachment is formed and this gives the individual an 'internal working model' of relationships to carry into the future. Several sources of evidence support this hypothesis.

Ethological evidence

Imprinting
In many species of mammal and some birds, imprinting attaches the young animal to its parent during a *sensitive period* early in life. This is the only chance an individual has to imprint. If the process fails, there are problems relating to others in adulthood. Bowlby noted a similar, but not identical, process in human infants who attach at about six months and show fear of strangers soon after. He thought that, if attachment had not occurred by two to three years of age, it would probably be too late and there could be long-term damage.

Animal studies
Harlow and Harlow (1958) separated infant rhesus monkeys from their mothers soon after birth and reared them in isolation, providing some with surrogate mothers to feed from. When given contact with normal monkeys the monkeys were either very distressed and withdrawn or extremely aggressive. When mature, their social behaviour towards other monkeys was dysfunctional or inappropriate. If they mated successfully, they seemed unable to parent their own young and were often abusive to them. Later studies showed three months of isolation could be remedied but six to twelve months of isolation did irreversible damage. The presence of the surrogate made little difference.

Watch out!

Early work in this area focused on mothers, hence the use of the term 'maternal'.

Checkpoint 1

Even when caregivers and infants are not separated, attachment may still fail. What characteristics of caregivers and infants might lead to attachment failure?

> *"Mother love in infancy and childhood is as important for mental health as are vitamins and proteins for physical health."*
>
> John Bowlby (1953)

The jargon

A *surrogate mother* is a substitute for the real thing. In this case, the Harlows provided monkey-like wire and/or terry towelling models of mothers.

Watch out!

Some of the Harlows' studies, such as the one described here, subjected young monkeys to privation rather than deprivation.

Short-term effects in human infants and children

Protest, despair and detachment

This is a recognisable sequence of reactions in children aged between about seven months to three years following separation from an attachment figure. At the time, detachment was viewed as a sign of recovery but the Robertsons' (1967) films of young children supported Bowlby's idea that even brief separations are acutely distressing and that detachment is associated with damage to the mother-child bond.

Long-term effects in human infants and children

Later attachments

Attachment problems in human infants may be linked to problems forming relationships later in life. Bowlby thought that such people would suffer from increased 'separation anxiety' and be especially vulnerable if they did form a relationship that later broke down.

Problems in development

Studies of children in the 1930s and 1940s, who had experienced long-term care in orphanages, tend to show long-term problems in language, social and cognitive development. Goldfarb (1947) showed that children fostered early on made better educational progress and had better social skills than those who received institutional care from six months to three years of age.

Juvenile delinquency

In 1946, Bowlby studied the family histories of 44 juvenile thieves. Seventeen of them had been separated from their mothers for six months before their fifth birthday. He compared these with 44 adolescents who had emotional problems but were not thieves and found only two had experienced such separation. Of the 'thieves', Bowlby noted that fourteen showed affectionless psychopathy, having no feelings of affection, warmth or concern for anyone. Bowlby concluded that these problems linked directly to early separation.

Deprivation and privation ●●●

In many studies used by Bowlby to support his hypothesis it was likely that deprivation was occurring. A few involved privation but the distinction was often uncertain. There are rare cases of privation in humans:

→ The case of Genie, a girl who was discovered at the age of eleven after being kept in virtual isolation all her life.
→ Skeels and Dye's (1939) study of children raised in unstimulating orphanages.

The problems indicate the impact of privation relative to deprivation.

Exam questions   answers: page 30

1 What is meant by the terms 'deprivation' and 'privation'? (4 min)

2 Outline two research studies that have explored the long-term effects of deprivation in the child. (12 min)

Example

During 'protest' the child might cry and scream. During 'despair' the child appears to be apathetic, sad and indifferent to others. At the detachment stage, they may respond more to others but rather coolly.

Checkpoint 2

Why do you think children tolerate separation better after they reach about three years of age?

Deprivation and privation 2

Researchers agree that a secure attachment in early life gives the child a safe base from which to explore and helps adults to develop secure relationships. For some children, however, early experience is less than ideal. Psychologists differ in the extent to which they think this matters.

Assessing Bowlby's 'maternal deprivation' hypothesis ●●●

Ethological evidence

Imprinting

There are doubts about whether it is appropriate to talk of imprinting in humans. The sensitive period seems to be very flexible. Children start to attach as late as two or three years old, and there are several studies of successful later attachment following adoption (e.g. Tizard and Hodges 1978).

Animal studies

The extreme privation experienced by Harlow's monkeys is not often seen in humans. Later research has shown how monkey therapists (younger peers) can undo much of the early damage. They cling to the deprived monkeys and seem to make up for the early loss of contact comfort. Effects of early deprivation do appear to be reversible.

Short-term effects in human infants and children

Robertson and Robertson (1967) found that children could overcome the problems of brief separation if they were cared for in a familiar environment by familiar people who made an effort to keep to familiar daily routines. (This challenges Bowlby's idea of **monotropy** since the child can attach to more than one person, which protects them in the event of separation.) Attempts to maintain contact with the absent parent were also helpful.

Long-term effects in human infants and children

Later attachments

There is plenty of evidence that people can overcome early attachment problems and form trusting relationships later in life.

→ Koluchova (1972) studied Czechoslovakian twin boys whose mother had died when they were born in 1960. The first few months of their lives were in an institution where they progressed well. At eighteen months they were removed to live with their father and stepmother at whose hands they suffered isolation and neglect until they were discovered at the age of seven. At eight years old they were put into high quality foster care provided by two sisters. They attended a special school at first but at fourteen had transferred to mainstream school and had normal IQs for their age.

→ Tizard and Hodges (1978) made a longitudinal study of 64 children who had been placed in residential nurseries before four months of

Links

See Deprivation and privation 1 (pages 20–1) for the evidence on which this hypothesis is based.

Checkpoint 1

In what other important way are human infants' capabilities different from animals that imprint?

Watch out!

Think carefully about whether a study concerns deprivation or privation. Sometimes it can be difficult to decide which of these has occurred, if at all.

The jargon

Monotropy is the tendency to favour one attachment figure over others.

Watch out!

Good quality care before and after deprivation appeared to undo the damage to these boys, but it is important to note that they had also had each other's company throughout.

age. The nursery environment was stimulating but staff were discouraged from forming attachments with the children. Children were later adopted, returned to their mothers or left in the nursery. At eight and sixteen years of age some emotional and behavioural problems at school were evident. Some children in all groups were able to make attachments if their caregivers were sensitive and understanding.

Problems in development

Skeels and Dye (1966) followed thirteen American orphans who were removed from an unstimulating orphanage to the care of subnormal girls in a well-equipped school for the mentally retarded. Comparisons with twelve children who remained in the orphanage showed significant IQ gains for the removed group and losses for the controls. A number of other persistent differences were noted in adulthood. Dowdney et al (1985) and Rutter and Quinton (1985) followed up 89 women in their 20s who had experienced several years of institutional care during childhood. Compared to controls, there was a higher incidence of broken relationships, criminal records and personality disorders in this group. There was also evidence that, while institutionalization may put the individual at risk, other experiences, such as supportive schooling and good relationships, can mitigate some of the negative effects.

Juvenile delinquency

Rutter (1981) questioned the link between maternal separation and delinquency suggested by Bowlby. In his study of nine- to twelve-year-old boys on the Isle of Wight, he found that it was not separation that caused problems. Instead he found a positive correlation between antisocial behaviour in these boys and the extent to which there was a stressful family atmosphere in their early years. He found no correlation between separation experiences and delinquency.

Lessons from research ●●●

The work of Bowlby and others gave rise to a great deal of research which has had important, beneficial consequences.

→ Improvements in institutional care and fostering and therapy for children who have been affected by adverse early experiences.
→ Better understanding of how to reduce the factors that put children at risk from deprivation and privation.
→ Reassurance to working parents that Bowlby's initial ideas of monotropy and the need for mothers to stay at home with young children were probably overstated. Parents can now feel more confident about providing the right quality of substitute care.

Checkpoint 2

Children who were adopted might have differed in important ways from those who were not adopted. What differences could there have been and why would they matter?

Example

Children who had experienced greater intellectual stimulation were more likely as adults to have completed high school, continued to college and be economically independent.

Watch out!

Extreme privation can result in profound problems later on, but even these might be overcome to some extent provided there are no abnormalities that would prevent recovery.

Exam question   answer: page 30

'Mother love in infancy is vital for later development.'
To what extent has psychological research supported this view? (12 min)

Day care 1

Checkpoint 1

What other day care patterns might British children experience?

Checkpoint 2

How do you think the relevant authorities are reacting to increases in day care in the UK and USA?

Watch out!

The majority of children in both these groups were securely attached.

Links

Such pre-existing differences might become 'confounding variables'. See Experimental design 2 (pages 78–9).

Since Bowlby proposed his 'maternal deprivation hypothesis' in the 1950s, much research has been carried out into the impact upon young children of care outside the home environment. This section considers some patterns of day care and touches on its likely emotional impact on the child.

Alternative child-care patterns

Nursery care and child-minding

Working parents in the UK who cannot call on family or nannies to help, will probably use one of two common alternatives:

→ **Nurseries** can be private or run by the state. Some nurseries take children from babyhood until they start school; others specify a starting age. Children can attend part-time or full-time and are cared for alongside other children by trained nursery nurses.

→ **Child-minders** are most often mothers who care for up to two or three other children, often fitting the care around their own family life. In the UK they should be registered, which means that the home where a child will be cared for is checked for agreed standards of health, safety and facilities.

Research into day care

Much research on the effects of day care has been carried out in the USA where concern has been expressed about whether working parents are damaging their attachment relationship with their children by not being with them until they begin school. Reassuringly, researchers in the 1980s concluded day care would not be damaging if:

→ care was of high quality
→ there was a good carer-to-child ratio
→ there was low staff turnover
→ there were plenty of stimulating activities.

However, in 1988, Belsky compared children who went into day care for 20 hours or more per week with children who had no day care or less than 20 hours before one year of age. Using the **strange situation** test, he concluded that 41% of the first group were insecurely attached compared with 26% of the second group. Such findings should be treated with caution because:

→ reactions to the strange situation may not be an accurate indication of the child's general emotional security
→ children of working mothers have more separation experience to start with so are not the same as children of non-working mothers
→ there might be other differences between families with working and non-working mothers that can account for the findings.

On child-minding there have been several UK studies. Mayall and Patrie (1977) studied minders in London, and Bryant et al (1980) studied minders in Oxfordshire. Both studies found that:

- ➜ children's physical needs were adequately met
- ➜ minders tended to put their domestic and family duties first
- ➜ children seemed less secure in the minder's home than in their own
- ➜ minders did not feel it necessary to develop a close bond with the children
- ➜ children scored lower than expected on tests of language and cognitive ability.

We cannot draw any firm conclusions from this because:

- ➜ there were no matched controls of non-minded children for comparison. The standard of care in the child's own home could have been the same, better or worse.
- ➜ problems experienced by some children could have resulted from being minded or could have been already present.

It is still unclear whether child-minding causes problems for children. There are 50 000 registered child-minders in the UK and, probably, three times that number who are not registered. It is not possible to make general statements about them because there are wide variations. Many parents find child-minding an excellent solution to the care problem, especially for very young children.

Across cultures ●●●

These are just two examples of the many ways in which child-care practices differ within and between cultures.

Uganda
Ainsworth (1967) compared Ugandan mothers with American mothers. Ugandan mothers and children have a great deal of physical contact. Infants are carried everywhere by their mothers in slings; they sleep with their mothers and are typically breastfed for two years. This greater contact seems to result in more anxiety on separation and earlier fear of strangers than in American babies. These babies seem to attach earlier than babies in the Western world.

Israel
In Israeli kibbutzim (agricultural communes) mothers stay with their newborn babies for a few weeks and then gradually return to full-time work. By about one year of age a child will be cared for mainly by a children's nurse, called a metapelet, in the 'Children's House'. Children usually return to their parents at the end of the working day. They have high quality day care and good quality time with their parents. Such children seem to have multiple attachments to a number of caregivers but their strongest attachments are still to their parents.

> **Watch out!**
>
> Care of the very young is inevitably shaped to suit the needs and circumstances of particular cultures. However, in the majority of cases, children appear to be very adaptable and will, under most circumstances, develop healthily.

> **Checkpoint 3**
>
> Why do you think infants developed their strongest attachment to their parents?

> **Check the net**
>
> www.cabri.org.il/kibbutz.html
> Use this site to find out more about the Israeli kibbutz.

> **Exam question** answer: page 30
>
> Outline the aims and conclusions of one research study that has explored the effects of day care on children. (6 min)

Day care 2

Research into day care for babies and young children is multi-faceted. Day care 1 noted patterns of care and some of the research into the effects of this on security of emotional attachment. Here the emphasis is on those aspects of cognitive and social development included in such research.

The impact of day care on cognitive development ●●●

Positive and negative effects of day care

In the UK, Melhuish (1990) compared the effects on children of care by relatives, child-minders and private nursery care. The children had started the care arrangements before nine months of age. Results showed no differences in the type of attachment to the mother (an important control) but:

→ communication abilities at eighteen months were best in children cared for by relatives, followed by minded children, then nursery children. By three years of age the differences had all but disappeared.

→ there were no differences in other aspects of cognitive development.

Research into day care and aspects of cognitive development elsewhere yields very mixed results, for example:

→ Scarr and Eisenberg (1993) found that good quality care did not affect cognitive abilities in children from economically advantaged American families but did affect disadvantaged children.

→ Andersson (1992) followed up thirteen-year-old middle-class children in Sweden who had begun day care in infancy and found that they performed better in school than controls who had experienced little or no day care.

→ Baydar and Brookes-Gunn (1991) and Caughy et al (1994) followed up a large sample of American children with different day care experiences at three to four years of age and five to six years of age respectively. They compared those who had experienced home care only with others who had different day care experiences. Poverty levels and age when day care began were influential. Children from poor families who had started day care before one year of age scored better than home care children on reading and maths tests but the effect was reversed for middle-class children.

A possible explanation

Clarke-Stewart et al (1994) proposed that the setting for day care mattered less than the level of 'cognitive enrichment' it provided in comparison to the home. Home and day care settings could be very good for stimulating children's cognitive abilities just as they could be poor. Where children's home background is poor, a stimulating day care environment is likely to be beneficial, but where home is good and day care is poor, it could have the opposite effect.

Checkpoint 1

Why is the fact that there were no differences in attachment type important in Melhuish's study?

Watch out!

Swedish day care is very well established and closely monitored by the authorities for quality. Comparisons with other cultures should, therefore, be made with great caution.

The jargon

Cognitive enrichment refers to how many opportunities and how much encouragement is provided for children to think, read, question, learn from and converse with other adults and children.

The impact of day care on social development

Again, the findings about day care and social development are mixed. A number of studies indicate increased social skills result from day care:

→ Melhuish (1990) found that British nursery children showed more understanding of pro-social behaviour such as sharing and co-operation.
→ Andersson (1992) found that Swedish children with day care experience were more socially skilled and played with others more harmoniously.

Some small negative effects have been found:

→ Bates et al (1994) found that children who had spent the most time in day care from infancy through to pre-school, regardless of when care began, were more aggressive than children with little or no such experience. They were also less likely to take notice of adults in authority such as teachers and parents.

As with cognitive development, the key to understanding these results appears to lie in the quality of care, e.g. higher levels of aggression and non-compliance are linked with poorer quality day care settings where the levels of stimulation might not engage children sufficiently. Researchers now recommend that the focus should not be on whether or not parents should work – for many it's essential – but on how to ensure that the day care their children receive is appropriate and of good quality.

Characteristics of good day care

Bredekamp and Copple (1997), amongst others, have identified several characteristics of good day care based on current research findings.

→ Physical setting – clean, colourful, well-lit and ventilated space which is not crowded. Outside play space also available.
→ Carer to child ratio – no more than 1:3 for babies and 1:5 for toddlers.
→ Small group size within a unit – no more than six infants with two caregivers and twelve toddlers with two caregivers.
→ Caregiver style – positive, involved, responsive, informed.
→ Daily plan – structured but flexible familiar daily routine with a variety of activities, both quiet and active.
→ Play materials – appropriate, accessible indoor and outdoor toys.
→ Parental involvement – frequent, constructive contact with carers.

Links

In Day care 1 (pages 24–5) the importance of a secure bond was noted. This will underpin all other aspects of a child's social interactions with others.

Checkpoint 2

Why might increased aggression in this context not be necessarily a bad thing?

Checkpoint 3

The issue of day care should be regarded as only one element amongst many that determine a child's behaviour. What others are involved? (For example, consider reasons why the child is in day care and the impact of long working hours on parents.)

Exam question   answer: page 30

To what extent can day care be said to have beneficial effects on the cognitive and social development of children? (12 min)

Answers
Cognitive and developmental psychology

Models of memory 1

Checkpoints

1 The two-process model is so named because of the model's emphasis on the two processes of encoding and rehearsal.
2 A common way to remember a long telephone number is to make it into three or four more memorable chunks and rehearse it. This avoids overloading the STM and makes transfer to LTM more likely.
3 HM could remember events from before the surgery but all new information could only be held in STM and not transferred to LTM. HM lived in the immediate present and would have to repeatedly be told new information and introduced to the staff caring for him.

Exam questions

1 STM and LTM differ in terms of their encoding, capacity and duration characteristics. Select two of these and illustrate how STM and LTM differ in these aspects of memory. For example, STM memory traces are maintained by *rehearsal* whereas in LTM memories are maintained almost indefinitely. Remember that you are only asked for two of these, and that you are being asked to illustrate the *differences* between STM and LTM.
2 This is a reference to Atkinson and Shiffrin's model that is described on pages 4–5. You should concentrate on the STM and LTM.

Models of memory 2

Checkpoints

1 Baddeley and Hitch's working memory model elaborates on the two-process idea of STM. Craik and Lockhart's model offers an alternative.
2 Structural processing of the word 'dog' would simply involve noting the appearance of the word (i.e. upper/lower case letters). Phonemic processing would involve noting what other words it rhymed with. Semantic processing would involve noting its meaning.

Exam questions

1 You should start with a simple definition ('memory depends on how we *process* information when it comes in'). You should then describe the nature of *shallow* processing and *deep* processing.
2 There are really three criticisms suggested on page 7. These are that the model *describes* rather than *explains*; the model is difficult to test; and it has needed to be modified to fit subsequent research findings.

Forgetting

Checkpoints

1 If you learn two foreign languages, first French and then later German/Spanish etc., both kinds of forgetting are possible. The 'new' German word could be retrieved when you want the French word (retroactive interference) or the 'old' French word could be retrieved when you want the 'new' German word (proactive interference).
2 A good way to remember a mass of written information is to put it into the form of a brain map or flow diagram. This organizes the material but also creates links between chunks of information and encourages deep processing.

Exam question

This is an open invitation for you to choose any *two* explanations of why we forget. You may choose two from STM (e.g. trace decay and displacement) or two from LTM (e.g. interference and retrieval failure) or one from each. You may also choose explanations from the material on pages 10–11.

Emotional factors in forgetting

Checkpoints

1 People often have flashbulb memories of meeting the 'love of their life', or of the birth of a child, or of receiving good news about such events as success in exams.
2 Psychologists have a duty to protect research participants. Inducing negative emotions, especially for prolonged periods of time, may mean that participants experience distress. In addition, it may prove difficult to restore the participants to the mood they were in when they began the study.

Exam question

'Flashbulb memories' are those memories that accompany a particularly significant emotionally arousing event. You might explain the analogy of the 'flashbulb' and mention that for such memories to be formed, both a high level of surprise and a high level of emotional arousal must be present.

The term 'repression' refers to the expulsion from the conscious mind of thoughts and memories that might provoke anxiety (primary repression), and secondary repression, where anything that might remind the individual of what has been repressed is also excluded from conscious thought.

Eyewitness testimony 1

Checkpoints

1 Real-life examples of constructivist memory at work include rumour and gossip, folklore and legends.
2 Important though Bartlett's work was, his test materials bear little resemblance to anything we might encounter in everyday life. In the real world we are more likely to witness complex sequences of events and actions.
3 Most of us can recall school subjects that we enjoyed more easily than those we disliked. Some people have encyclopaedic memories for things such as sporting or historical events.

Exam question

This question requires an evaluative response. You might draw upon the sources of bias in EWT (page 13) or the research findings that challenge the effectiveness of EWT (pages 14–15). Either of these could be used in the construction of either a defence of EWT, or supporting the claims of the quotation used in the question.

Eyewitness testimony 2

Checkpoints

1 To stage a crime such as a hold-up convincingly would necessitate deception of participant witnesses and is likely to cause them distress. It may not be possible to fully debrief people afterwards. We should question whether other, less distressing, ways of presenting such a scene could be found.
2 Corroborative evidence is an important way of ensuring reliability in eyewitness accounts. Corroborative evidence of different kinds is a form of triangulation which, again, should improve the veracity of eyewitness accounts.

Exam question

Your answer should be carefully balanced so that you spend an equal amount of time on each of your chosen research studies. It is well worth looking up each of these studies in your textbook – this active research will help make the information you include more memorable.

You might describe Loftus and Palmer's 'car-crash' study, or Loftus and Zanni's study on the same theme. Alternatively you may, after your own personal research, describe some of the later studies.

Remember, the question only asks for a *description*, so do not waste time evaluating.

The development of attachments

Checkpoints

1 Proximity promoting behaviours that develop with time are social smiles, stranger anxiety, rudimentary language and increasing mobility.
2 Infants' conversations involve eye-contact, movements and vocalizations inserted into interactions with the caregiver and resembling turn-taking in communication.
3 Sweeping generalizations about cultures should be avoided because, as Clarke-Stewart (1988) warns, variations within cultures are greater than between cultures.

Exam questions

1 Your answer will almost certainly concentrate on Ainsworth's 'strange situation' research. This part of the question only gives you six minutes of writing and thinking time, so be prudent about the amount of detail you include when describing the three different types of attachment Ainsworth discovered.
2 This is a beautifully straightforward question that can be answered by using the information at the bottom of page 17. Try to find out more about each of these cultures and studies – it makes the material more interesting and memorable.

Explanations of attachment

Checkpoints

1 Breastfeeding is not critical in attachment formation as long as the feeding situation is a pleasant interactive experience for parent and child. Note that the 'burst-pause' pattern of infant feeding is unique to humans and is especially suited to fostering communication between mother and infant.
2 Caregivers may attend to the infant's signals for attention equally often but some caregivers may be better able to read the infant's signals and so make the quality, pace or intensity of their response more contingent on those signals.

Exam question

A very straightforward question. The question asks for *explanations* of attachment, so you might choose two from: psychodynamic, learning theory and ethological explanations. You do not have the luxury of adding research evidence (this is not required in this question) and do not evaluate here either.

Deprivation and privation 1

Checkpoints

1 Attachments may fail because of factors to do with the infant, the caregiver or both. Premature babies or those with birth defects (e.g. congenital blindness) may not be as responsive as others to the caregiver. Some infants

may be temperamentally difficult and drain the caregiver's coping resources. Some caregivers may lack attachment skills because they had poor attachment experiences when they were young.

2 Older children seem better able to tolerate separation because of their growing cognitive abilities to understand the absence of the attachment figure and hold an image of them in their minds.

3 The lack of an emotional bond with the mother, or with anyone else, would affect their moral development (i.e. ideas of right and wrong). The lack of concern for anyone would result in their having no empathy with any victim of crime. Both of these could make them more likely to commit crimes.

Exam questions

1 These terms are defined on page 20. Use your textbook to read about examples of each so that you can illustrate your answer with them.

2 It is important to select studies that have explored the *long-term* effects of deprivation. You may choose to outline the Goldfarb (1947) and Bowlby (1946) studies, or some other studies that you have read about. You would only have six minutes for this.

Deprivation and privation 2

Checkpoints

1 An obvious difference between human infants and animals that imprint in the true sense is that infants cannot follow the parent at will so attachment depends far more on being able to maintain the proximity of the caregiver in other ways.

2 Children selected for adoption might have been more appealing in particular ways to prospective parents and so different from the outset from children who were not adopted.

Exam question

This is a very open-ended question, and one that invites you to consider all the evidence (explanations, research studies, lessons from research etc.) and come up with some conclusions about whether mothers are as indispensable as the quotation suggests. Whatever material you choose, it should fit into a carefully constructed argument.

Day care 1

Checkpoints

1 Other day care arrangements include day or live-in nannies, au pairs, care by grandparents or other relatives, pre-schools or any mixture of these.

2 Day care facilities are increasingly under the scrutiny of social services. Child-minders and pre-schools are regularly assessed, the latter by Ofsted.

3 The stronger attachment of kibbutz children to their parents may happen because there is higher quality of interaction between them than between the child and its daily caregivers.

Exam question

There are several research studies included in this section. Although the aims and conclusions do not need to be equally weighted you do need to address both in this question. When you have chosen your study, think carefully about what the researchers were trying to find out (the aims) and what conclusions they drew from this study.

Day care 2

Checkpoints

1 If the three groups of children had differed in the quality of attachment they would not have been equivalent at the outset of the study, making it difficult to decide where the differences between them lay.

2 Children in day care may well have to compete more with other children for attention and/or playthings. Aggression in this context could be an adaptive way of protecting oneself!

3 Children may differ temperamentally and so adapt to day care with different degrees of success. Children may be in day care because of financial pressures on the parents to work. Parents (and children), exhausted from long hours, may not interact with each other or may be irritable when together.

Exam question

This is an evaluative question. As it asks 'to what extent . . .' this should be in your mind as you construct your answer. There is research evidence on pages 26–7 that examines research evidence on the *impact* of day care. It is for you to use this evidence. Show that you have *thought* about the material available.

This section concentrates on the study of stress and the study of abnormality. The study of stress is of great importance, not just because it is a key part of the specifications for all examination boards, but also because it has such a potentially devastating effect on our health. As well as looking at the sources of stress and its effects on our health, we will also review some of the major techniques of stress management.

The concept of abnormality is one that divides psychology and psychologists. We will examine the major models of abnormality, and the critical issue of eating disorders.

Exam themes

→ The nature and effects of stress

→ Stress management

→ Defining abnormality

→ Models of abnormality

→ Eating disorders

Topic checklist

○ AS ● A2	AQA/A	AQA/B	OCR	EDEXCEL
Stress as a bodily response	○	○●	●	●
Stress and illness	○	●	●	●
Sources of stress	○	●	●	●
Individual differences in stress	○	●	●	●
Stress management 1	○	●	●	●
Stress management 2	○	●	●	●
Definitions of abnormality	○	●	○	●
Problems with defining abnormality	○	●	○	●
Models of abnormality 1	○	●	○	●
Models of abnormality 2	○	●	○	●
Eating disorders 1	○	●		●
Eating disorders 2	○	●		●

Stress as a bodily response

The beginning of stress research is normally attributed to Hans Selye in the 1930s. Selye believed that the body reacts to psychological and physical stressors with the same pattern of physiological activation (the general adaptation syndrome). Although this response is an adaptive one, in some circumstances it can lead to illness and disease.

What is stress?

The term 'stress' has a number of meanings.

→ As a *response*, it may be seen as a physiological reaction to something in the environment.
→ As a *stimulus*, it can refer to those aspects of our environment that are considered stressful (usually known as *stressors*).
→ The *transactional* definition sees stress as an imbalance between our perceptions of the stressful nature of our world and our ability to deal with those demands.

The role of the adrenal gland

The adrenal cortex
The adrenal cortex is under the control of the *pituitary gland*, which in turn is under the control of the hypothalamus. The pituitary releases ACTH into the bloodstream. This travels to the adrenal cortex and stimulates the release of hormones known as *corticosteroids*. These have a range of effects on different parts of the body. This is known as the *hypothalamic-pituitary axis*.

The adrenal medulla
The adrenal medulla is controlled by the *autonomic nervous system* (ANS). The autonomic nervous system has two divisions, the *sympathetic nervous system* and the *parasympathetic nervous system*.

→ When the sympathetic division dominates, the body is in a state of arousal.
→ Parasympathetic dominance produces the opposite effect, with heart rate and blood pressure returning to normal; a state of bodily relaxation.

Stimulation by the sympathetic division of the ANS causes the adrenal medulla to release the hormones adrenaline and noradrenaline into the bloodstream. These stimulate heart rate and blood pressure and mobilize energy reserves.

This and the hypothalamic-pituitary axis are the main components of the body's response to stressors. Corticosteroids, adrenaline and noradrenaline mobilize our energy reserves, sustaining heart rate and blood flow in order to get oxygen to the muscles. This pattern of bodily arousal is generally referred to as the 'fight or flight' response.

Watch out!

Stress has many meanings.

Example

Although exams are generally perceived as stressful, you can decrease your levels of stress by increasing your perception of your ability to cope (i.e. better study skills).

The jargon

ACTH = *adrenocorticotrophic hormone*

Test yourself

After reading about the role of the adrenal cortex and the adrenal medulla, close this book and make a list of bullet points that describe the different stages in the stress response.

Checkpoint 1

What do you think is the *adaptive* value of the stress response?

The general adaptation syndrome (GAS) ●●●

Selye (1956) proposed the general adaptation syndrome as a way of explaining the short-term effects of stressors on the body. The GAS model can also account for the development of some stress-related illnesses such as gastric ulcers.

The GAS has three stages:

Alarm

The presence of a stressful event is registered and the body goes into a state of shock. Body temperature and blood pressure are lowered. In the latter part of this stage the body initiates the arousal response.

Resistance

The physiological systems in the body try to maintain normal functioning; body temperature and blood pressure return to normal.

Exhaustion

If the stress is intense or prolonged, the demands made are too great for the body to deal with and the characteristics of the first stage reappear. The body is no longer able to deal with them, and physiological symptoms such as gastric ulcers start to appear.

Evaluation of the general adaptation syndrome ●●●

→ The GAS has been extremely useful in explaining the relationship between exposure to stressors and physical illness. Many illnesses can be viewed as the result of the body's prolonged exposure to a perceived threatening stressor.
→ Because Seyle's work was focused on reactions to physical stressors among animals, it failed to acknowledge the importance of *psychological* aspects of stress in human beings (such as the cognitive appraisal of the stressful situation).
→ Patients with the same illnesses or injuries do not all react by developing stress-related disorders; there are individual differences (e.g. personality differences, gender differences and cultural differences).
→ Among those people who do develop stress-related disorders, some develop heart disease, some gastric ulcers and some asthma. Although the same bodily arousal systems are involved, the precise way that these lead to illness must involve other physiological or psychological processes.

Action point

Think about the adaptive evolutionary advantages of the body's response to stressors (e.g. fight or flight response).

Don't forget

It is at the exhaustion stage that the body becomes susceptible to stress-related illness.

Checkpoint 2

In what other ways might the value of this work be affected by the use of non-human animals?

Links

Individual differences in stress (pages 38–9).

Links

Stress and illness (pages 34–5).

Exam question   answer: page 56

Describe the main ways in which the body responds to stress. (12 min)

Stress and illness

When Seyle developed his general adaptation syndrome, he believed that the constant production of stress hormones eventually led to their exhaustion. It was this exhaustion of essential hormones that led to stress-related illness. This view has changed, as it is now the action of these hormones that is held responsible for the negative effects of stressful situations.

Action point

Psychosomatic disorders are now more commonly known as 'psychophysiological disorders'.

Checkpoint 1

Why is physical exercise so good as a stress buster?

Psychosomatic illness

This refers to physical symptoms that are not produced through physical damage or infection, but through more psychological processes such as fear and anxiety. Chronic stress may contribute to the development of illness *indirectly* by damaging the body in such a way that psychosomatic illnesses are more likely to develop.

Stress can damage the body in different ways (Green 2000).

Direct mechanical effects

The body's stress response increases heart rate, pumping blood around the body faster and at higher pressure. This increased mechanical pressure may lead to increased damage and a shorter life. Scarring of the blood vessels acts as a 'collection point' for fatty acids in the bloodstream, and may lead to the formation of plaques which slowly block the blood vessel – a process known as *atherosclerosis*.

Energy mobilization

The bodily response to stress evolved because of its adaptive advantages (the fight or flight response). With most contemporary stressors, however, physical activity is rarely the appropriate coping response. As part of the stress response, corticosteroids, adrenaline and noradrenaline release stored carbohydrates and fats into the bloodstream. When the stressful situation passes, these are reabsorbed. If the stress is prolonged, reabsorption cannot cope and these remain in the bloodstream, where they fur up the cardiovascular system. This can lead to raised blood pressure (hypertension) and atherosclerosis.

Checkpoint 2

Make a list of some of the different ways in which stress might damage the body.

Suppression of the immune system

The immune system protects the body from infection by harmful viruses and bacteria (the immune response), and helps in the repair of tissue damage. Short-term stress leads to the suppression of the immune system (through the action of corticosteroids released by the adrenal cortex), as all resources are diverted in order to deal with the stressful situation. Corticosteroids stop the production of lymphocytes (white blood cells) which destroy infectious agents. Short-term suppression of the immune system is not dangerous, but long-term suppression may leave the body vulnerable to infection and disease. The immune system is a self-regulating system, so it will recover from suppression when the stressful situation is resolved.

The jargon

The *immune response* is the reaction of the body to the introduction of harmful toxins.

Research evidence ●●●

Research evidence for the relationship between stress and illness has come from different types of study. These tend to be correlational, where scores on life-events scales are correlated with illness. The main problem with this approach is that cause-effect relationships between the two cannot be identified. In experimental studies this is possible.

Kiecolt-Glaser (1984)

Kiecolt-Glaser believed that although many people exposed to prolonged stress may not display obvious illness, they may have lowered immune functions (known as *immunosuppression*) caused by stress, which would make them more vulnerable to illness.

She measured the activity of the immune system from blood samples taken from volunteers. This enabled her to compare immune function in groups believed to be under chronic stress with control groups. Results showed significant immunosuppression in the groups under chronic stress. These included:

→ unhappily married women
→ long-term carers for Alzheimers patients
→ students taking examinations.

In recent studies Kiecolt-Glaser (1998) has found decreases in immune system functioning in couples undergoing episodes of marital conflict.

Cohen et al (1993)

Using men and women volunteers, Cohen et al measured their level of stress in three ways:

→ a scale measuring life events in the previous year
→ a perceived stress scale indicating the level of stress the person believed themselves to be under
→ a negative-effect scale measuring their levels of, for example, anxiety, fear, depression and irritation.

The scores on these three scales were combined to produce a measure of overall psychological stress (the psychological stress index) for each person. The researchers then exposed these volunteers to respiratory viruses (e.g. the cold virus) and measured whether associated infections developed. Participants high on the stress index were more likely to develop the respiratory infections. This study is particularly important because it demonstrates a cause and effect relationship between stress and illness.

Watch out!

Correlational studies cannot tell us anything about cause and effect.

Links

Quantitative methods (see pages 72–3).

The jargon

Immunosuppression – the partial or complete suppression of the immune response of an individual.

Checkpoint 3

What do you think these groups have in common that makes them so vulnerable to the adverse effects of stress?

Action point

You should not try to replicate this study at home!

Examiner's secrets

Questions such as this require a précis of the studies rather than a full description.

Exam question   answer: page 56

Outline research that has explored the relationship between stress and illness. (6 min)

Sources of stress

The sources of stress lie primarily in what individuals perceive as stressful, therefore there are considerable individual differences in the sources of stress. Whether certain things are considered 'stressful' depends on our coping abilities. However, there are some situations that are consistently seen as stressful – we shall review them here.

Stress and life events ●●●

These are events that necessitate a significant transition or adjustment in various aspects of a person's life. This classification would include events such as widowhood, divorce, retirement etc. Research into the effects of life events has attempted to explain the development of stress and stress-related disorders (such as depression) in terms of exposure to these 'critical' life events.

The Social Readjustment Rating Scale (SRRS) (Holmes and Rahe 1967)

In this scale, respondents indicate those events that they have experienced in the previous 24 months. Each event is given a score determined by its potential stress for the person. As a guide, marriage is given a score of 50 and death of a spouse the highest score at 100. By totalling up the scores, Holmes and Rahe were able to construct an index of the recent life stress of their respondents. They used the scale *retrospectively* (using people who already had stress-related illnesses) and *prospectively* (assessing life stress and following respondents over the next eighteen months). They found that the higher the score the more likely that the person would develop, or had developed, stress-related illness.

Evaluation of the SRRS

→ The stressful nature of specific events varies from person to person. Certain events are stressful for some but not for others.

→ Some life events are undoubtedly positive (marriage is presumably one of them) yet the model does not distinguish between positive and negative life events, seeing them all as potentially stressful.

→ Studies that have tested the reliability of self-reports of life events have found that agreement between reports from the same person declines significantly over time. Reports may also be affected by the attributional style of the individual. Those who see illnesses such as heart disease and cancer as purely medical problems may under-report the incidence of life events in the previous 24 months. Others may habitually associate illness with psychological stressors, therefore may over-report such events.

→ The relationship between SRRS scores and illness is only correlational, not causal. We do not know whether the life events (such as divorce) led to illness (such as depression), or were caused by it.

Action point

A 'life events' model of stress sees our life punctuated by events that present us with major transitional challenges.

Watch out!

There are major variations in the impact of these life events for different people. For some people the death of a dog may have a profound effect.

Action point

Marriage is the baseline by which the potential impact of other events is judged.

The jargon

Attributional style – an individual's style of assigning causal explanations to the good and bad things that happen to them.

Checkpoint 1

How might life disorders such as depression *cause* the life event in question?

Workplace stress ●●●

Stress in the workplace can affect psychological and physical health.
The type of workplace stress depends very much on the type of job,
but there are some sources of stress that apply to most work situations
(Green 2000):

→ relations with co-workers (workmates, subordinates and superiors)
→ the physical work environment (space, lighting, office layout etc.)
→ career progression (or lack of it)
→ workload (including long hours and ability to cope)
→ job insecurity (long-term security is difficult to find)
→ lack of control (work patterns may be determined by others).

These sources of stress may affect not only the workers themselves,
but also the organization they work for. The physical and psychological
consequences of stress may cause increases in absenteeism and
decreases in motivation and productivity.

Research evidence (Johansson et al 1978)

These researchers investigated employees in a Swedish timber mill.
One type of worker was highlighted as being especially vulnerable to
stress – the 'finishers' who were the workers at the end of the assembly
line responsible for the final stages of the timber preparation process.
The rate at which these individuals completed their part of the job
determined the overall productivity of the sawmill, and therefore
everyone else's wages. The job was also repetitive and, being part
of an assembly line, the work was machine-paced.

Johansson et al measured levels of stress hormones during work
days *and* rest days, as well as looking at other measures such as
sickness and absenteeism. This is what they found:

→ these workers had raised levels of stress hormones on work days
→ they had a higher incidence of stress-related health problems
→ there was a higher rate of absenteeism for this group than a control
   group of workers from other jobs in the sawmill.

The researchers concluded that the work environment of these workers
was particularly stressful because:

→ they were responsible for the wages of the whole factory
→ their work was highly skilled but boring and repetitive
→ the work was machine-paced, therefore they lacked control over
   their work environment
→ they worked in social isolation.

Action point

Make a note of what aspects of your
school, college, or workplace you find
most stressful.

Check the net

www.stress.org.uk/
This site is full of useful information
about the occupational effects of stress.

Example

Many aspects of modern production-line
work are organized in this way and
therefore impose similar levels of
occupational stress.

Examiner's secrets

When describing studies, it is better
to concentrate more on their findings
than on their procedures.

Exam question   answer: page 56

Outline the findings and conclusions of one research study that has explored
the sources of workplace stress. (6 min)

Individual differences in stress

Don't forget

Some people don't experience much stress because they perceive stressful situations as *challenges* to be overcome.

Action point

Find out more about chronic heart disease.

Check the net

Take an online personality test to see if you display Type A behaviour at: www.queendom.com/tests/eng/typea_frm.html

Action point

Summarize, in your own words, the relationship between Type A behaviour and coronary heart disease.

It is generally believed that stress is bad for us. However, we have seen previously that there are wide variations in the way different people *perceive* stressful situations, as well as differences in the way they are affected by them.

Personality – Type A behaviour

Friedman and Rosenman (1974) studied the behaviour of patients who were suffering from coronary heart disease (CHD) and discovered that they displayed a particular type of behaviour pattern, characterized by:

→ constantly being under time-pressure
→ being intensely competitive at work and in social situations
→ being easily frustrated by the efforts of others.

They called this pattern of behaviour the 'Type A' behaviour pattern. A number of studies have investigated the link between Type A behaviour and coronary heart disease. Significant correlations *have* been found, but these tend not to be very high. Some studies have also reported *negative* findings, with people displaying the Type A behaviour pattern being *less* vulnerable to stress.

Mediating factors in the Type A and CHD relationship

→ Individuals high in *hostility* combined with Type A behaviour are more vulnerable to CHD than Type A behaviour alone.
→ Correlations between Type A and CHD are higher when hostility is *repressed* rather than *expressed* (Matthews and Haynes 1986).

Evaluation of the relationship between Type A and CHD

Although individuals displaying Type A behaviour appear to be more at risk from coronary heart disease (particularly when combined with hostility), they often survive without significant signs of illness. There are a number of reasons why they appear able to manage their stress even when their behaviour appears destined for stress-related illness.

→ A key aspect of our experience of stress and our ability to manage it is our sense of *control*. Type A individuals typically believe nobody else can do the job as well – i.e. they have a strong sense of control.
→ Other factors such as physical exercise and social support are effective buffers against the negative effects of stress – these may help minimize the harmful effects of stress for the Type A individual.

Gender

Although social, familial and occupational roles may differ somewhat for males and females, there is no evidence that there is a gender difference in the levels of stress that each experience. There is, however, evidence that the genders react differently to stressful situations.

Research evidence for gender differences in reaction to stress

Frankenhauser et al (1976) measured levels of stress hormones in boys and girls who were taking an examination. Boys showed a more rapid increase in levels of hormone, and these took longer to return to normal after the examination. Girls' levels of stress hormones increased more slowly, and in smaller increments, and returned to normal more quickly. The reported levels of subjective stress were the same for both males and females. This finding has been confirmed in other studies. Possible explanations for this difference include (Green 2000):

→ the hypothalamic-pituitary and ANS pathways are more reactive in males than in females
→ males and females vary in their attitude to examinations. This *psychological* difference may then influence the stress response.

If, as research suggests, males show more stress-related physiological arousal than females, then does this mean that males are more vulnerable to stress-related illness? Two effective buffers against the negative effects of stress are *exercise* and *social support*. There may well be gender differences in the *type* of buffer used by the two sexes, but both of these serve to make predictions about who will develop stress-related illness more problematic. Frankenhauser was more confident – females live longer because they experience less stress-related arousal.

Culture ●●●

Stress is found in all cultures. The *sources* of stress, on the other hand, may be different depending on the nature of the culture. As we have already seen, stress is experienced when the perceived demands on an individual are greater than their perceived ability to cope (the *transactional model* of stress).

Social support appears to be a very important factor that protects people against the negative effects of stress. Kim and McKenry (1998) found strong cultural differences in the degree to which members of different cultures relied on family or other close relationships (such as the church) for social support.

It is difficult to disentangle the effects of stress from other factors that may prolong or shorten life. Weg (1983) in a study of the Abkarsian people of Georgia found that their longevity (4 in 1 000 live to over 100) could be explained by a combination of factors including genetic inheritance, high levels of social support, physically active lifestyles, no alcohol or smoking and low reported stress levels.

The jargon

Reactive – the stress response in these individuals is more easily activated by events around them.

Checkpoint 1

Why is this conclusion a speculative one?

Checkpoint 2

In what ways might other people *lower* our levels of stress?

Examiner's secrets

Remember that when asked to explain *two* things in a question, you must balance the amount of time you spend on each.

Exam question   answer: page 56

Explain *two* types of individual differences that might modify the effects of stress. (12 min)

Stress management 1

Don't forget

This is an important distinction and will be reflected in exam questions.

The jargon

Beta blocker is a drug that prevents the stimulation of increased cardiac action.

Checkpoint 1

This technique works on an important psychological principle. Try to find out what this is.

Check the net

For advice on understanding, recognizing and managing stress:
www.mindtools.com/smpage.html

Action point

Relaxation techniques can be very useful ways of lowering your stress levels.

The potentially harmful effects of stress means that effective techniques for stress management are essential. Some techniques are physical (such as the use of drugs) whilst others are psychological (such as meditation).

Physical approaches

Drugs

Commonly used drugs that are used to combat stress are:

→ Benzodiazepine (BZ) anti-anxiety drugs such as Librium and Valium. These drugs work by reducing the activity of the neurotransmitter *serotonin*. This has an inhibitory effect on the brain producing muscle relaxation and an overall calming effect.
→ Beta-blockers such as Inderal. These drugs work by reducing activity in the pathways of the sympathetic nervous system, and, therefore, are effective against raised heart rate and blood pressure.

Biofeedback

This is a technique for controlling physiological responses by receiving information about the body's stress response as it occurs. Monitoring devices track physiological responses such as heart rate and blood pressure. These provide the person with feedback in the form of a light or audible tone whenever they change the response in the desired direction. The aim of this technique is to find a strategy to reduce a particular stress-related response (such as increased heart rate) which can then be transferred to the outside world and used regularly to relieve stress.

Psychological approaches

Psychological approaches to stress can either be *general* such as using relaxation techniques or meditation to reduce the body's state of arousal, or *specific*, using cognitive and behavioural training.

Relaxation techniques

Progressive muscle relaxation is an active approach to reducing bodily arousal. In a typical relaxation session a client would be trained to progressively tense and relax muscles, working up the body from the legs to the facial muscles. Eventually the person can use the technique as a way of reducing bodily arousal. During the relaxation state, stress response mechanisms are inactive and the parasympathetic nervous system is dominant (see Stress as a bodily response, page 32).

Meditation

This technique is similar to relaxation in that the aim of the technique is to reduce bodily arousal and achieve a state of inner calm. During meditation, a person is trained to repeat their mantra (a sound or single word) while breathing deeply and regularly. By doing this, the person is able to rid their mind of the arousing thoughts that activate the body's stress response system.

Meichenbaum's stress-inoculation training

This technique has three phases.

→ *Conceptualization* – the cognitive element, in which the client is encouraged to relive stressful situations, analyzing what was stressful about them and how they attempted to deal with them.
→ *Skills training and practice* – the client is taught a variety of techniques (e.g. relaxation, social skills, time management) in the therapeutic setting.
→ *Real-life application* – following training, the client can put what they have learned into practice in the real world. Reinforcement of techniques learned in therapy makes the practices self-sustaining.

Hardiness (Kobasa and Maddi 1977)

The concept of 'hardiness' is taken to mean resistance to illness, or ability to deal with stress. From studies of highly stressed executives, Kobasa et al were able to identify the characteristics of those who handled stress well from those who did not. Those who reported the fewest illnesses showed three kinds of hardiness.

→ They showed an openness to change, i.e. life changes are seen as *challenges* to be overcome rather than threats or stressors.
→ They had experienced a feeling of involvement or *commitment* to their job, and a sense of purpose in their activities.
→ They experienced a sense of *control* over their lives, rather than seeing their life controlled by outside influences.

Kobasa found that the most important of these factors was the first, openness to change. Those who perceived change (such as the loss of a job) as a challenge rather than a devastatingly personal event, were more likely to interpret the event positively and show fewer signs of stress. Kobasa proposed three ways in which hardiness could be improved.

→ *Focusing* – the client is trained to recognize stressful situations and therefore to identify the sources of stress.
→ *Reliving stressful encounters* – the client analyzes past coping and realizes their techniques are more effective than they thought.
→ *Self-improvement* – a central aspect of hardiness is that we *can* cope with life's challenges. Clients are encouraged to take on challenges that they *can* cope with, thus reinforcing feelings of *control*.

Action point

The same psychological principle underlies this final aspect of stress-inoculation as underlies biofeedback.

Watch out!

Kobasa's original studies were of highly stressed executives. This may not generalize easily to other occupational groups.

Checkpoint 2

What other factors might determine whether these stress management techniques are effective?

Watch out!

This question makes a clear distinction between physical (such as drugs) and psychological (such as relaxation) approaches. Your answer must do the same.

Exam question   answer: page 56

Outline *one* physical and *one* psychological approach to stress management. (12 min)

Stress management 2

While it is clear that some attempt at stress management is better than no attempt at all, it is also clear that the techniques described on the previous pages are not without their problems. The effectiveness of a particular technique is also determined by a range of other factors.

Evaluation of physical approaches ●●●

Problems with the use of drugs

→ Long-term use of BZs can lead to physical and psychological dependency, therefore should only be used for short periods.
→ All drugs have side-effects. BZs can cause drowsiness and adversely affect memory (Green 2000).
→ Drugs treat the symptoms of stress not the causes. Most stressors are psychological, therefore physical measures do not address the real cause of the problem.

Limitations of biofeedback techniques

→ It is claimed that biofeedback techniques can have significant positive effects in the reduction of generalized anxiety disorders. The use of this technique and the related efforts to reduce heart rate in sufferers of anxiety disorders has had only limited success.
→ Biofeedback may be no more effective than muscle relaxation in the absence of biofeedback. This is a critical issue as biofeedback can be expensive as a technique.
→ This technique may be more effective with children who treat it more as a game and are more optimistic about its effects (Attanasio et al 1985).

Evaluation of psychological approaches ●●●

Relaxation

→ It is fairly easy to practice relaxation, even in unusual situations. These techniques may also involve cognitive strategies that help reduce arousal in unpleasantly arousing circumstances.
→ Although relaxation techniques can be useful by reducing the levels of stress response, their action is non-specific. Effective long-term stress reduction requires focused intervention on the source of the stress.

Meditation

→ Meditation has the advantage of 'portability' and may give individuals more confidence to deal with stressful situations (Green 2000).
→ As with relaxation techniques, the action of meditation techniques is non-specific rather than focused on effective intervention at source.

Examiner's secrets

Exam questions invite more than a list of bullet points when evaluating specific techniques. Make sure you can elaborate on each of these points – why are each of them so important?

Checkpoint 1

In what ways are progressive muscle relaxation and biofeedback techniques similar?

Don't forget

Relaxation techniques could be useful in exam settings and when stuck in traffic jams, but should not be practised while actually driving!

Evaluation of Meichenbaum's stress-inoculation training

→ Meichenbaum's model focuses on both the nature of the stress problem (enabling clients to more realistically appraise their life) and the ways of coping with stress (giving clients more under-standing of the strengths and limitations of specific techniques).

→ The combination of *cognitive* strategies and *behavioural* techniques makes stress-inoculation a potentially effective way of managing stress. Despite this potential, few controlled studies have confirmed its predictions.

Evaluation of hardiness

→ The relative importance of the three aspects of hardiness (control, commitment and challenge) is uncertain, although it is likely that control is the most significant of these.

→ Kobasa's studies have tended to involve middle-class businessmen – results cannot reliably be generalized to other social and cultural groups.

Effectiveness – the importance of other factors ●●●

→ *Previous experience* – once we have experienced a particular stressful situation, we are usually able to cope better with it if it reoccurs. The experience provides us with knowledge about the situation and makes it more predictable.

→ *Individual differences* – some people try to protect themselves from the full impact of the stress by denying, playing down, or emotion-ally detaching themselves from the situation. Providing information to these people may actually increase their stress levels, rather than decreasing them.

→ *Social support* – the impact of stressful events is affected by our social systems. Response to stress can be eased by support from either the family or the community. For example, studies have shown that women who have close, confiding relationships are less likely to develop stress-related psychiatric disorders.

→ *Control* – the degree to which we believe we can control a situation has an important impact on the degree to which that situation is likely to cause us stress. The most harmful and distressing situations are those in which we feel entirely helpless, believing that nothing we can do will alter the outcome.

Action point

It is important to note that different techniques are supported by scientifically controlled studies – the absence of these weakens the value of a particular technique.

Checkpoint 2

In what situations are we most likely to feel 'entirely helpless' and therefore more likely to experience stress?

Exam question   answer: page 56

'Physical approaches to stress management are ineffective given the fact that the source of our stress is inevitably psychological.'
To what extent is this statement a fair reflection of the role of physical approaches in the management of stress? (12 min)

Watch out!

Questions such as this require a more thoughtful, considered response rather than a list of points for and against.

Definitions of abnormality

How do we decide that somebody has a mental disorder? There are currently a number of different approaches to abnormality which manage to co-exist. The model to which a psychologist subscribes has an important part to play in both the explanation and treatment of a mental disorder.

Deviation from statistical norms

Many human characteristics fall into a frequency pattern known as a normal distribution (see graph below). In a normal distribution, scores cluster around the central point or mean. The further away from this point a score is, the rarer it is. If we could measure the characteristic in question, e.g. frequency of hand-washing, most people would be placed in the middle section of this distribution and very few at the extremes. Statistically, then, abnormality is defined as those behaviours or personality traits that are extremely rare. For the statistical model to be useful we must be able to:

→ measure the behaviour in question on a continuum
→ establish norms against which comparisons can be made
→ decide on cut-off values for abnormality at both ends of the scale.

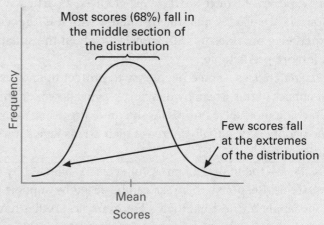

The normal distribution curve

Eysenck's (1975) personality inventory measures extraversion and neuroticism and is based on the assumption that scores on these are normally distributed. Extreme scores can be considered abnormal. Eysenck proposed that psychopaths score high on both while neurotics score low on extraversion and high on neuroticism.

Watch out!

Eysenck also proposed a third dimension called psychoticism. This is a special case as it yields a skewed distribution whereby most people score low and only a few score high.

Deviation from social norms

In this view, abnormal behaviour is not a large deviation from a statistical norm but from a social one. Social norms are implicit rules about how one 'ought' to behave and anything that violates these is abnormal. Having a child when unmarried, for example, is not statistically rare, but acceptance in the current climate is not total because some may see it as immoral or undesirable. This model overcomes the problem of desirable extremes which dog the statistical model since it is implicit

Checkpoint 1

Think up one example of:
→ behaviour that is acceptable in one culture but not in another
→ behaviour that was once unacceptable but is now acceptable.

that normal is desirable and deviation is wrong or undesirable. It allows for value judgements where the statistical model does not.

Failure to function adequately

In judging our own or someone else's mental state we often use practical criteria of adequate functioning and see mentally healthy people as being able to operate within certain acceptable limits. This model is the one most lay-people and some mental health professionals use in the initial stages of judging abnormality. Sue, Sue and Sue (1994) suggest that the presence of one or more of the following may impair our ability to function adequately:

→ *Discomfort* – this can be psychological (e.g. depressed mood) or physiological (e.g. fatigue) or both and may be intense, prolonged or exaggerated.

→ *Bizarreness* – vivid or unusual behaviour or experiences that grab the attention, e.g. hallucinations, delusions, inappropriate exposure of the body.

→ *Inefficiency* – difficulty in adequately fulfilling one's everyday duties and roles and/or failure to reach one's potential.

Rosenhan and Seligman (1984) also suggest that we tend to see behaviour that is *unpredictable* and *incomprehensible* as abnormal.

Deviation from ideal mental health

This approach takes us one step further than the failure to function adequately model and asks what characteristics mentally healthy people possess. Abnormality, then, is judged as deviating from this ideal picture. Atkinson et al (1993) say a healthy person has:

→ efficient perception of self and reality
→ self-esteem and acceptance
→ voluntary control over own behaviour
→ ability to form affectionate relationships
→ ability to be productive.

Humanistic psychologists such as Rogers (1902–1987) go on to suggest that mentally healthy people can strive for personal growth, achievement of potential and eventual **self actualization**. In this view, abnormal people not only fail to function positively but also fail to grow psychologically.

Watch out!

Discomfort may also be caused to others.

Checkpoint 2

Try to come up with your own list of what a mentally healthy person is like. Compare your list with attributes identified by others in the text.

Exam question   answer: page 57

Outline *two* ways of defining abnormality. (12 min)

Problems with defining abnormality

The decision to seek help for abnormality is rarely a straightforward matter. As we saw in Definitions of abnormality, psychologists have proposed a number of approaches but there are pitfalls with all of them. Added to this, abnormal conditions vary greatly in nature, intensity and duration, making definition problematic.

Checkpoint 1

Who actually defines a person as in need of help?

Deviation from statistical norms

The statistical model, which views abnormality as statistically rare behaviour or personality traits, can be a useful objective measure but it has problems with:

→ determining the cut-off points between normal and abnormal
→ explaining the origins of abnormalities and so making recommendations for treatment
→ specifying which behaviours should be considered, e.g. exceptional musical ability is rare but not considered to be aberrant in the same way as exceptional aggression or activity
→ the universality of some abnormal conditions, such as depression, which means that they do not fit the criterion of rarity
→ taking into account the influence of time, place or culture.

Watch out!

Some symptoms of mental disorder seem to be culturally universal but the way they are regarded and dealt with may differ.

Deviation from social norms

Some of the problems of the statistical model can be overcome by adopting the deviation from social norms definition. This model is often a useful starting point from which lay-people might consider seeking professional help with a problem, however:

→ on its own it is rather weak, although it can be used alongside other models to help build a complete clinical picture of an individual case. (The same is also true of the statistical model.)
→ social norms are not static but are affected by time, place and the dominant culture.

Checkpoint 2

Think of an example of behaviour that is not necessarily statistically rare but that violates social norms.

Failure to function adequately

The judgement that a person is unable to function within certain acceptable limits is intuitively appealing and this model provides a starting point for mental health professionals, however:

→ notions of adequate functioning are affected by time, place and culture.

Example

Context matters in judging adequacy of functioning. What is considered adequate is very different during war or after an earthquake compared with other times.

Deviation from ideal mental health

Models that see abnormality as deviating from an ideal of positive mental health provide a refreshing change from approaches that emphasize the negative, however:

→ by these definitions too many people are excluded
→ they assume that it is possible to assess potential – something which is notoriously difficult to do
→ the 'ideal' is not static but is affected by time, place and culture.

Cultural considerations

All of the approaches described so far share one key problem, that is, how to take account of the undeniable influence of culture in defining abnormality. Berry et al (1992) noted that abnormal conditions can be:

→ absolute (same nature and incidence in all cultures)
→ universal (found everywhere but with varying frequency)
→ relative (unique and meaningful only to certain cultures).

Culturally absolute conditions may or may not be organically caused. The others, especially culturally relative disorders, call into question the role of sociocultural factors in determining abnormality. These highlight how culturally set norms or ideals not only lack objectivity but also should not be applied universally.

Culture bound syndromes (CBSs)

Some conditions seem to appear only in particular cultures. They are recognized as illnesses but do not fit any recognized Western category. These are examples of culture bound syndromes. An example is *koro*, a condition observed in South East Asian cultures in which the sufferer fears fatal retraction of the genitals into the abdomen. Simons (1985) however, disputes that *koro* is a CBS. Similar sensations of genital shrinkage are experienced in other cultures but labelled differently. Simons believes they are triggered by different cultural stresses.

Subcultural issues

Within cultures there may be sub-groups or 'subcultures' e.g. those defined by race, class or gender.

→ *Gender* – women receive more diagnoses than men of anxiety and depression and much more attention has been paid to PMS than to the role of males' hormones in mental health (Sampson 1993).
→ *Race* – in the UK, Cochrane (1977) noted higher rates of diagnosis of schizophrenia in African Caribbean immigrants than in whites.
→ *Social class* – Hollingshead and Redlich (1958) showed that members of lower socioeconomic classes in the USA appear more in state mental hospitals than middle-class people.

Differences in diagnosis rates within these subcultures could indicate real differences, or that the dominant cultural group is failing to recognize the possibility that it might be biased.

Action point

Write your own definitions of culturally absolute, relative or universal abnormality.

Links

To refresh your memory, see Definitions of abnormality (pages 44–5) as well as the criticisms in this section.

Watch out!

Don't confuse this with fatal attraction!

Checkpoint 3

Could *anorexia nervosa* be considered to be culturally relative?

Exam question   answer: page 57

'Problems of defining abnormality means that we can never be confident that what we are experiencing is truly "abnormal".'
To what extent is this statement a fair reflection of the problems faced in defining abnormality? (12 min)

Models of abnormality 1

The jargon

Remember that *somatic* or *biomedical* are sometimes used in place of medical.

Watch out!

'Systemic' means 'to do with a system'. Do not make the mistake of using the word 'systematic'.

Checkpoint 1

Name another mental illness in which neurochemical factors have been implicated.

Watch out!

These causes need not be mutually exclusive.

Links

See Biological therapies (pages 156–7).

Psychologists draw on a number of different ways of explaining abnormality and ideas about causes will influence how it is dealt with. Here we look at two contrasting explanations: the biological (medical) model and the behavioural model.

Assumptions of the biological model

The biological model of abnormality proposes that psychological disorders have underlying biological or biochemical causes.

Psychological disorders are referred to as mental illnesses. These are thought to arise from one of four main causes.

→ *Infection* by germs or viruses leading to a cluster of symptoms or a syndrome. Early work on general paresis established that this condition was brought about by untreated syphilis infection.

→ *Inherited systemic defect*   A number of mental disorders run in families and may be transmitted down the generations. It is possible that schizophrenia results, at least partly, from an inherited dysfunction of the nervous system.

→ *Neurochemical factors*   Some disorders may be caused by the action of neurochemicals in the brain. Schizophrenics, for example, show a characteristically high level of dopamine (a brain neurotransmitter). Treatment of schizophrenia normally involves using drugs that block the action of dopamine, thus limiting the symptoms of the disorder.

→ *Effects of trauma*   Trauma can be physical (e.g. brain damage or poisoning) or psychological (e.g. bereavement, rape). Korsakov's syndrome is an alcohol-related condition that can lead to memory disturbances, confusion and apathy. Bereavement is closely linked to depression.

Evaluation of the biological model

→ The biological approach has led to relatively humane and effective treatment of the mentally ill with some astounding successes.

→ Its scientific status, and its links with medicine, give it popularity and credibility.

→ Anti-psychiatrists such as Szasz, Laing and Goffman have argued that labelling people as 'ill' allows society to see them as scapegoats, remove them from mainstream life and treat them accordingly.

→ This approach tends to use classification systems such as DSM and ICD, which have inherent problems of reliability and validity.

→ Armed with the disease analogy, a classification system and a whole battery of treatments, there is a danger of over-diagnosis of mental illness.

Implications for treatment

Disorders with biological causes can be treated by biological means.

Assumptions of the behavioural model ●●●

The behavioural model of abnormality makes two major assumptions:

→ all behaviour is the product of learning even if it is maladaptive
→ what has been learned can be unlearned.

It follows that symptoms (abnormal behaviour patterns) are the whole problem. There is no need to look for deeper causes. Abnormal behaviour is mainly attributed to the following types of learning.

Classical conditioning

In the classical conditioning process, a neutral stimulus is paired with one that naturally evokes anxiety and thus also becomes capable of eliciting anxiety. The classic case of eleven-month-old Little Albert (Watson and Rayner 1920) demonstrated how fear of a white rat could be conditioned by pairing its presentation with a startling noise.

Operant conditioning

Operant conditioning models emphasize the role of reinforcement, punishment and extinction in shaping and maintaining behaviour. Behaviours that have pleasant consequences are more likely to be repeated than those that do not, e.g. a person who disrupts the class by their behaviour is reinforced by welcome attention from others.

Observational learning

The work of Bandura in the 1960s demonstrated that we can learn by observing significant others (models). He also showed that we sometimes imitate that behaviour if we perceive that the consequences have been desirable for the model. Bandura argued that behaviour could thus arise without any direct need for reinforcement.

Evaluation of the behavioural model

→ Behavioural explanations are parsimonious.
→ They are also based in scientific research.
→ Much of the behaviourist model is based on demonstrations of learning in laboratory animals leading some to question the validity of the approach for explaining human learning in natural settings.
→ Ethical questions arise about how people are regarded and treated. Some say the approach is dehumanizing and mechanistic.

Implications for treatment

Abnormal behaviour patterns acquired by the processes of learning outlined above can be unlearned by applying the same principles.

Watch out!

Present day approaches sometimes mix behaviourist principles with others, e.g. in cognitive behavioural therapy.

Checkpoint 2

Give a new example of a classically conditioned fear.

The jargon

A *parsimonious explanation* is one that adequately accounts for something in the most economical way possible.

Links

See Behavioural therapies (pages 158–9).

Exam question   answer: page 57

'The many successes of the biological model means that it is the most valid way of explaining abnormal behaviour.'
To what extent is the biological model a more acceptable model than any other way of explaining abnormal behaviour? (12 min)

Models of abnormality 2

Links

See Alternative therapies (pages 160–61).

Watch out!

Freudian psychoanalysis is just one example of the psychodynamic approach.

Checkpoint 1

What characteristics might be displayed by an anally fixated character?

The jargon

A *trauma* is an event which is so shocking that it can cause long-term damage.

Example

Little Hans was afraid to go out in case a horse bit him. Freud saw this symptom as symbolizing Hans' unconscious fear that his father might castrate him.

This section addresses two further models of abnormality – the psychodynamic approach and the cognitive approach. Within these broad approaches, several varieties of therapy may be practised. A selection is outlined here.

Assumptions of the psychodynamic model

To illustrate the psychodynamic approach the psychoanalytic theory of Sigmund Freud (1856–1939) is used here. Freud's followers (e.g. Jung, Erikson, Klein) developed his theory and changed some of its emphases but continued to share some of the original assumptions:

→ Much of our behaviour is biologically determined by the *unconscious* operation of instinctive forces.
→ Early experiences are also important. They can have a profound effect on later behaviour.
→ Personality develops in stages. The sequence is universal but the individual's early experiences result in a unique personality.
→ The fully developed personality consists of an id, ego and superego. Psychological problems can arise from a number of sources.
→ Psychic energy may be fixated at an early stage of development and unbalance the adult personality.
→ The concept of *anxiety* is central. This can be:
  → anxiety about real dangers
  → moral anxiety: the result of conflict between the ego and superego
  → neurotic anxiety: the result of conflict between the id and ego.

Anxiety that threatens to go out of control could be *traumatic*. The ego can employ a number of *defence mechanisms*, such as repression or displacement, to protect itself. Repressions usually form in childhood when the ego is weak but may not show themselves until later, perhaps during adolescence when sexual maturation is occurring or as a result of a personal crisis. Symptoms are often symbolic of internal conflicts.

Implications for treatment

→ The clinical interview and case study are favoured methods.
→ Symptoms are over-determined (have a number of sources) so the only thorough way to treat them is by psychoanalysis.
→ Radical restructuring of the personality is necessary.

Evaluation of the psychodynamic model

→ It can be difficult to test psychodynamic ideas scientifically because the central forces are unconscious, therefore not directly observable. The theory can also account for seemingly contradictory findings.
→ The theory is deterministic and therefore pessimistic. Normal development is a struggle against inevitable biological forces.
→ The model is the origin of modern-day 'talking cures'.

Assumptions of the cognitive model ●●●

Like the psychodynamic approach, the cognitive approach to abnormality has a number of forms, for example:

➔ The *information processing approach* which views the person as similar to a computer and abnormality as a malfunction in processing at one or more of the stages of input, storage, manipulation or output.
➔ The 'faulty cognitions' approach, e.g. Beck (1976), talked of cognitive errors, Meichenbaum (1976) of counterproductive self-statements and Ellis (1962) of irrational thoughts. Such cognitions are distortions of reality and can lead to people feeling worthless, unhealthy or unhappy and being unrealistic about the future.

Implications for treatment

The aim of cognitive therapies is:

➔ either to correct the malfunction in the cognitive system
➔ or to uncover and alter a person's faulty cognitions.

Maladaptive behaviour should disappear once a person understands the mismatch between the reality of a situation and how they construe it. Changes in cognition should also bring about changes in feelings. Examples include Beck's cognitive restructuring therapy, Meichenbaum's stress-inoculation therapy and Ellis's rational emotive therapy.

Evaluation of the cognitive model

➔ Behaviourists have criticized the model for re-introducing unobservable mental processes into psychology, arguing that this moves away from the scientific ideal.
➔ Humanistic psychologists have criticized it for not being human enough and reducing the person to no more than a string of cognitive processes.
➔ Clients are responsible for their own progress, which many view as desirable because it is empowering. Client and therapist work as a team.
➔ (Ironically) cognitive behavioural therapy has grown out of cognitive approaches.
➔ Alteration of cognitions is often recognized as an important part of more eclectic therapies.

Checkpoint 2

Give an example of a counterproductive self-statement.

Example

Life should be fair.

The jargon

Cognitions are thought processes – in this case, ways of construing the world and ourselves.

Checkpoint 3

What other major approach did behaviourists originally criticize in this way?

Exam question   answer: page 57

Describe the psychodynamic model of abnormality. (6 min)

Eating disorders 1

The two main classes of eating disorder – anorexia nervosa and bulimia nervosa – are described in ICD-10 (International Classification of Disorders) as behavioural conditions linked to both psychological and physiological factors. Here, some psychological explanations of these potentially fatal conditions are considered.

Some characteristics of eating disorders

Anorexia nervosa is 'nervous loss of appetite' characterized by:

→ prolonged refusal to eat
→ deliberate weight loss
→ distorted body-image
→ cessation of menstruation in women (amenorrhoea).

Some anorectic individuals are also **bulimic**, i.e. they binge eat then control their weight by causing themselves to vomit afterwards (purgers) or by vigorous exercise (non-purgers).

Most sufferers are young, white, Western, middle-class women although there is evidence that more black women are becoming anorexic. Five to ten per cent of sufferers are men and half of these are homosexual (Petkova 1997). Onset of the condition is usually between twelve and eighteen years of age. Anorexia is diagnosed when the sufferer reaches 85% of the weight clinically defined as normal for them. Other physical complications are also likely.

Anorexia nervosa and bulimia nervosa compared

These two disorders have much in common – a drive to be thin, a pre-occupation with food, depression, anxiety, a need to be perfect and difficulty with 'reading' internal states such as hunger or anxiety. However, some believe that there are also some important distinctions.

Anorexia nervosa	*Bulimia nervosa*
→ Refusal to maintain healthy body weight	→ Under- or overweight or in between
→ Hunger and disorder denied	→ Awareness of hunger and disorder
→ Less antisocial behaviour	→ More antisocial behaviour
→ Amenorrhoea common	→ Irregular menstruation common
→ Family conflict denied	→ Intense family conflict perceived

Comer (1995)

Psychological explanations of eating disorders

These explanations have been applied to both anorexia and bulimia because of the way in which they can overlap.

Psychodynamic explanations

These explanations focus on the girl's relationship with her parents and the requirement that, during adolescence, she needs to develop her own identity and become separate from them. Three themes have emerged from this.

Watch out!

Eating disorders are not 'all or nothing' conditions. Many people have problematic ideas about food and their weight so professionals tend to think in terms of a continuum of eating disorders.

Checkpoint 1

What other symptoms and problems are sufferers of eating disorders likely to have?

The jargon

The term *bulimarexia* has been introduced to cover those cases where the two conditions overlap.

Watch out!

Some psychologists (e.g. Garner 1986 and Bee 1992) think it is a mistake to view these conditions as distinct.

1 Anorexia nervosa is symptomatic of an unconscious desire to remain pre-pubescent and thus escape the responsibilities of adulthood such as sexual maturity and independence.
2 Anorectic girls may unconsciously fear facing up to their sexuality in general and pregnancy in particular. Controlling food intake ensures a 'boyish' appearance and amenorrhoea.
3 Some parents can be domineering and thus foster dependence in their offspring particularly if they are good, obedient and conscientious children (Bemis 1978). Anorectic symptoms are, therefore, the unconscious expression of the need to control one's life and assert individuality and independence from parents.

Problems with these explanations are:

→ General principles about avoiding independence and sexual maturity can apply equally to males and females but avoidance of pregnancy and amenorrhoea are only overtly relevant to females.
→ Anorexia can begin after adolescence when problems of identity and independence should be resolved. (However, according to psychodynamic theorists, unresolved problems from earlier stages can emerge as symptoms in times of crisis.)

Behaviourally related explanations

Behaviourists focus on learning processes as the most important determinant of behaviour and see anorexia as *weight phobia*. Western cultures tend to idealize images of slender women and link thinness with good health. Uncontrolled eating and weight gain cause anxiety, which anorectics can avoid by controlling their weight.

A related idea is that of *ineffective parents*. Bruch 1973 found that many parents of anorectics control the child even to the point of deciding when, what and why they eat so that the child never learns to respond appropriately to their own sensations of hunger and satisfaction or emotions and, thereafter, eats dysfunctionally.

A *feminist perspective* on behaviourist explanations asks why certain images of body types are idealized. Petkova (1997) suggests that images of women originate from dominant (male) discourses about what is feminine and attractive. These discourses are reflected back to women and control them so that the power imbalance between the sexes is maintained. Differing cultural ideals and the prevalence of eating disorders in Western cultures provide some support for this view. One finding difficult to explain from this perspective is the onset of anorexia in blind individuals (Yager et al, 1986) who cannot see idealized images.

Watch out!

Psychodynamic theorists say that symptoms are often 'over-determined', i.e. they have a number of underlying causes rather than one simple explanation. The analysis of an individual anorexic is, therefore, likely to be very complex.

Checkpoint 2

List some of the ways in which idealized images of women's bodies and links between health and thinness are presented to the world at large.

Example

Ineffective parents may offer a child food when it is anxious or upset so that, later, these emotions become signals to eat.

Checkpoint 3

How might blind individuals gain an impression of ideal body shape? What factors other than psychological ones might be at work here?

Exam question   answer: page 58

Outline *two* psychological explanations of anorexia nervosa. (12 min)

Eating disorders 2

Biological explanations for eating disorders are of two main types. These are explanations based on genetic inheritance, and explanations based on biochemical dysfunction. As yet there is no clear evidence that either type of explanation is better able to explain the causes of eating disorders than the psychological theories described in the last topic.

The influence of genes

There is no evidence, as yet, for the *genes* that cause anorexia nervosa or bulimia nervosa. Researchers have turned their attention to an investigation of the degree to which eating disorders run in families.

→ Results from *family studies* (APA 1994) have shown that there is an increased risk of eating disorders among first-degree relatives (parents, children, siblings) than among the general population.

→ Results from twin studies involve comparing MZ (i.e. genetically identical) twins with DZ (i.e. alike as siblings but not identical) twins. As MZ twins are genetically identical, a higher concordance rate (the percentage of twins who, where one twin has an eating disorder, so does the other) would indicate a significant influence of genetic factors.

→ Holland et al (1984) found a 55% concordance rate for MZ twins compared with only 7% for DZ twins. Wade et al (2000) found similar levels in their study of 2 163 female twins. The authors of this study were unable to rule out the possibility that the greater concordance rate for MZ twins might have been caused, at least in part, by the contribution of a shared environment.

Evaluation of genetic explanations

→ Although there are significantly higher concordance rates for MZ twins compared with DZ twins, this still leaves a large percentage of twins where the 'other' twin of an affected individual does not develop an eating disorder (Prentice 2000).

→ Bulik et al (2000) suggest that although twin studies are powerful tools, their results are easy to misinterpret, which has implications for our understanding of the causes of eating disorders. In their review of twin studies research, they found it was not possible to draw firm conclusions about the precise contribution of genetic and environmental contributions to *anorexia*. However, they found that there was evidence that *bulimia nervosa* is familial with genetic factors more prominent than the effects of shared environment.

→ Hsu (1990) suggests that the genetic element of eating disorders may relate more to personality traits such as emotional instability, which makes such individuals more susceptible to life events. Wade et al (2000) found evidence for a relationship between anorexia and major depression that could be traced to the influence of genetic factors that influenced the risk for both disorders.

Biochemical explanations

The role of the hypothalamus

An alternative biological explanation for eating disorders focuses on the role of a brain region known as the *hypothalamus*, and the concept of a *weight set point*. Research with animals has shown that when the hypothalamus is damaged, it can lead to starvation.

There are two major areas of the hypothalamus that control eating.

→ The lateral hypothalamus (LH) produces hunger when it is activated. If the LH of an animal is stimulated, it begins to eat.
→ The ventromedial hypothalamus (VMH) depresses hunger when it is activated. If the VMH is stimulated an animal stops eating. If it is destroyed the animal eats more often and becomes obese.

It is believed that the LH and VMH work together to set up a 'weight thermostat' which maintains a set point for weight (the normal weight for that person, determined by genetic inheritance, early eating practices etc.). If the 'thermostat' rises above this point, the VMH is activated, if weight falls below the weight set point, the LH is activated. The action of the LH and VMH sends messages to other areas of the brain that in turn initiate thoughts and behaviours which will satisfy whichever is activated. It is possible that a malfunction in the hypothalamus might explain eating disorders.

Evaluation of the role of the hypothalamus

→ Although the role of the hypothalamus in the eating behaviour of animals is well documented, there is little conclusive evidence that eating orders might be influenced in the same way in humans.
→ According to this model, once the person's weight drops below the weight set point, the brain and body begin compensatory activities to return the weight to the correct level. It is not clear why some people manage to gain control over these compensatory mechanisms, while others are caught in a cycle of bingeing and purging. It seems likely that the psychological differences between anorexic and bulimia sufferers are important in this respect.

The role of serotonin

Recent research (Walsh et al 1997) has implicated the neurotransmitter serotonin in patients with bulimia. Low levels of serotonin were found to be associated with binge eating. This association is supported by evidence that selective serotonin-active anti-depressants are effective in the treatment of binge eating.

> **The jargon**
>
> *Hypothalamus* – a part of the brain that helps maintain various bodily functions, including hunger and eating.

> **Checkpoint 2**
>
> What other factors might control eating in humans?

> **Action point**
>
> Chocolate contains a chemical that has a mild anti-depressant action, which may explain why chocolate products are popular in binge eating.

Exam question   answer: page 58

'Biology, as yet, has no answers to the puzzle of eating disorders.'
To what extent is this statement true? (12 min)

Answers
Physiological psychology and individual differences

Stress as a bodily response

Checkpoints

1 For our ancestors, threats tended to be external (e.g. large animals) and the fight or flight response enabled them to take the most effective form of action. Nowadays, physical responses tend not to be particularly effective in dealing with stressors.

2 There are many other aspects of stress and stress appraisal that might not apply to animals. As you read through the rest of this section, ask yourself whether each of these might be exclusive to humans.

Exam question

This question allows only 12 minutes, so you need to be pretty well focused on the right sort of material.

- The role of the adrenal cortex (stimulated by the pituitary gland, causes the release of corticosteroids) – part of the hypothalamic-pituitary axis.
- The role of the adrenal medulla (stimulated by the sympathetic nervous system) causes the release of adrenaline and noradrenaline and the mobilization of energy resources.

Stress and illness

Checkpoints

1 Exercise removes excess fats and glucose that are mobilized as part of the stress response.

2 There are many ways in which stress is thought to affect the body – including atherosclerosis, immunosuppression, coronary heart disease and gastric ulcers.

3 All are in stressful situations where their degree of perceived control over the source of their stress is low.

Exam question

There are two obvious studies which could be outlined in response to this question. These are Kiecolt-Glaser and Cohen. Remember to write in paragraphs, not bullet points when describing these studies. A small number of studies in detail is better than many in less detail.

Sources of stress

Checkpoints

1 It is possible that experiencing a disorder such as depression might place strains on a relationship or a job, thus leading to a consequent life event.

Exam question

The study included here is the Johansson et al study. It is important to stress the main *findings* and *conclusions* rather than the procedures used. This study showed there was a clear relationship between the nature of work and the amount of stress experienced. It is also important to give *reasons* for these findings.

Individual differences in stress

Checkpoints

1 It is speculative because the study is only correlational – it tells us nothing about cause and effect.

2 Other people provide a way of re-appraising the way we view the stressful nature or our situation as well as being a valuable source of social support.

Exam question

This section covered the role of personality, gender and culture. You should select just two of these. Try to include:

- in what ways does this individual difference modify the effects of stress?
- *why* should this individual difference modify the effects of stress?
- what evidence is there to support this claim?

Stress management 1

Checkpoints

1 Operant conditioning – the consequences of an action determine the likelihood of it being used again in the future.

2 These are included on page 43.

Exam question

With just 12 minutes to answer this, your response must be highly focused. You should select two techniques (one psychological and one physical) that you feel competent to describe effectively in just 6 minutes each. Remember you are only required to *describe* these here, not to evaluate them.

Stress management 2

Checkpoints

1 Both rely on the reinforcing consequences of an action increasing the frequency with which it occurs in the future.

2 These might include coping with a terminal illness, prolonged unemployment or even trying to cope with an impossible relationship.

Exam question

You should consider problems with using physical approaches to stress management (e.g. drugs and biofeedback) and weigh these up against the claimed advantages of psychological techniques. Are the latter demonstrably more effective than the former?

Definitions of abnormality

Checkpoints

1 Venezuelan Penare Indian fathers take an emetic immediately following the birth of their child and vomit continually for some time afterwards. Such behaviour would be very unwelcome in British fathers! Homosexuality was once far less acceptable than it is now.

2 According to Atkinson et al (1993), mentally healthy people perceive reality efficiently, have accurate self-knowledge, can exercise voluntary control over behaviour, have self-esteem and accept themselves, can form affectionate relationships and are productive.

Exam question

This question asks only for an outline of two ways of defining abnormality. These should be taken from:
- deviation from statistical norms
- deviation from social norms
- failure to function adequately
- deviation from ideal mental health.

There is no need to evaluate these definitions in this question, merely to offer a summary description.

Examiner's secrets

Don't write in bullet points in your answer. Try to be precise, and use the same language as the descriptions given here.

Problems with defining abnormality

Checkpoints

1 With certain forms of mental disorder, the sufferer may be aware enough to refer themselves for help. In other cases, referral may be recommended by friends or relatives. In extreme cases, there is provision for a person to be 'sectioned' under the Mental Health Act.

2 In her autobiography, the feminist Jill Tweedie describes a period of time that she spent in Canada as a teenager. She was struck by the far greater frequency with which her contemporaries there took baths and showers compared with those in England – a norm from which, at first, she deviated!

3 Anorexia nervosa appears to be a condition that strikes teenage, white, Western, middle-class females most of all. This suggests a cultural effect as, relative to males and young women in other cultures, its incidence is high.

Exam question

It is essential that any material used in this answer is used effectively. As the question asks 'to what extent', it is expected that you would review the adequacy of the different definitions of abnormality, together with the consideration of cultural factors in the definition of abnormality, *and then reach a conclusion*. It would not be sufficient just to replicate the material on pages 46–7 without comment or argument.

Models of abnormality 1

Checkpoints

1 Neurochemical factors have also been implicated in certain forms of depression and in anxiety disorders.

2 A dog might be a neutral stimulus to a small child until it barks in their face or bites. The dog then becomes a conditional stimulus that evokes an unconditional response of anxiety.

Exam question

In order to assess whether the biological model is a more valid model of abnormality than any other, you should consider whether its advantages outweigh its disadvantages and the advantages of other models. The major advantages of the biological model are its scientific status and the proven applications derived from it. Against this must be offset the problems of labelling people as mentally 'ill' and the claims of other models that mental disorders can be 'learned'.

Models of abnormality 2

Checkpoints

1 According to Freud the anally fixated character is typically orderly, obstinate and parsimonious (dislikes wasteful behaviour and enjoys economical solutions to things).

2 Your list may closely resemble Atkinson et al's, but check again. Have you fallen into the trap of saying 'a mentally healthy person does not/is not . . .'? Make sure you say what they *do/are* rather than what they *do not/are not*.

3 Behaviourists were critical of psychoanalytic theory which, like the cognitive model, proposed the existence of unobservable mental processes. In the case of psychoanalytic theory the unobservable unconscious mind is central to understanding behaviour.

Exam question

With only 6 minutes to answer this question, it is easy to go astray. Your answer should focus on those parts of psychoanalytic theory (the most obvious choice of a psychodynamic approach) that illustrate the development of abnormal behaviour. In particular you should stress the concept of anxiety and the development and use of defence mechanisms.

Eating disorders 1

Checkpoints

1 Other symptoms of eating disorders could be emaciation, low body temperature and blood pressure, body swelling and reduced bone density. Repeated vomiting is associated with damage to the wall of the oesophagus, acid damage to the teeth and potassium deficiency leading to *hypokalaemia* (associated with weakness and paralysis, gastro-intestinal disorders and irregular heart rhythms).

2 Idealized images of women's bodies are abundant throughout the mass media, e.g. in adverts, magazines, on films and even in computer games. Many health education

campaigns link being overweight with health problems such as heart disease, diabetes and high blood pressure and encourage people to restrict their intake of certain foods.

3 It is conceivable that young blind people can gain an impression of the 'ideal' through touch experience of dolls and or other models of beauty. Visual images alone are not the only way in which idealized body type can be conveyed. Conversations about weight loss dieting, exercise and health are common everyday occurrences. If none of these sources of information proved important, a physiological basis for eating disorders is implicated.

Exam question

There are three important points to bear in mind when answering this question.
- The question asks for *explanations* of anorexia nervosa, not symptoms of this disorder.
- The explanations should be *psychological* not biological.
- You are not required to *evaluate* these descriptions, merely to offer a summary *description*.

Psychodynamic explanations focus on an individual's relationship with their parents, and the need to develop a separate identity from them.

Behavioural explanations focus on learning processes as the most important determinant of behaviour, with anorexia being seen as 'weight phobia'.

Eating disorders 2

Checkpoints

1 As MZ twins are genetically identical, they are bound to be the same sex, and look physically identical. This increases the likelihood that other people will treat them as identical, and that they themselves will see themselves as being identical.

2 Eating is interwoven with a vast number of other factors, including social etiquette, habit, time of day, opportunity, attractiveness of food and so on.

Exam question

Biological explanations of eating disorders have emphasized the role of genetics (e.g. the leptin gene) and the role of biochemicals. As we have seen, there are a number of problems with these explanations. For example, when one identical twin develops an eating disorder, this does not automatically mean that the other will also develop the disorder. This shows that the environment is also important as an explanation of eating disorders. Genetics may give an individual a *vulnerability* to an eating disorder, but through some other route, rather than the disorder being the direct product of genetic inheritance.

The study of social influence represents one of the most important areas of social psychology – the influence of other people on our behaviour. Up to the late 1960s, this influence was thought to be caused by exposure to the views of a majority, but research since then has also emphasized how exposure to the views of a persuasive minority may also have considerable influence. In particular, we appear to have a strong tendency to obey the orders of an authority figure. The work of Stanley Milgram in this area was particularly important in the light of the terrible events of the Second World War. Because of the nature of research in this area, there is a need for careful consideration of the ethical issues that underlie research with human participants. We will review these here and examine how psychologists have responded to them in the days since Milgram's research. Scientific psychology used to be thought of as purely number crunching, but interest in the more qualitative methods has changed the way that psychologists view the nature of the research process. We will consider both quantitative and qualitative methods in this section.

Social psychology and research methods

Exam themes

→ Minority and majority influence (conformity)

→ Obedience

→ Ethics

→ Quantitative and qualitative research methods

→ Experimental design

→ Data analysis

Topic checklist

O AS ● A2	AQA/A	AQA/B	OCR	EDEXCEL
Conformity	O	O	O	O
Minority influence	O	O	O	O
Obedience to authority	O	O	O	O
Explaining and resisting obedience	O	O	O	O
Ethical issues	O●	O●	O●	O●
Dealing with ethical issues	O●	O●	O●	O●
Quantitative methods	O	O	O●	O●
Qualitative methods	O	O	O●	●
Experimental design 1	O	O	O●	O●
Experimental design 2	O	O	O●	O●
Data analysis 1	O	O	O●	O●
Data analysis 2	O	O	O●	O●

Conformity

Conformity is a form of social influence which results from exposure to the opinions of a majority. Zimbardo et al (1995) define it as a 'tendency for people to adopt the behaviour, attitudes and values of other members of a reference group'.

Research studies of conformity

Asch (1956)

In Asch's study, he showed a series of lines to participants seated around a table. All but one were confederates of the researcher. In each trial, participants were shown a 'test' line, and asked which of three other lines was the same length. On six neutral trials, the confederates gave correct answers; on the other twelve they unanimously agreed on the same incorrect answer. The main results were:

→ on 32% of the trials where confederates had unanimously given a wrong answer, naïve participants conformed to the majority view
→ 74% of the naïve participants conformed at least once (compared to a figure of only 5% when making decisions in private)
→ some conforming participants went along with the majority because they believed that their perception must be inaccurate and the majority's accurate. Some yielded because they did not want to be in the minority and risk being ridiculed by the rest of the group.

Subsequent variations of Asch's procedures found that conformity could be raised or lowered according to certain conditions such as:

→ the size of the majority – conformity levels were close to zero when only one confederate was used, 12.8% when two were used, and 32% with three confederates. Further increases in the size of the majority did not produce significant increases in conformity.
→ a non-unanimous majority – the presence of another participant who also gave a response different to that of the majority caused a dramatic decrease in the levels of conformity in real participants
→ mode of response – when participants were required to write their answers down instead of calling them out, the levels of conformity dropped significantly.

Criticisms of Asch's research

→ Harris (1985) argues that as the majority of trials in the Asch studies produced *non-conforming* responses, this was more a demonstration of *independence* than *conformity*.
→ Perrin and Spencer (1981) claim that the Asch studies reflect a particular historical and cultural perspective (the American era of McCarthyism) and suggest that such conformity effects are no longer evident in similar experimental studies.
→ Smith and Bond (1998), in a review of 31 studies of conformity, suggest that conformity to a majority is more likely in collectivist cultures than in individualist cultures (like the UK and USA).

The jargon

Conformity is also referred to as 'majority influence'.

Watch out!

Students frequently claim that 32% of *participants* conformed whereas it should be 32% of *trials* produced conforming responses.

Checkpoint 1

How are these two explanations of conformity usually described?

Checkpoint 2

The level of conformity dropped when answers were written down. What does this tell you about conformity?

Action point

Perrin and Spencer referred to the Asch effect as a 'child of its time'.

Checkpoint 3

What is the main difference between a collectivist and an individualist culture?

Zimbardo's prison simulation study (Zimbardo et al 1973)

Zimbardo used a prison simulation to investigate to what extent people would conform to new social roles when they took part in a role-playing exercise. Zimbardo used 24 male volunteers, judged to be both physically and mentally healthy, allocated randomly to the roles of prisoners or guards. The prisoners were 'arrested' at their homes and, after being initially processed by the police, handed over to the guards. Although Zimbardo intended the study to last for two weeks, he had to stop it after six days. The guards continually harassed and humiliated the prisoners. Some guards behaved in a brutal and sadistic manner. The prisoners initially revolted, but became increasingly passive and docile. Some prisoners had to be released from the study before its conclusion because they showed symptoms of severe emotional disturbance.

Criticisms of Zimbardo's study (Savin 1973)

→ Savin believed that 'the ends did not justify the means' in this study. However, the study has had a great deal of impact on the way in which prisons (and mental institutions) are run, and the film of the study is used in the training of prison officers.
→ The reality of this study contributed greatly to the distress experienced by participants. Zimbardo claimed that studies such as this are criticized because they 'open our eyes' to the possibilities that all of us are capable of conformity to destructive social roles.

Why do we conform? ●●●

Insko et al (1985) claim that there are two main reasons why we conform to social norms (i.e. the views of the majority).

→ *Normative social influence* – we conform so that others will approve of us and accept us.
→ *Informational social influence* – we look to others to provide information about ambiguous situations.

These two processes do not necessarily operate independently, but frequently operate together. Turner (1991) claims that belonging to a social group makes us conform to its social norms. We observe how other members of the group behave and we behave in the same way. He describes this as *referential informational influence*. Using others as a reference group sets the scene for normative and informational influence to be most effective.

Check the net

www.zimbardo.com/
includes a full slide show of the prison simulation study.

Action point

Even studies that appear to be extremely unethical can have positive consequences.

Watch out!

This question is asking *why* people conform rather than asking you to describe research into conformity.

Exam question answer: page 84

Outline two reasons why people conform. (6 min)

Minority influence

The jargon

Minority influence – a form of social influence where people reject the established norm of the majority of group members and move to the position of the minority.

Checkpoint 1

In what ways does 'majority influence' differ from 'minority influence'?

> *"When great changes occur in history, when great principles are involved, as a rule the majority are wrong. The minority are right."*
>
> E. V. Debs (1918)

Test yourself

After reading about this study, put the book to one side and try to explain to someone else what happened and what the main findings were.

There are many situations where social influence can be attributed to exposure to the persuasive influence of a minority position, or even a lone dissenter. Thus, although initially dismissed as eccentric or unacceptable by the majority, the views of the minority may become increasingly influential.

Research into minority influence

Research into this form of social influence has generally found that in order for a minority to have an influence over the majority, a number of conditions are necessary.

→ They must express a clear position at the outset.
→ They must hold firmly to that position despite pressure exerted by the majority to change it, but at the same time must be seen as flexible by other group members.
→ The minority must hold a consistent line with each other.

Moscovici et al (1969)

In this study, participants were required to estimate the colour of 36 slides. Of the six participants, two were confederates of the experimenter. The slides used were all blue, but the use of different filters varied their brightness.

→ In the *consistent* condition of this experiment, the two confederates called all 36 slides green. Participants yielded to this influence in 8.42% of all trials.
→ In the *inconsistent* condition, the two confederates called 24 of the slides green and the remaining 12 slides blue. Participants yielded to this influence in only 1.25% of the trials.
→ In an extension to this study, both experimental groups showed a lower threshold for green than a control group, i.e. they were more likely to report ambiguous blue/green stimuli as green.

Clark (1994)

Clark studied how minority influence might work in jury settings. Student jurors read a summary of the film *Twelve Angry Men* in which one juror (played by Henry Fonda) gradually changes the minds of the other members of the jury concerning the innocence of a man accused of murder. There were three conditions in this study.

→ Some read the whole script of *Twelve Angry Men*.
→ Some were made aware of the fact that the character played by Fonda was unconvinced of the man's guilt but were not aware of his arguments to support this position.
→ Some knew of Fonda's arguments but did not receive information about other jury members changing their opinions.

Knowing both the arguments *and* the behaviour of other group members affected the student jurors' decision regarding the man's guilt. Reading the arguments was sufficient to persuade many of the student jurors, but knowledge that others had also changed their decisions increased this effect.

Evaluation of Moscovici's research

→ Nemeth (1986) found that participants tended to converge on the views of the majority. Exposure to minority influence, however, stimulated more active information processing that increased the probability of correct answers.

→ Maas and Clark (1983) studied the effects of exposure to majority and minority opinions about gay rights. Participants conformed *publicly* to the views of the majority whereas exposure to the views of a minority produced change in *privately* expressed attitudes.

→ Moscovici and Personnaz (1986) found participants reported an *after-image* that corresponded to minority rather than majority judgements. If the minority called 'green' but the majority 'blue', the complementary colour (purple or yellow) reported suggested that participants had *seen* the same colour as the minority.

Explanations of minority influence

A consistent finding of research in this area is that minority influence is only felt after a period of time. This suggests that a consistently expressed opinion by the minority sets up a number of interpersonal processes that lead to the gradual defection from the majority position.

→ According to Kelley's co-variation theory of attribution (Kelley 1967), the majority will make a 'dispositional attribution' in that they will see the minority as being confident in their position. This is enhanced if this position is expressed consistently over time.

→ If the minority opinion continues to be expressed despite the inhibitory pressure of majority disagreement, its impact is increased and thus causes the majority to take the minority view seriously. If some 'defect' to this position, it may set up a 'snowball' effect where minority influence becomes more pronounced.

→ Self-categorization theory explanations emphasize the role of in-groups in shaping our attitudes. David and Turner (1996) found that messages from in-groups were more influential than those from out-groups. Messages from 'deviant' out-groups tended to entrench in-group positions. This challenges the claim that deviant minorities produce more innovative thinking in majority group members.

Action point

Minority influence may produce more changes in privately expressed attitudes, whereas exposure to the views of a majority produces public compliance.

Checkpoint 2

What does this final point tell you about minority influence?

The jargon

A *dispositional attribution* means that other people believe the minority are expressing their own views rather than being influenced by other people.

Action point

An in-group is the group with which we identify. The out-group is effectively everyone else.

Exam question   answer: page 84

'Exposure to the views of a persuasive minority may, it appears, be more influential than the views of the dominant majority.'
To what extent has research shown this to be true? (12 min)

Obedience to authority

Obedience refers to a type of social influence whereby somebody acts in response to a direct order from another person. There is also the implication that the person receiving the order is made to respond in a way that they would not otherwise have done without the order.

Watch out!

Make sure you don't confuse obedience with conformity.

Links

Ethical issues (see pages 68–9).

Action point

No shocks were really being delivered in this study. However, participants *believed* they were giving real electric shocks.

Checkpoint 1

As the 'learner' was brought closer to the 'teacher', the level of obedience dropped. How would this be explained?

The jargon

Experimental validity is whether the observed effect really was caused by the experimental manipulation.
Ecological validity is whether these results could be generalized out to other situations and settings.

Milgram's research into obedience (1963)

Milgram deceived 40 male volunteer participants into thinking they were giving gradually increasing electric shocks to another participant (an actor) during a word association task. The 'real' participant acted as the 'teacher' and the 'learner' was in fact an actor. In the 'baseline' condition, the learner was in another room, with no voice contact with the teacher. After each wrong answer an electric shock was delivered (although none were really given) with an increase of 15 volts each time up to 450 volts.

→ All 40 participants continued to at least the 300-volt level.
→ 65% continued to the full 450 volts.

Milgram extended his research to explore the different situational factors that led participants to obey or disobey. He found that the closer the 'teacher' was to the 'learner', the more likely they were to refuse the experimenter's command to deliver the shocks. Milgram also discovered that obedience levels were lower when the experimenter was not physically present and gave orders over the telephone.

Criticisms of Milgram's research

Milgram's research was criticized on two main counts.

1 It was not a *valid* research study, in that the deception had not worked (experimental validity) and the study had little relevance outside of the experimental setting (ecological validity).
2 The study was *unethical*; it should not have been carried out because it compromised the trust between researchers and their participants. We can now look at each of these criticisms in turn.

Experimental and ecological validity of Milgram's research

→ Orne and Holland (1968) claimed that Milgram's research lacked experimental validity; participants had not been deceived at all. Therefore conclusions drawn from the study were inappropriate.
→ Milgram defended his original claim through evidence from debriefing sessions (participants admitted they had believed they *were* giving shocks), and through film evidence where participants appeared in considerable distress when delivering the shocks.
→ Orne and Holland's second claim was that the study lacked ecological validity, having been carried out in the psychology lab of a prestigious American university (Yale).
→ Milgram carried out a replication in some run-down office buildings, and found that obedience levels, although lower, were still far higher than predicted at the beginning of the research.

Ethical criticisms of Milgram's research

Baumrind (1964) criticized Milgram's research on the grounds that it was not ethically justified. She claimed that:

→ participants suffered considerable distress that was not justified given the aims of the research
→ participants would suffer permanent psychological harm from their participation in the study, including a loss of self-esteem and distrust of authority
→ Milgram failed to obtain *informed consent* from his participants – they may not have volunteered had they known what they had to do.

Milgram responded to each of these criticisms in turn.

→ In a follow-up survey, 84% of his participants indicated they were 'glad to have taken part', and felt they had learned something extremely valuable about themselves.
→ Psychiatric examinations one year later showed no sign of psychological damage attributable to participation in the research.
→ At no point were participants *forced* to do anything, and the fact that some had withdrawn meant that all were free to do so.

Other research on obedience (Hofling et al 1966)

Hofling et al arranged for nurses in a hospital ward to receive a telephone call from an unknown doctor. Each unsuspecting nurse was asked to administer a drug to a patient before the doctor arrived. To have done so meant breaking a number of hospital rules, including:

→ giving twice the maximum dose for the drug
→ accepting a telephone instruction from an unknown doctor
→ acting without written instructions from a doctor.

Despite this, 21 out of 22 nurses agreed to administer the drug (a harmless placebo), thus lending some support to Milgram's claim that obedience would also be evident in natural settings.

Criticisms of Hofling et al's research

Rank and Jacobson (1977) criticized the Hofling et al study because:

→ the nurses had no knowledge of the drug involved (Astroten)
→ they had no opportunity to seek advice before giving the drug.

In a replication of the study where the common drug, Valium, was used, and nurses were able to speak to other nurses before proceeding, only 2 out of 18 nurses gave the drug as requested by the absent doctor.

Checkpoint 2

If you were Milgram, how might you answer this second criticism?

Action point

By the use of experimental 'prods' – such as saying 'You must continue' – Milgram applied pressure on participants to continue.

Action point

This research is important as it involved obedience in a more natural setting than was the case in Milgram's study.

Examiner's secrets

When revising a research study, it is a good idea to revise the main aims, procedures, results and conclusions of the study.

Exam question   answer: page 84

Describe the findings and conclusions of two studies that have investigated obedience. (12 min)

Explaining and resisting obedience

In the light of Milgram's findings, psychologists have explored the reasons *why* people obey. A number of psychological processes operate that appear to both remove personal *agency* (freedom to direct our own behaviour) and *bind* people to an obedient relationship with the authority figure. Research in this area has also been important in highlighting how people might *resist* the influence of destructive obedience (that which harms others).

Explaining obedience

Socio-cultural explanations

A socio-cultural perspective suggests that we learn to obey authority and expect to encounter legitimate authority in many different contexts. The role of legitimate authority figures tends to be defined by society. This gives them the right to exert power over others, who in turn tend to accept the legitimacy of their power and act accordingly. Those who took part in Milgram's research had a long history of rewarded obedience.

Binding factors

Once subjects are actually in the experimental condition, *binding factors* begin to operate. Various cues (the experimenter's status and manner, the volunteer status of the subject and the learner's apparent willingness to receive punishment) increase the pressure on the participant to continue their role in the study. The gradual increase in shocks may be made more likely through a combination of factors ('foot in the door', embarrassment at non-continuation). It is perhaps this slow progression towards violence that explains destructive obedience in the real world.

Agentic shift

The participant shifts the responsibility for their actions onto another person (in this case the experimenter) through the process of *agentic shift*. They now see themselves as the *agents* of another person (the authority figure) and no longer responsible for their own actions. This claim that the actual responsibility for actions lay elsewhere has been a common defence throughout the war crimes trials.

The role of buffers

A 'buffer' is defined as any aspect of a situation that protects people from having to confront the consequences of their actions (Meldrum 2000). In Milgram's original study, the teacher and learner were in different rooms, with the teacher protected (i.e. *buffered*) from having to see his 'victim', and the consequences of his electric shocks. When the learner was in the same room, this buffering effect was reduced, as was the tendency to obey the commands of the experimenter.

Watch out!

Make sure that you are clear about the distinction between conformity and obedience.

"Under conditions of tyranny it is far easier to act than to think."

H. Arendt (1970)

Checkpoint 1

What does 'foot in the door' mean in this context?

Action point

In all conflicts, war criminals make use of this defence. Look out for it when reading or watching stories about war atrocities.

Checkpoint 2

Think of some different ways in which military personnel are 'buffered' from the consequences of their actions during wartime.

Resisting obedience ●●●

→ Individuals can be reminded that it is they who are responsible for their actions, not the authority figures. Hamilton (1978) found that under these conditions, agentic shift was reversed and sharp decreases in obedience could be obtained.

→ The presence of *disobedient* models (which might suggest that obedience was inappropriate) can also serve to reduce obedience. In Milgram's research the presence of two disobedient peers was sufficient to override all the binding and agentic shift dynamics that usually produce an obedient response.

→ There is growing evidence (e.g. Sherman 1980) that knowledge of results such as Milgram's may change people's behaviour. Knowing about the process of obedience may enhance people's ability to resist destructive obedience.

→ Kohlberg (1969) found that people who used more advanced stages of moral reasoning were more likely to disobey the commands of the experimenter than those who reasoned at lower levels.

Obedience research – the legacy ●●●

Research such as Milgram's has changed the way in which we view the nature of destructive obedience.

→ It appears from these research studies that many of us are capable of committing destructive acts, and that we fail to recognize our susceptibility to such influence. Prior to this research, it was traditional for social scientists to explain behaviour such as the Nazi war crimes in World War II in terms of the actions of deviant personalities.

→ The current view is that destructive obedience may be produced in the majority of people purely by situational factors (i.e. the orders of an authority figure). The capacity for moral decision-making may be suspended when an individual is embedded within a powerful social hierarchy. This has led some to comment upon the 'ordinariness' of such evil acts rather than seeing them as the product of pathological (i.e. 'disturbed') personalities (Arendt 1963).

Action point

Ask yourself *why* the presence of disobedient peers would override binding and agentic shift dynamics.

Links

Development of moral understanding (see pages 138–9).

> "It was though . . . he [Eichmann] was summing up the lessons that this long course in human wickedness had taught us – the lesson of the fearsome, word-and-thought-defying banality of evil."
>
> H. Arendt (1963)

Exam question answer: page 84

'Obedience research has only provoked controversy because of the *results* rather than the procedures used to gain them.'
To what extent might obedience research, such as that carried out by Milgram, be considered worthwhile? (12 min)

Ethical issues

Historically, the role of ethics has been in the promotion and maintenance of competence in a particular discipline or activity. One consequence of research such as Milgram's work on obedience has been the development of ethical guidelines for the treatment of human participants. The 'role' of these ethical guidelines is summarized in the BPS Code of Conduct: 'To preserve an overriding high regard for the well-being and dignity of research participants.'

Ethical issues in social influence research

Deception

One of Baumrind's main objections to Milgram's study of obedience was that he had *deceived* the participants on two counts.

→ First, he had led them to believe they were taking part in a study of the effects of punishment on learning.
→ Second, he had then led them to believe they were actually delivering electric shocks.

In order to understand why *deception* is such an important issue in psychological research we need to examine, from the participants' point of view, the impact of such practices.

→ Deception may make participants suspicious about a research investigation, or they may develop negative feelings about any future research participation.
→ It may reduce support for psychological research in general.
→ It may undermine the commitment of researchers to always telling the truth.

Probably the most serious consequence of deception is that it removes the ability of research participants to give their full informed consent to take part in an investigation. This does create dilemmas for the researcher, especially since complete openness may decrease the effectiveness of the investigation. In Milgram's research complete honesty would have made the research untenable.

Informed consent

The essence of the principle of informed consent is that research participants should be allowed to agree or refuse to participate in the light of comprehensive information concerning the nature and purpose of the research. Homan (1991) suggests that there are two elements implied in being 'informed', and two that constitute 'consent'.

→ 'Informed' suggests that all relevant aspects of what is to happen and what *might* happen are disclosed to the participant and that they should be able to understand this information.
→ 'Consent' suggests that the participant is competent to make a rational and mature judgement and that their agreement to participate should be voluntary, free from coercion and undue influence.

Watch out!

Ethical guidelines are just one way in which psychologists try to resolve ethical issues.

Action point

Critics of Milgram's study did not believe that the deception had worked. Milgram provided compelling evidence that it had.

Checkpoint 1

In what way would complete honesty have made Milgram's research 'untenable'?

Checkpoint 2

Can you think of situations where consent might not be 'voluntary' or free from 'undue influence'?

Even if researchers have sought and obtained informed consent, that does not guarantee that participants really do understand what they have let themselves in for. Another problem is the requirement for the researcher to point out any likely benefits and risks of participation. Researchers are not always able accurately to predict the risks of taking part in a study. Milgram claimed that he could not have foreseen the severity of the stress experienced by his subjects (Milgram 1974).

Protection of participants from harm

A further concern is that participants should be protected from undue risk during psychological research. The definition of undue risk is based on the risks that individuals might be expected to encounter in their normal lifestyle. Thus, the risks that an individual may be exposed to during a psychological investigation should not be greater than the risks they might already be expected to face in their everyday life.

→ One of Baumrind's main criticisms of Milgram's research was that participants would suffer permanent psychological harm from the study, including a loss of self-esteem and distrust of authority (Baumrind 1964).

→ Milgram responded by providing evidence that in psychiatric examinations one year after the study, there was no sign of psychological damage that was attributable to the experiment.

Was Milgram's research *really* so unethical?

Diana Baumrind claimed that the benefit to humanity of Milgram's work was not sufficient to justify the anxiety and distress felt by those who took part. Baumrind also claimed that Milgram violated the basic human rights of his participants by exposing them to a potentially harmful experience without first getting their *informed* consent to do so. Milgram's response to these criticisms provided a powerful defence of his actions, showing that although most participants did indeed suffer distress during the experiment, a follow-up survey showed that the vast majority were glad to have taken part and some actually volunteered to take part in further research. Erikson (1968) wrote of the 'momentous contribution' that Milgram had made, and suggested that the ethical criticisms arose simply because Milgram had 'opened our eyes' to the possibility that such blind destructive obedience may be possible in all of us.

Action point

Only a minority of research participants appear fully to understand what they have volunteered to do when they agree to take part in an experiment.

"Milgram, in exploring the external conditions that produce such destructive obedience . . . seems to me to have done some of the most morally significant research in modern psychology."

Elms (1986)

Exam question   answer: page 85

Using *one* research study into social influence as an example, consider the extent to which this study might have been seen as unethical. (12 min)

Dealing with ethical issues

Ethical codes are standards of conduct or rules of behaviour adopted by various professions. Ethical codes help to guide conduct within that profession and establish guidelines for standard practice and competence. Ethical codes are quasi-legal documents that have specific functions within professions; they are not abstract ideas or theories.

Ethical guidelines for research with human participants ●●●

→ Ethical guidelines tend to be based on a 'cost-benefit' approach – scientific ends are sometimes seen as justifying the use of methods that *sometimes* sacrifice individual participants' welfare, particularly when the research promises 'the greatest good for the greatest number'.

→ The BPS Code of Conduct (1995) is unique in that it gives primary attention to research. It recognizes that psychologists owe a debt to the individuals who participate in research, and that in return those 'participants' should expect to be treated with the highest standards of consideration and respect.

→ Each section consists of a series of statements clarifying appropriate conduct (e.g. deception, consent). It is acknowledged that many people view the use of research deception as unacceptable conduct, *but* it is recognized that many psychological processes could not be studied if individuals were fully aware of the research hypothesis in advance. Therefore, a distinction is made between withholding some details of the research hypothesis and deliberately providing false information to participants.

Dealing with specific ethical issues ●●●

Deception
Withholding information or misleading participants is unacceptable if the participants are typically likely to show unease once debriefed. Where this is in any doubt, appropriate consultation must precede the investigation. Intentional deception of the participants over the purpose and general nature of the investigation should be avoided whenever possible, although it may be impossible to study some psychological processes without withholding information about the true object of the study or without deliberately misleading the participants.

Informed consent
Whenever possible, the investigators should inform all participants of the objectives of the investigation. The investigators should inform the participants of all aspects of the research that might reasonably be expected to influence their willingness to participate. Research with children or with other vulnerable participants requires special safeguarding procedures.

Protection of participants

Investigators have a primary responsibility to protect participants from physical and mental harm during the investigation. Normally the risk of harm must be no greater than in ordinary life. Where research may involve behaviour or experiences that participants may regard as personal and private, the participants must be protected from stress by all appropriate measures, including the assurance that answers to personal questions need not be given.

Limitations of ethical codes for resolving ethical issues

→ All codes imply an obligation to behave in a particular way, which in turn implies that a professional group is definable and that there is a clear dividing line between members and outsiders (Homan 1991). A number of researchers (e.g. A-level students and undergraduates) do not belong to a professional organization such as the BPS and are therefore not professionally bound by its codes.

→ Most professional codes, particularly those in the social sciences, have very little power of censure over their members. Exclusion from a professional body does not exclude social scientists from continuing to carry out research. The BPS have introduced a professional 'qualification' – Chartered Psychologist status. This is a further way in which the BPS can assure good practice among their members.

→ Some researchers have argued that the ethical decision-making should also involve a consideration of the costs and benefits of *not doing* the study. Social psychologists such as the late Stanley Milgram have an ethical responsibility to society as a whole, and we might argue that they would not be fulfilling that responsibility if they did not carry out such important research to the best of their ability.

→ Elliot Aronson (1995) suggests that psychologists face a particularly difficult dilemma when their wider responsibility to society conflicts with their more specific responsibilities to each individual research participant. This conflict is greatest when the issues under investigation are issues of great social importance.

> **Action point**
>
> In a study of ethical codes across nine countries, Shuler (1982) found that 'protection' was of primary importance in all of them.

> **Watch out!**
>
> Ethical codes are not foolproof and may not always deal adequately with the ethical issues faced in research.

> **Checkpoint 3**
>
> What would have been the costs of *not* carrying out Milgram's research?

> **Example**
>
> This would include 'socially sensitive' research where the results of the research (e.g. on drug-taking behaviour) have far reaching implications for many people.

Exam question   answer: page 85

Consider how effective psychologists have been in dealing with ethical issues in psychological research. (12 min)

Quantitative methods

Watch out!

Qualitative (non-numerical) data can sometimes be converted to quantitative data.

Test yourself

List and define the four different kinds of variables named in bold type on the right.

Checkpoint 1

Some people argue that we can only call some of these true experiments. Why is that?

Links

See Ethical issues (pages 68–9) and Dealing with ethical issues (pages 70–1).

Quantitative methods involve measurement and the collection of numerical data. Such data can be treated descriptively in the form of statistics, such as averages, or in the form of visuals, such as graphs and charts. They can also be treated inferentially by the application of statistical tests.

Experiments

An experiment is a research method in which the experimenter changes some influence on the participants (an **independent variable** or **IV**) and observes and measures the effects of the changes on some aspect of their behaviour (the **dependent variable** or **DV**) while keeping all other sources of influence (**extraneous variables**) constant. Uncontrolled extraneous variables which interfere systematically with the influence of the IV on the DV are called **confounding variables**.

	The experimental environment is controlled by the experimenter	The experimental environment is not controlled by the experimenter
The IV is directly manipulated by the experimenter	Laboratory experiment	Field experiment
The IV varies naturally (or fortuitously)	Quasi-experiment	Natural experiment

Strengths of experiments

→ The amount of control possible in some experiments makes it possible for the experimenter to make causal statements about behaviour. Understanding cause is one of the key aims of science. This cannot be done so readily with other methods.

→ Knowing what causes behaviour to change puts the experimenter in the position of being able to control it.

Problems with experiments

→ Lack of realism in certain kinds of experiment, especially the laboratory experiment, so that findings do not apply to real life.

→ Loss of control in the more 'true to life' experiments, such as the natural experiment, means it is more difficult to be confident about what causes what.

→ In spite of rigorous control, there is always the chance that behaviour is not affected by the IV but by a confounding variable.

→ Ethical considerations are as relevant here as in any other form of psychological research.

Correlation

Correlation is used to detect linear relationships between samples of paired data. It can be expressed pictorially as a scattergram, or numerically as a correlation coefficient which will range from +1 through 0 to −1. The sign (+ or −) gives the direction of the relationship and the number (0 to 1) gives the strength of the relationship (e.g. a correlation of +0.6 is weaker than a correlation of −0.7). Correlation coefficients have to be tested for statistical significance.

Patterns of correlation

Correlation analysis will reveal one of the following patterns:

→ perfect positive correlation (+1.0)
→ imperfect positive correlation (e.g. +0.6)
→ no correlation (0)
→ imperfect negative correlation (e.g. −0.7)
→ perfect negative correlation (−1.0)

Scattergrams

These scattergrams show a perfect positive, a zero and an imperfect negative relationship.

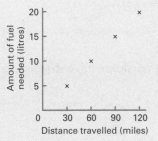 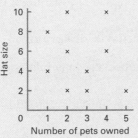 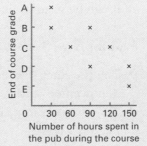

Strengths of correlation

→ It allows us to see how two variables *relate* to each other.
→ It allows us to *predict* the likely value of one variable when we only have information about the other one.
→ It is useful in checking certain kinds of reliability and validity.

Limitations of correlation

→ It is purely a *description* of relationships between variables. It does not allow us to say one variable *causes* changes in another.

Exam question   answer: page 85

Give one advantage and one disadvantage of each of the following methods:
→ laboratory experiment
→ field experiment
→ natural experiment.
(12 min)

Watch out!

Correlation is not a research method. It is a method of data analysis.

Action point

Sketch scattergrams to show an imperfect positive and a perfect negative relationship. Identify variables that might correlate in these ways.

Checkpoint 2

Give a real-life example of one variable being predicted from another.

Qualitative methods

Qualitative and quantitative methods should be seen as complementary and equally valuable.

Qualitative methods are less concerned with objective measurement than are quantitative methods. Their emphasis is on systematically observing, describing, exploring, interpreting and making sense of an issue or problem. Researchers and participants tend to be seen as collaborators in a process of discovery.

Naturalistic observation

→ *Naturalistic* means that the researcher studies participant(s) in a setting which is familiar to them; e.g. home, classroom, playground.
→ *Observation* means that the researcher systematically watches and records behaviour. Manipulation of an IV does not occur.
→ The researcher may observe from the outside (non-participant observation) or from within a group (participant observation).
→ Observations differ in focus, timescale and structure.
→ The method of data collection can vary from simple note-taking to sophisticated recording techniques.

Strengths of naturalistic observation

→ It produces rich and detailed descriptive accounts of behaviour.
→ It often provides ideas for further research.
→ It can be used when other methods might be unethical.

Action point

In your own words, write a definition of naturalistic and observation.

Problems with naturalistic observation

→ The presence of the observer may influence participants' behaviour in unwanted ways.
→ The observer must be able to identify and acknowledge possible personal biases.
→ There are many uncontrolled influences, which may affect participants' behaviour, making it hard to know which are the important ones.

Checkpoint 1

Find two actual examples of psychological research that used naturalistic observation.

Questionnaire surveys

Questionnaires usually comprise a standard set of questions about an issue and are presented to participants in exactly the same way.

→ Questions can be open or closed and be answered face-to-face, by post or by telephone.
→ A survey is usually a large-scale study of a representative sample of a relevant population.
→ Surveys can measure attitudes, opinions and behaviour patterns.

Strengths of questionnaire surveys

→ Useful for gathering data from large numbers of people about the issue of interest.
→ Anonymity or lack of face-to-face contact with the researcher can encourage more honest responses.

Links

See 'selecting participants' in Experimental design 1 (page 76).

Problems with questionnaire surveys

→ Difficulties with devising unambiguous questions that avoid bias, 'leading' the respondent or cause offence.

→ Respondents may answer to give a socially favourable impression. (Guaranteeing anonymity might help avoid this.)

→ Good sampling is vital if the results are to be of general use.

→ There may be low rates of return.

→ Respondents may participate because they have a special interest in the issues being surveyed, thus the sample becomes 'self-selected'.

Interviews

Interviews usually involve one-to-one, face-to-face contact between researcher and interviewee. Types of interview include:

→ structured – fixed questions and fixed answers for the participant to choose from

→ semi-structured – specific questions are asked but flexibility is allowed in responses

→ clinical – often used in therapeutic settings where the participant and interviewer may explore an issue with a view to helping the participant understand their problems.

Strengths of interviews

→ Interviews can provide detailed information about the individual's subjective view.

→ They can permit the exploration of complex ideas and issues which do not readily lend themselves to measurement.

→ They can be more flexible than other methods.

Problems with interviews

→ Interviews can yield a large amount of information which is open to misinterpretation, over-interpretation or partial interpretation (Banister et al 1994).

→ The interviewee may feel unable to be totally open and honest particularly if the issue of interest is sensitive.

→ Certain kinds of interview might exclude people who have difficulty articulating their thoughts.

Links

Some of the strengths and problems with using questionnaires apply here also.

Checkpoint 2

Identify an actual example of psychological research that used the questionnaire survey and another that used interviewing.

Exam question   answer: page 86

A researcher decided to join a religious cult to investigate the particular form of social influence that it had over its members. She was able to observe members in their daily behaviours and then wrote up her notes in the evening.

(a) What specific form of investigative method is being used here?

(b) Give one advantage and one disadvantage of this method.

(c) Explain two ethical problems with this method.

(12 min)

Experimental design 1

This section covers preliminary considerations when designing research, i.e. formulation of research aims and hypotheses, selection of participants and the importance of the relationship between researchers and participants.

Aims and hypotheses

Experimental research usually begins with a *question*. For example, 'Do boys and girls differ in their ability to spell?' This gives rise to:

→ an **aim** (e.g. to devise research to help answer the question)
→ a **hypothesis** – a testable statement, based on theorizing and/or research, that predicts the outcome of a study, e.g. boys and girls differ in spelling ability. Correlational hypotheses predict a relationship. Experimental hypotheses predict a difference. These become **alternative hypotheses** when the terms in them are precisely defined (operationalized) and can be statistically tested e.g. age of boys/girls and the spelling test specified.
→ a **null hypothesis** which predicts that a difference or relationship will be zero.

Directional hypotheses predict the direction of a difference (e.g. girls' spelling is superior to that of boys) or correlation (e.g. there is a positive relationship between weight and height). Non-directional hypotheses allow for differences or correlation in either direction. Hypotheses are retained or rejected on the basis of research findings.

Selecting participants

Psychologists begin research with a particular target population in mind. **Population** refers to the total number of individuals who qualify to participate because they have the certain characteristics, e.g. all the couples marrying at a particular town in a given year. If it is possible to test all members of a population, the study constitutes a **census**. If not, a representative group called a **sample** is selected. The sample should be large enough adequately to represent the population.

Reasons for sampling

→ It is usually only practical to study a selection of the population.
→ It helps to ensure that the sample is representative of the population.
→ Findings from a representative sample can be generalized to the population from which it was drawn.

Sampling techniques

→ **Random sampling** – each member of the population has an equal chance of being chosen. Population members are assigned a number and the required number of participants selected using random number tables or computer-generated random numbers.
→ **Stratified random sampling** – the population is organized into sub-groups (strata) and random samples are taken from each stratum in the same proportions that appear in the population.

Action point

Distinguish between a research question, aim, alternative hypothesis and null hypothesis.

Watch out!

Note that certain kinds of qualitative research, such as naturalistic observation, may only have aims and no quantitatively testable hypotheses.

Checkpoint 1

Write out a directional, a non-directional and a null hypothesis for either an experimental study or a correlational study.

Action point

Write your own definitions of population, sample and census.

- → **Opportunity sampling** – the researcher decides on the type of participant needed and approaches anyone who appears suitable.
- → **Quota sampling** – the population is organized into sub-groups (strata) and opportunity samples are taken from each stratum in the same proportions that appear in the population.

The relationship between researchers and participants ●●●

The influence of the participant
Weber and Cook (1972) identified four roles, which participants being studied might adopt:

- → the **faithful** participant tries to react to the situation as naturally as possible
- → the **co-operative** participant tries to discover the hypothesis being tested so that they can do their best to help support it
- → the **negativistic** participant tries to discover the hypothesis in order to disprove it
- → the **evaluatively apprehensive** participant is concerned about the impression they are creating or that the experimenter might discover something about them.

The influence of the investigator
Rosenthal (1969) discovered three key influences, which could affect participants' behaviour in experiments and other kinds of research:

- → **Biosocial or physical characteristics** of the experimenter such as age, sex, race and appearance.
- → **Psychosocial factors** which have to do with the experimenter's social skills in dealing with participants.
- → **Experimenter expectancy effects**. Experimenters who have a hypothesis in mind may end up validating it simply because of their belief about how the results will turn out. The hypothesis then becomes a self-fulfilling prophecy.

The influence of the situation
Human participants are often affected by the knowledge that they are being observed. Orne (1962) said that they are influenced by **demand characteristics** by which he meant cues in the experimental situation (e.g. the physical set-up of the experiment or the experimenter's behaviour) might alert the participants to the hypothesis being tested.

". . . science is a social business . . ."

Richardson (1991)

Action point

Name and define the four kinds of participant identified by Weber and Cook (1972).

Watch out!

The importance of participant, investigator, and situational influence varies according to the research method being used.

Checkpoint 2

What classic research study claimed to demonstrate the operation of teacher expectancy effects?

Exam question   answer: page 86

Without using your book, suggest two ways that:

(a) the participants might affect the outcome of an experiment (other than their reaction to the IV)

(b) the experimenter might affect the outcome of an experiment.

(12 min)

Experimental design 2

This topic covers some of the technicalities of good research design, concentrating in particular on experimental research design and techniques of control.

Links

Good research design always takes ethical considerations into account. See Ethical issues (pages 68–9) and Dealing with ethical issues (pages 70–1).

Checkpoint 1

How might you operationalize aggression?

Variables

Researchers sometimes need to define precisely (operationalize) what they mean by the terms they use in hypotheses and put them into a measurable, or quantifiable, form. This is a problem for psychologists who often deal with concepts such as aggression, fatigue or anxiety. In a study investigating the hypothesis that fatigue impairs driving ability, fatigue may be operationalized as a numerical measure of sleep quality and driving ability as a score in a standardized test of driving skill.

Experimental designs

Simple experiments involve collecting scores from participants under two different conditions to see if there are differences between them. In a laboratory or field experiment, it is usual to have:

→ a **control group** which lacks the influence of the IV and provides baseline data
→ an **experimental group** which is influenced by the IV.

All **extraneous variables** need to be controlled so that the only systematic difference between groups is the presence or absence of the IV. A systematic difference that interferes with the effect of the IV on the DV is called a **confounding variable**. In a natural or quasi-experiment the researcher compares two levels of the IV. There are three ways of collecting the two sets of data. These help to control variation due to participants.

The repeated measures design
Participants take part in both conditions. Advantages include:

→ it is economical in the number of participants used
→ there are fewer individual differences affecting the DV.

Problems with it include:

Watch out!

If order effects are a real possibility, counterbalancing is not the solution. In such cases, a different design should be used.

→ participants may become used to being tested and carry over the effects of practice or fatigue from one condition to the other. These are called **order effects**. **Randomized presentation** can guard against them, so can **counterbalancing**, i.e. half the participants do condition A first and half do B first (ABBA design)
→ participants may not return to be tested a second time.

The matched pairs design
Participants are put into pairs on the basis of variables relevant to the investigation. One member of the pair is then randomly assigned to condition A and the other to condition B. Advantages include:

→ no order effects
→ fewer individual differences between conditions.

Problems with it include:

→ good matching can be difficult to achieve
→ some individual differences will remain uncontrolled
→ more participants are needed
→ loss of one person means you lose a pair of data.

The independent groups design

A sample of participants is randomly divided between conditions or the groups arrange themselves on the basis of a naturally occurring IV. Advantages include:

→ it is relatively quick and easy to set up
→ it avoids order effects
→ random allocation should balance out individual differences.

Problems with it include:

→ it takes more participants than the repeated measures design
→ differences between the two groups are likely to be greater at the outset than in the other two designs.

Further aspects of experimental control

→ The **single blind procedure** is when steps are taken to ensure participants do not know the research aim or hypothesis. This helps to guard against participant reactivity.
→ The **double blind procedure** helps to guard against researcher and participant influences – the researcher instructs someone else to collect the data but neither that person nor the participants know the hypothesis.
→ **Standardized instructions** are the same for all participants in a particular condition and given in the same way. This should avoid favouring some over others.

Pilot studies

With any research project, it is often a good idea to carry out a small-scale 'dummy run'. This usually enables the researcher to identify any problems and correct them in advance of the main study. But note that problems can still occur. Although Milgram (1963) piloted his well-known obedience to authority research design he ran into problems in the main study.

Checkpoint 2

How would you match drivers into pairs for a test of driving ability?

Watch out!

Single and double blind procedures raise particular ethical problems because participants are not fully informed about the study before they take part in it.

Links

See Obedience to authority on page 64.

Exam question   answer: page 86

A researcher was interested in whether students revised better when listening to music than when revising in silence. Using an AS class, he randomly split them into two groups – the music group and the silence group, and played music to the former whilst they revised.

(a) What type of experimental design has been used here?
(b) Give one advantage and one disadvantage of this design.
(c) Suggest two extraneous variables that should be controlled.
(12 min)

Data analysis 1

This topic concerns simple descriptive analysis of quantitative data. Such data can be described in the form of summary statistics and in the form of 'visuals' such as graphs. The correct use of these requires an understanding of how the data have been measured.

Types of measurement

Measurement differs in its level of sophistication:

→ nominal measurement – frequency counts into named categories
→ ordinal measurement – values on this scale represent rankings, ratings or placings
→ interval and ratio measurement – these scales are more sophisticated and measure quantities or numbers of fixed units with equal distances between all the points on the scale.

Measurement scales can also be:

→ discrete – i.e. whole units such as numbers of children
→ continuous – values can be subdivided *ad infinitum* e.g. a timescale.

Speed learning

The initial letters of these scales spell the French word *noir*.

Checkpoint 1

Give an example of nominal, ordinal, interval and ratio measurement scales.

Measures of central tendency

These are used to summarize a sample of data using one typical score.

→ **Mean** – the arithmetic average. Its sensitivity is a strength and a weakness (an extreme score can distort the mean).
→ **Median** – the central value found when scores have been arranged in order of size. It is immune to extremes but affected by small changes in the number of scores.
→ **Mode** – the most frequently occurring value. It is immune to extremes and good for relatively large amounts of homogenous data.

Choosing between them depends both on the measurement scale:

→ interval or ratio – mean preferred if appropriate
→ ordinal – median preferred but means are sometimes used
→ nominal – mode can be used;

and on the shape of the frequency distribution:

→ normal – mean preferred
→ skewed – median preferred
→ bi- or multimodal – mode preferred.

Checkpoint 2

When might a mean be inappropriate for interval/ratio data?

Measures of dispersion

These indicate how varied scores are around the measure of central tendency.

→ **Range** – the difference between the largest and smallest score.
→ **Standard deviation** – a more complex measure which takes into account every score and its deviation from the mean. It is useful with interval and ratio data.

Watch out!

Measures of dispersion are sometimes called measures of variability or spread.

Frequency diagrams ●●●

Choice of the appropriate type of frequency diagram depends on knowing whether data are:

➔ shown on a nominal, ordinal, interval or ratio scale: nominal are qualitative, interval and ratio are quantitative and ordinal fall in between
➔ discrete or continuous.

The diagrams below provide some illustrative examples.

Links

Correlation can be presented in the form of scattergrams. See Quantitative methods (pages 72–3).

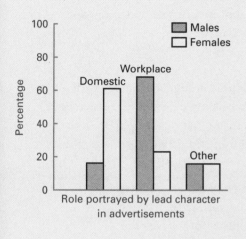

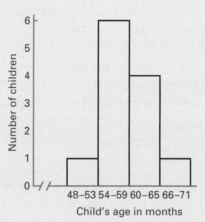

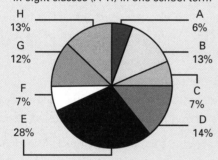

Pie chart showing percentage of lateness in eight classes (A–H) in one school term

Watch out!

Note that there should be gaps between bars when data are nominal or ordinal.

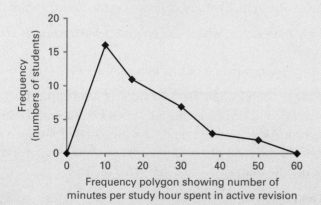

Frequency polygon showing number of minutes per study hour spent in active revision

---

Exam question   answer: page 86

(a) When would a median be preferable to a mean?

(b) What extra information is achieved by using a measure of dispersion?

(12 min)

Data analysis 2

Links

See Data analysis 1 (pages 80–1).

Action point

Make sure that you can provide a definition of each of the emboldened terms under 'Observations'.

Checkpoint 1

What other advantage do you think diarists might have?

Qualitative methods yield a wide variety of data. These may be quantitative or in the form of written accounts which can sometimes be converted to quantitative data and treated with descriptive and inferential statistical techniques. Researchers use the method that suits their purpose best.

Observations

In both participant and non-participant observation, the observer may choose to make a written record of events or take video or tape recordings for more detailed analysis later.

Observation techniques

Diary description – an observer who is in regular contact with a participant makes a written account of any changes in behaviour as they occur. Piaget (1896–1980) made diary descriptions of the development of his own three children and, from these, was able to identify developmental changes. Diary descriptions:

→ give a rich and full account of behaviour on all levels
→ are a fertile source of hypotheses for further research
→ are limited in their generalizability to other cases
→ may lack objectivity if the observer is closely involved with the subject.

Specimen description – the observer makes as full an account as possible of behaviour in a chosen segment of the subject's life, e.g. Barker and Wright (1951) who made a record of an American boy's day. Specimen descriptions:

→ can be very time-consuming
→ require special attention to the reliability of the observations
→ can be a useful starting point for more detailed research.

Event sampling – a specific type of behaviour is identified and the number of times it occurs, its context and events surrounding it are recorded, e.g. Bell and Ainsworth's (1972) study of infant crying. Event sampling is:

→ particularly time-saving where the type of behaviour to be recorded occurs infrequently
→ is good for preserving the context in which the event occurs.

Time sampling is useful when the behaviour of interest occurs relatively frequently. The researcher observes for a specified time and then records for a specified time. The presence or absence of the behaviour during each observation interval can be recorded to give an idea of how frequently it occurs. This method:

→ is quick and efficient
→ tends to lose the continuity of behaviour
→ may give a fragmented picture, not the full context.

In all these methods, it is good policy to have more than one observer watching and recording the same thing or analyzing the same written account. This leads to greater **inter-observer reliability** and helps to guard against biased or subjective interpretation.

"Two heads are better than one."

Proverb

Case studies ●●●

A case study is an in-depth study of a particular instance of something. It can be about an individual or a school, a married couple or a family. The method of data collection and analysis is fitted to the case.

Classic examples

→ Freud's clinical case-histories and analyses of his neurotic clients
→ Piaget's clinical interviews and diary descriptions of children's intellectual development
→ Ebbinghaus's (1885) tests of his own memory for nonsense syllables
→ Gregory and Wallace's (1963) interviews and perception tests used on 'SB' who recovered his sight after decades of blindness.

Case studies:

→ are as open to bias on the part of the observer as any other research technique which involves interpreting information
→ benefit from inter-observer reliability checks
→ sometimes depend on unreliable retrospective data which may be incomplete or distorted
→ are not always generalizable to others
→ are a rich source of ideas for further research.

Watch out!

Case studies are not always of people with problems.

Checkpoint 2

What is the general meaning of the term 'reliability'?

Interviews ●●●

The type of data gathered by interview depends on the type of interview conducted and its purpose.

→ Structured interviews tend to yield responses which can be treated quantitatively using descriptive and inferential statistics.
→ Semi-structured interviews may also yield some quantifiable information but generally generate a great deal of verbal information. The analysis of this 'discourse' or 'text' can be for a number of things including meanings or recurring themes.
→ Clinical interviews can be sharply focused or wide-ranging depending on the context and may include, amongst many other things, clinical notes, recordings and test results.

Links

See Qualitative methods (pages 74–5) for more details about interviews.

Triangulation ●●●

Triangulation in qualitative research involves checking the reliability of findings by scrutinizing them from different vantage points:

→ method triangulation – use of two or more methods
→ data triangulation – data collection from different sources
→ investigator triangulation – use of two or more researchers
→ theory triangulation – use of two or more theoretical viewpoints.

Exam question   answer: page 86

Describe two advantages that qualitative data might have over quantitative data. (6 min)

Answers
Social psychology and research methods

Conformity

Checkpoints

1 The former is known as 'informational influence' and the latter as 'normative influence'.
2 This suggests that many people engage in *public compliance* rather than *private acceptance*. Conformity, therefore, does not necessarily mean *agreement*.
3 In an individualist culture, self-interest and individual rights are promoted rather than the rights and interests of the community (as in a collectivist culture).

Exam question

The two most obvious reasons why people conform are because of 'normative influence' and 'informational influence'. An alternative explanation is 'referential social influence'.

You should begin your answer by explaining each of your chosen reasons, then perhaps show how each of these might have contributed to the conformity found in (for example) Asch's research.

Remember this is only an outline injunction, so requires a concise, highly focused description of the two reasons.

Minority influence

Checkpoints

1 Conformity to majority influence is often unthinking or may produce conformity merely to 'fit in'. It frequently results in *public compliance*. Reactions to minority influence may be more considered and it is more likely to lead to *private acceptance* of the views of the minority.
2 It tells us that previous exposure to a consistent minority had produced actual changes in the way participants perceived ambiguous colour slides.

Exam question

This question requires an evaluative response ('to what extent . . .') therefore requires more than just a description of studies. You might structure your response in the following way:
- a discussion of conclusions that can be drawn from the Moscovici and Clark studies
- Nemeth's finding that participants tend to converge on the views of the majority but minority influence stimulates more active information processing
- Maas and Clark found that although participants conform publicly to the views of the majority, exposure to the views of a minority produces change in privately expressed attitudes.

Obedience to authority

Checkpoints

1 If the learner is physically removed from the teacher, the latter is psychologically 'buffered' from the consequences of their actions. As this distance decreases, buffers are removed, the consequences become more obvious and obedience levels drop.
2 Milgram did, in fact, point out that most of his participants felt they had learned something valuable about themselves. Distrust of an authority figure who ordered them to engage in destructive acts would be socially desirable.

Exam question

Twelve minutes to answer this question gives you about 200 words (or about 100 words per study).

This might involve Milgram *and* Hofling's studies, or two studies carried out by Milgram. You should only describe, not evaluate either of these studies.

Explaining and resisting obedience

Checkpoints

1 'Foot-in-the-door' refers to the gradual commitment to a course of action. By initially agreeing to give a low level of shock it was more difficult for participants to refuse to deliver subsequent higher levels of shock.
2 The use of cruise missiles does not require visual contact with the victim, attacks at night, the dropping of bombs from high altitudes or the use of landmines where victims are harmed at some later date.

Exam question

This question is not asking you to *defend* Milgram's research, but to consider whether it was 'worthwhile'. This might be achieved by examining the ethical problems of the work and balancing these against any lessons learned from this research (i.e. the *legacy*).

If such research was not *valid*, this would make it less worthwhile (see page 64). Milgram has challenged such claims.

Finally, there is the view that knowledge of Milgram's research may enhance people's ability to resist destructive obedience.

Ethical issues

Checkpoints

1 This research relied on a deception (that participants *believed* they *were* delivering shocks). Without this, Milgram would not have been able to explore the power of obedience with any degree of realism.

2 These might include situations where participants are paid or where participation in research is seen as compulsory in some way (e.g. schools or prisons).

Exam question

This appears to be quite a challenging question, but really isn't that difficult. A number of the studies that you have considered in this area might be seen as unethical *nowadays* (although perhaps not at the time). Milgram's study is the most obvious example. This might be addressed on three fronts.

- Baumrind's objections to Milgram's work (e.g. deception, lack of informed consent).
- Milgram's response to these criticisms.
- Valuable lessons learned as a result of Milgram's research (i.e. the legacy of the research, which offers some ethical justification of it).

Examiner's secrets

Make sure that claims you make about individual research studies are accurate. Milgram did not 'break BPS ethical guidelines' (he was American) and Zimbardo was careful to design his study within existing APA ethical guidelines.

Dealing with ethical issues

Checkpoints

1 Milgram's participants were led to believe that they were delivering real electric shocks as part of a study on the effects of punishment on learning.

2 Although they had *consented* to take part in the research, participants were not fully informed of the fact that they would be pressurized to continue.

3 It has been argued that Milgram's research has taught us valuable lessons concerning the power of situational factors in destructive obedience. This finding, that destructive obedience is common (rather than being a personality flaw in some people) is an important discovery that has clear social implications.

Exam question

It is important to remember that you are being asked to do more than simply *describe* how psychologists have attempted to deal with ethical issues, but to *consider* how effective these attempts have been. There is scope for *some* descriptive content here (e.g. describing the nature and purpose of ethical guidelines) but it is vital that you *engage* with this material in some way.

- You may begin by describing the purpose of ethical guidelines (primarily to protect the well-being of those who take part in research) and then show how these are applied to specific ethical issues.
- You can then move on to a critical consideration of whether these are actually *effective* given the nature and aims of psychological research. The limitations of ethical codes for resolving ethical issues are covered on page 71.

One technique for answering these critical questions is to think of yourself as a courtroom lawyer, presenting arguments and then showing their strengths and weaknesses to an uninformed audience. For example, you may state that within ethical codes, clear guidelines are given concerning what is unacceptable conduct *but*, as Elliot Aronson points out, sometimes psychologists' wider responsibilities to society may conflict with their specific responsibilities to individual research participants.

Quantitative methods

Checkpoints

1 Strictly speaking, an investigation only qualifies as an experiment if the IV is directly manipulable by the experimenter. By this definition, laboratory and field experiments are true experiments, but quasi- and natural experiments are not.

2 Places at university are often offered on the basis of predicted A-level grades because A-level performance is usually a reliable indication of how well an individual would cope with degree level work.

Exam question

Laboratory experiment:
Advantage – the experimenter has full control over the independent variable and other variables therefore causal statements are more certain.
Disadvantage – participants know they are in an experiment and may adjust their behaviour.
Field experiment:
Advantage – behaviour occurs in a naturalistic setting therefore is more true to life.
Disadvantage – because participants are not aware they are taking part in a research study, there may be some ethical problems, such as invasion of privacy.
Natural experiment:
Advantage – as the IV is manipulated by outside agencies, this enables psychologists to study issues that are of high natural interest (such as the effects of two types of child-rearing technique).
Disadvantage – experimenter lacks control over other variables that might affect the behaviour being studied.

Qualitative methods

Checkpoints

1 Piaget used naturalistic observation to provide material for his diary descriptions of his own children's intellectual development. Sylva et al (1980) used naturalistic observation in a time-sampling framework to study the patterns of play in children in Oxfordshire playgroups and nursery schools.

2 Shere Hite (1971) conducted an extensive survey of female sexuality using postal questionnaires. Sears, Maccoby and Levni (1957) carried out a classic study on child-rearing styles using interviews.

Exam question

(a) Participant observation.

(b) Advantage – enables a more in-depth study of the group in question. Disadvantage – impossible to write up notes 'in situ' therefore relies on memory.

(c) Invasion of privacy as people 'open up' without knowing of the researcher's other role. Deception, of researcher deceives the group as to her true reason for being there.

Experimental design 1

Checkpoints

1 A non-directional experimental hypothesis:
   There is a difference in the mathematical abilities of boys and girls.
   A directional experimental hypothesis:
   Girls' mathematical ability is superior to that of boys.
   A null hypothesis for an experiment:
   There is no difference in the mathematical abilities of boys and girls.
   A non-directional correlational hypothesis:
   There is a relationship between variable A and B.
   A directional correlational hypothesis:
   There is a positive (or negative) relationship between variable A and B.
   A null hypothesis for a correlational study:
   There is no relationship between variable A and B.

2 Rosenthal and Jacobson's (1968) study called 'Pygmalion in the Classroom' claimed to show the effects of positive teacher expectations on the behaviour and educational attainment of elementary school children.

Exam question

Turn to page 77 for some suggestions about how participants and investigators can affect the outcome of an experiment. Check your answers against the information there.

Experimental design 2

Checkpoints

1 Aggression is notoriously difficult to define. It can be verbal or physical, direct or indirect, directed towards people or objects. Some researchers use acts of physical violence as an indication of aggression and count the number of times they occur within set time periods.

2 To match drivers into pairs, a researcher might take into account bodyweight, sex, usual drinking pattern, previous driving experience, type of vehicle typically driven, timing of most recent meal and many other variables besides.

Exam question

(a) Independent groups design.

(b) See page 79.

(c) Possible extraneous variables include the nature and loudness of the music, the material being revised, the motivation of the students and so on.

Data analysis 1

Checkpoints

1 Most physical measurements of weight, time, speed etc. qualify as ratio measurement. Interval measurement scales are similar in that they involve quantities of things but these scales do not have absolute zero so °C and °F scales are good examples. Rank positions in a race are an example of ordinal measurement. Frequencies of male and female newsreaders on TV constitute nominal data.

2 Although the mean is preferred for interval or ratio data, it might not give an accurate impression of central tendency in a skewed sample of data. In this case, the median would be preferable.

Exam question

(a) When there are extreme scores that might distort the mean or where the data is ordinal.

(b) It measures the degree of spread around the mean (i.e. how varied are scores in the sample).

Data analysis 2

Checkpoints

1 Diary descriptions of the kind carried out by Piaget are unlikely to be distorted by participant reactivity to being observed. Piaget was a familiar figure to his children so they were unlikely to be affected by being observed by him.

2 Another word for reliability is 'consistency'. There are several kinds of reliability. The example given here is of inter-observer reliability, which is used to minimize bias in observations. To establish this, two or more observers would record their observations independently of each other and then crosscheck them to ensure that they matched.

Exam question

• Qualitative methods tend to give a rich and full account of behaviour at all levels rather than a 'snapshot' of behaviour at only one level.

• They can generate data that can be explored for meaning and underlying themes.

This section covers three key areas of social psychology – an attempt to understand and explain how the thoughts, feelings and behaviour of individuals are influenced by the actual, imagined or implied presence of others (Allport 1985). Relationships are formed, maintained, and often they break down. We will examine some of the major explanations of these processes. Although social psychologists have tended to focus on the more 'traditional' heterosexual Western relationships, a growing body of research has explored other 'understudied' relationships. Psychologists have fought to explain aggression in psychological terms against a growing body of evidence that has identified its biology. Of major interest in this respect are the potential effects of media violence.

Why do people help in an emergency? Explanations are divided between those that see such helping behaviour as purely altruistic and those that see more selfish reasons as the most likely explanation.

Exam themes

→ Formation, maintenance and dissolution of relationships

→ Cultural and sub-cultural differences in relationships

→ Aggression

→ Altruism and bystander behaviour

→ Media violence and its effects

Topic checklist

O AS ● A2	AQA/A	AQA/B	OCR	EDEXCEL
Interpersonal relationships	●	●		●
Maintenance and dissolution of relationships	●	●		
Cultural and sub-cultural differences in relationships	●	●		●
The causes of aggression	●			●
Altruism and bystander behaviour	●			
Media influences on behaviour	●			●

Interpersonal relationships

People are initially attracted to each other for a number of reasons. Theories of attraction stress the initial factors that are important in drawing people together. Theories of relationships explain why attraction may sometimes lead to more enduring partnerships.

Interpersonal attraction

Interpersonal balance theory (Newcomb 1961)

This is a cognitive theory which predicts that people like to see the world in a balanced way. We are attracted to people who share our attitudes as this makes for a balanced cognitive world. If these attitudes are not shared, or if one person behaves towards the other in a manner inconsistent with friendship, this creates an inconsistency in the relationship, which must be removed either cognitively (reinterpreting the inconsistency) or behaviourally (changing or ending the relationship). The more attracted we are to someone, the more the pressure for our attitudes to be similar to maintain this consistency.

Evaluation of interpersonal balance theory

→ The original theory suggested that people needed **cognitive consistency** at all costs. This is now seen as a product of the time in which Newcomb was writing, as it is now known that people can put up with a great deal of inconsistency in their relationships.

→ Balance in a relationship can be achieved in many ways, making it difficult to predict what will happen in any one given situation.

→ Balance theory describes relationships in an almost mathematical manner, ignoring other important factors, such as the nature and content of any interaction, and the nature of the people themselves.

The repulsion hypothesis (Rosenbaum 1986)

Rosenbaum suggested that rather than being attracted to people who hold similar attitudes to ourselves, we are initially attracted to all strangers, and only start to dislike them if we discover *dissimilarities* between them and us. Rosenbaum's research involved comparing 'liking ratings' given to photos of other students in a 'no information condition' with those given to students expressing similar attitudes to the raters. He found no differences between the two conditions.

Evaluation of the repulsion hypothesis

→ It is difficult to create a true 'no information' condition. In the absence of information to the contrary, people will resort to the **false consensus effect**, i.e. they assume similarity, and given the nature of the student raters, it is probable that they did just that.

→ Subsequent research (Smeaton et al 1989) found clear evidence to the contrary. As the perceived similarity of attitudes increased, so did the attraction, thus failing to support this view of attraction.

Action point

Make your own notes on the words shown in bold in the text.

"My life is spent in a perpetual alternation between two rhythms, the rhythm of attracting people for fear that I may be lonely, and the rhythm of trying to get rid of them because I know that I am bored."

C. E. M. Joad (1948)

Checkpoint 1

In what different ways might partners attempt to achieve 'balance' in a relationship?

Take note

Proximity/nearness often determines who you are likely to meet, and is also important in determining our choice of friends (Festinger et al 1950).

The jargon

False consensus effect is the tendency to over-estimate the degree to which our opinions and beliefs are shared by others.

The formation of relationships

Evolutionary theories

Evolutionary theorists suggest that human beings select mates according to criteria that are important from an evolutionary point of view. The sex investing more in offspring will be *selected* to exert stronger preferences about mating partners. Buss (1989) found evidence that females seek to mate with males who have the ability and willingness to provide resources related to **parental investment**. Females should value attributes in potential mates that signal the likely possession of resources. Furthermore, females should compete to display the reproductively linked cues that males desire in mates.

Evaluation of evolutionary theories

→ Evolutionary explanations of human relationships presume hetero-sexuality. Attempting to explain homosexual relationships in such a way is more problematic.
→ Evolutionary theories presume that relationships are solely about 'reproduction'. For many people (particularly in the case of later life relationships), relationships are *not* about having children.
→ These explanations may be seen as endorsing 'natural' behaviours such as sexual promiscuity in males and 'coyness' in females.

Reinforcement and need satisfaction

This theory suggests that we are attracted to, and form relationships with, people who **reinforce** us in some way. The model proposes:

→ our social environment contains experiences that can be evaluated as either 'good' or 'bad'
→ we like things that make us feel good
→ we associate *people* with these experiences, and are thus attracted to, or repelled by, them.

Evaluation of the reinforcement and need satisfaction model

→ Partners in relationships are frequently more concerned with equity and fairness than maximizing their own rewards.
→ Many relationships in non-Western societies show little concern for personal reinforcement in relationships.
→ It is easy to find examples of things that might be considered reinforcing in existing relationships, but we cannot be sure that these are the factors that led to their original formation.

Exam question   answer: page 100

Outline and evaluate *two* explanations of interpersonal attraction. (30 min)

Test yourself

When you have finished reading these pages, take a blank piece of paper and, in your own words, make a list of the key aspects of each area, and the critical points associated with each.

"The cost of indiscriminate mating will be less for the sex investing less and the benefits greater."

Buss (1989)

Checkpoint 2

Why would homosexual relationships pose a problem for theories that explain the formation of relationships in this way?

Checkpoint 3

In what ways might other people 'reinforce' us?

Checkpoint 4

In what ways do personal relationships in the West differ from those in non-Western societies?

Examiner's secrets

Be prepared to illustrate these theories with research studies that support or challenge the main assumptions.

Maintenance and dissolution of relationships

Explaining why some relationships succeed and others fail has been a major challenge for social psychologists in this field. Research has focused on the strategies used by people to maintain relationships, and the factors involved in the dissolution of relationships.

Maintenance strategies

A study by Ayres (1983) identified three types of strategy used by individuals in the maintenance of relationships.

→ Avoidance strategies – used to resist attempts made by another person to alter the relationship in some way (e.g. trivializing a partner's concerns).
→ Balance strategies – exerting more or less effort in an attempt to change the relationship. The amount of effort tends to reflect the direction of change (i.e. continuation or dissolution).
→ Directness – confronting issues (usually by talking about them) in an attempt to maintain the status quo.

Dindia and Baxter (1987) identified two categories of maintenance strategies – the *maintenance* strategies (aimed at preventing problems) and *repair* strategies (aimed at making good problems in a relationship). The former strategies tend to revolve around 'doing things together' whereas the latter strategies are more analytical about the relationship.

Stages of relationship breakdown (Duck 1988)

→ **The intra-psychic phase** One partner becomes increasingly dissatisfied with the relationship as it is. This may, if the dissatisfaction is sufficiently great, lead on to the next phase.
→ **The dyadic phase** The other member of the relationship is now involved. If the source of the dissatisfaction is not resolved (by one or both partners changing), it may lead to the third phase.
→ **The social phase** The break-up becomes 'public'. Partners are forced to consider the possibility and potential impact of the break-up. If problems are not resolved here it leads to the final stage.
→ **The grave-dressing phase** Each partner now organizes their post-breakdown lives and creates their own version of who was responsible for the breakdown of the previous relationship and why. During this phase, each partner may attempt to minimize their own blame for the breakdown within their *version* of events.

Theories of the maintenance and dissolution of relationships

Social exchange theory (Thibaut and Kelley 1959)

This is referred to as an 'economic' theory because it proposes that we run our relationships like a balance sheet, i.e. we aim to maximize our profits and minimize our losses. Thibaut and Kelley proposed a four-stage model of relationships.

"Being a husband is a whole-time job. That is why so many husbands fail. They cannot give their entire attention to it."

A. Bennett (1918)

→ **Sampling** – partners explore the rewards and costs in a number of relationships.
→ **Bargaining** – partners identify profits and losses in their own relationship.
→ **Commitment** – the relationship becomes stable, the exchange of rewards between partners becomes predictable.
→ **Institutionalization** – interactions become established as the partners 'settle-down'.

This theory proposes that we engage in a comparison process, involving a comparison of our current relationship with the same relationship in the past (CL) and alternative relationships we might be in (CL alt).

→ **Comparison level (CL)** – a comparison of the current state of the relationship with the rewards and costs of this relationship in the past. If this comparison is favourable, the relationship is healthy.
→ **Comparison level for alternatives (CL alt)** – if we feel we might be better off in another relationship, we might be motivated to end our current relationship in favour of the alternative.

Equity theory (Walster, 1978)

Equity theory is a development of social exchange theory and is also an 'economic' theory. It focuses on the importance of *balance* in relationships. There are four principles in this theory:

→ individuals attempt to maximize rewards and minimize losses in their relationships
→ rewards are 'distributed' within a relationship to ensure fairness
→ inequitable (i.e. unfair) relationships lead to dissatisfaction
→ the 'loser' is motivated to re-establish the equity in the relationship. The greater the inequity, the greater the effort needed

Evaluation of economic theories of relationships

→ Many of the studies supporting exchange and equity theories have taken place in artificial 'laboratory' situations that have little relevance to relationships in the real world.
→ Clark and Mills (1979) have identified two types of couple, the communal couple and the exchange couple. Only in the exchange couple is 'score-keeping' evident. Communal couples are more relaxed about what is rewarding or equitable in their relationship.
→ Moghaddam et al (1993) argue that the preoccupation with exchange and equity is a feature of North America rather than more collectivist cultures.

Take note

Levinger (1976) proposed a similar social exchange theory. It helps to explain why marital dissatisfaction is not a strong predictor of divorce.

Checkpoint 1

What is the main difference between CL and CL alt?

Action point

Both social exchange theory and equity theory explain relationships in terms of the profits and losses accrued, and each partner's motivation to maintain a balance between these.

Checkpoint 2

What is it about North American culture that makes exchange and equity a more conspicuous feature of relationships than in more collectivist societies?

Exam question   answer: page 100

Outline and evaluate research into the dissolution of relationships. (30 min)

Cultural and sub-cultural differences in relationships

Action point

Although there may be differences *between* cultures, there are also many differences *within* cultures.

Checkpoint 1

Give two examples of cultures that you consider to be 'individualistic' and two that you consider to be collectivistic.

Take note 1

People in collectivist societies tend to have fewer, but closer, friendships than people in individualist societies (Goodwin, 1995).

Take note 2

In some societies polygamy (where a man has more than one wife) is the norm.

Action point

You may know someone (or be such a person yourself) for whom such practices are the norm. Talk to them about arranged marriages and attitudes to divorce.

Example

Dating agencies are common in Western societies. They offer to help you find your 'ideal' mate.

Whereas interpersonal relationships in Western cultures tend to be individualistic, voluntary and temporary, those in non-Western cultures tend to be collective, obligatory and permanent. Sub-cultural differences include those represented by men and women, homosexuals and heterosexuals, Asians and Afro-Caribbeans.

Differences between Western and non-Western cultures

Individualist and collectivist cultures

In individualist cultures, the emphasis is on the individual and their personal rights and achievements. There is an emphasis on autonomy and the 'I' is more important than the 'we'. Where there is a conflict between the interests of the individual and the collective, individuals prioritize their own needs. In contrast, in collectivist societies, the needs of the collective are prioritized over the needs of the individual. A marriage may be seen as a union between families as much as a union between individuals (Humphreys 2000).

Voluntary and involuntary relationships

Although marriage arrangements vary from those where partners have no choice at all to those where the choice is totally determined by the partners themselves, the majority of cultures have characteristics of each. The commonest form of marriage is by arrangement, with parents having the most significant influence on the eventual choice (Ingoldsby 1995).

→ A study of Sikhs, Hindus and Muslims living in Britain found that arranged marriages were common. The most important factors in partner choice were caste, social class and religion (Ghuman 1994).

→ A study of Hindu Gujarati couples found that only a small percentage had completely arranged marriages. Most had been introduced by a third-party but had been given the option of refusal.

Permanent and impermanent relationships

Most cultures allow divorce although there is a greater stigma attached to divorce in cultures where marriages are arranged. There is considerable variation between different cultures for the main reasons for marital breakdown (Goodwin 1999).

→ In China (a collectivist culture) divorce rate is very low and is considered shameful for both the individuals concerned and their families.

→ In some African societies, increased urbanization and greater educational opportunities for women have led to increases in divorce rates. This is seen as a reflection of the preoccupation within individualist societies to search for the 'ideal partner'.

Evaluation of cross-cultural differences research

→ Smith and Bond (1999) argue that there are considerable problems faced by researchers when having to translate research designs into 'local' languages, and having to translate 'local' responses into a form where they make sense to the researchers. This may lead to a loss of the more subtle aspects of peoples' responses.

→ Some researchers (e.g. Buss 1989) have claimed that there are actually far more similarities among different cultures concerning those factors that are considered important for male-female relationships. In particular, Buss argues that there are strong male-female differences that are universal to most if not all cultures.

Understudied relationships ●●●

Gay and lesbian relationships

Homosexuality is still illegal in many cultures and was, until 1973, considered sufficiently 'abnormal' to be classified as a mental disorder on DSM (Diagnostic and Statistical Manual of mental disorders). There are some cultures where homosexuals are treated more sympathetically, and even some cultures where homosexuality is positively encouraged. Because gays and lesbians are exposed to so many negative stereotypes and prejudices, they may develop pride and dignity by maintaining privacy and secrecy about their sexual preference (Humphreys 2000). Humphreys identifies a number of problems faced by gay and lesbian couples.

→ The operation of pervasive stereotypes about gays and lesbians. These include the belief that they are incapable of sustaining long-term relationships and that they are inferior versions of heterosexual relationships.

→ Partners must continuously seek the support and sympathy of their partner rather than sharing the load with others (because of the fear of being 'outed').

→ Family and friends may hold unrealistic expectations about 'closeted' homosexuals and may continuously attempt to pair them off at social occasions.

→ They face a complex world of schools and other child-oriented networks. Those in shared custody arrangements with a former heterosexual spouse face losing custody of their children.

Action point

Buss tested this claim across 37 different cultures, and found strong support for these 'evolutionary significant' male-female differences.

Checkpoint 2

What do you think are the differences in male-female and female-male preferences that Buss found?

The jargon

Understudied relationships are those relationships such as gay and lesbian, relationships among the disabled, and internet relationships, that have traditionally been ignored by the majority of social psychologists.

The jargon

Outed means being 'exposed' as a homosexual by other people.

Don't forget

Only one type of 'understudied relationship' has been included here. There are others that can also be included under this heading e.g. relationships over the internet.

Exam question   answer: pages 100–1

Discuss research relating to understudied relationships (e.g. gay and lesbian relationships or internet relationships). (30 min)

Examiner's secrets

Although this question mentions gay and lesbian relationships and internet relationships, they are merely included as examples of appropriate content.

The causes of aggression

Social psychological explanations of aggression see the causes of our aggressive behaviour as located within our social world. This is in stark contrast to psycho-dynamic and biological explanations, which may see aggressive behaviour as a consequence of instinctual drives or biochemistry.

Social learning theory (SLT) explanations

SLT explanations claim that aggressive behaviour is learned either through:

→ direct experience – aggressive behaviour may be reinforced and is therefore more likely to reoccur in similar situations in the future
→ vicarious experience – the person observes a role model behaving aggressively and subsequently imitates the behaviour.

For behaviour to be imitated it must be seen to be rewarding in some way. The likelihood of a person behaving aggressively in any situation depends on:

→ their previous experiences of aggressive behaviour (both direct and vicarious)
→ the degree to which their aggressive behaviour was successful in the past
→ the likelihood of their aggressive behaviour being successful in this situation
→ other cognitive, social and environmental factors that are operating at the same time.

Evaluation of social learning theory explanations

→ Experimental studies that support SLT explanations (e.g. Bandura et al 1963) have been criticized as being artificial and lacking in **ecological validity** (i.e. not related to 'real-life' aggression).
→ SLT explanations can account for the lack of consistency in people's aggressive behaviour. It may be reinforced differently in different situations.
→ Biological factors, such as the male hormone **testosterone** may also have a causal role in aggression. Pre-menstrual syndrome has been cited in criminal trials as a reason for aggressive behaviour. These cast doubt on aggression being purely a learned response.

Deindividuation

Zimbardo (1969) distinguished between *individual* behaviour, which is rational and conforms to acceptable social standards, and *deindividuated* behaviour, which is based on primitive urges and does not conform to **social norms**. People usually refrain from acting in antisocial ways because such behaviours are easily identifiable in a society that has strong norms against such 'uncivilized' behaviour. In some situations (e.g. crowds) these restraints may become relaxed and aggression might follow as a consequence.

→ Mann (1981) used the concept of individuation to explain the **'baiting crowd'**. Distance from the potential suicide victim and crowd size produce a state of deindividuation in crowd members.

→ Milgram (1965) found that participants were likely to give higher levels of electric shock if they could not see their 'victim' (and when the 'victim' could not see them).

Evaluation of deindividuation

→ Deindividuation may not only produce antisocial behaviour. Evidence also exists (e.g. Diener 1980) that deindividuation may produce increases in *pro-social* behaviour.

→ The deindividuation perspective argues that when we *are* deindividuated we are less likely to conform to social norms. However, an alternative view is that individuals are conforming to 'local group norms', which may sometimes be antisocial and aggressive, and at other times prosocial and altruistic.

→ Marsh et al (1978) found that, in most cases, 'deindividualized' football violence is highly organized rather than undisciplined, and ritualized rather than physically violent.

Environmental stressors and aggression ●●●

Environmental stressors such as heat and noise may cause an increase in arousal, which may lead to negative emotions, and thus hostile thoughts and/or aggression. They may cause stimulus overload, interfering with task completion, leading to frustration. The effects of high temperatures on aggression have been demonstrated in a number of studies.

→ Hotter regions of the world tend to have more aggression than cooler regions, and hotter seasons and days more than cooler ones.

→ In laboratory studies, as temperature rises so does aggression, but beyond a certain temperature, aggression declines (Halpern 1995). At moderate temperatures we may be motivated towards hostility, but at high temperatures we are motivated to escape.

Intense levels of noise have also been shown to be antecedents of aggression, either by increasing arousal or decreasing our ability to deal with frustration. Evidence has shown that:

→ participants gave higher levels of electric shock when they were exposed to high levels of noise over which they had no control

→ if the person has control over the source of the noise or is not predisposed to aggress, noise has little or no effect on aggression.

Exam questions   answers: page 101

1   Outline and evaluate *two* theories of aggression. (30 min)

2   Discuss research relating to the effects of *one* environmental stressor on aggressive behaviour. (30 min)

Test yourself

When you have finished reading these pages, take a blank piece of paper and, in your own words, make a list of the key aspects of each area, and the critical points associated with each.

"Deindividuation may produce an orgy of aggressive, selfish and antisocial behaviour."

Hogg and Vaughan (1998)

Checkpoint 3

Hotter days are associated with higher levels of aggressive behaviour. Can you think of another reason for this relationship?

Action point

Environmental stressors may not necessarily produce aggression directly, but may change the way we interpret ambiguous situations, predisposing us to aggression.

Examiner's secrets

Pay particular attention to the different injunctions in these questions. 'Outline' only requires a summary description, but 'discuss' or 'describe' require a more detailed account.

Altruism and bystander behaviour

Altruism is a form of pro-social behaviour in which a person will voluntarily help another person at some cost to himself or herself. One of the major problems for psychologists has been determining what is truly altruistic and what might better be explained in terms of egoism (self-interest).

Action point

Make your own notes on the words shown in bold in the text.

The jargon

Empathy is feeling an emotional response that is consistent with another's emotional state or condition.

The empathy-altruism hypothesis (Batson 1991) ●●●

This explains altruistic behaviour as a consequence of **empathy**. Empathy consists of a number of different components including:

→ perspective-taking (the ability to take another's point of view)
→ personal distress (experiencing emotions such as sadness)
→ empathetic concern (feelings of compassion for another).

It is perspective-taking that leads to empathetic concern, otherwise helping would be based on **egoistic** motives. Research (Batson et al 1981) shows that people high in empathetic concern are more likely to help another in distress even when there was an easy way to escape. Participants who only experienced **personal distress** were less likely to help if there was an easier way to reduce their negative feelings.

Checkpoint 1

When would people be most likely to help out of empathetic concern?

"This contradicts the underlying assumption that human nature is fundamentally self-serving."

Batson (1991)

Evaluation of the empathy-altruism hypothesis

→ Research by Batson et al has shown that people do frequently help for reasons other than the reduction of their own personal distress.
→ Concern about the disapproval of others does not appear to explain why empathetic concern motivates helping (Fultz et al 1988).
→ People may help simply to avoid feeling bad about themselves. Research suggests this is not the case (Batson et al 1988).

Checkpoint 2

What do we mean by 'egoistic' helping?

The negative-state relief model (Cialdini 1987) ●●●

This proposes that when we are experiencing **negative states** we are motivated to reduce them by helping others. According to this view, therefore, the motivation for helping is egoistic. If we are able to reduce these negative states by a less costly route (e.g. ignoring the other person), we should, according to this hypothesis, take it.

Research by Cialdini et al (1987) found that when participants were led to believe they had been given a 'mood fixing' drug, they were less motivated to help another participant in distress.

Evaluation of the negative-state relief model

→ Both Batson and Cialdini agree that when we come across someone in need we feel sad, and helping them makes us feel happier. The subtle difference between the two is *why* we help.
→ Cialdini et al (1987) claim that when we feel empathy for another, we also feel sadness. However, raising the former did not increase the likelihood of helping, whereas raising the latter (a negative state) did increase the likelihood of a helping response.

Action point

Helping someone close to us may be an example of 'kin selection'. Try to find out more about kin selection and how it might affect altruistic behaviour in humans.

→ Batson (1991) suggests that we feel empathy when we feel a close attachment to another person; otherwise we feel personal distress.

Research into bystander behaviour ●●●

Latané and Darley (1968) have proposed two possible processes to explain why sometimes bystanders help in an emergency, yet at other times they do not.

→ **Diffusion of responsibility** – when one person is present, they have total responsibility to help. As the number of bystanders increases, so this responsibility becomes diffused among them.

→ **Pluralistic ignorance** – when making a decision whether or not to help, we look to others to see what they are doing. If other people fail to react we may conclude it is not an emergency and do not help either.

Research in the laboratory (Darley and Latané 1968) and in the natural environment (Latané and Darley 1970) have supported the proposal that help is less likely to be given, or is slower to happen, when others are present.

Latané and Darley's cognitive model (1970)

This is a five-stage model to explain why bystanders help or withhold help in an emergency. At each stage there is the possibility that the helping response will be inhibited. These possible inhibitions are:

→ the bystander may not notice the situation
→ the situation may be ambiguous and not seen as an emergency
→ the bystander assumes someone else will take responsibility
→ the bystander may feel they lack the competence to help
→ helping may be against their personal interests (e.g. it is dangerous).

Evaluation of Latané and Darley's cognitive model

→ Latané and Nida (1981) have shown that increasing the ambiguity of a situation inhibits people's likelihood of helping.
→ More 'competent' people (or those who *believe* themselves to be competent) are more likely to help in specific circumstances (Clark and Word 1974).
→ The presence of other observers appears to reduce the likelihood that a person will help in an emergency (Latané and Nida 1981).
→ Alternative models (e.g. Piliavin et al's **'arousal: cost-reward model'**) stress the importance of a series of calculations concerning the potential consequences of getting involved.
→ The likelihood of helping in an emergency is also determined by cultural factors. Culture also provides the rules and norms concerning when it is appropriate to seek and to offer help.

Exam questions

answers: page 101–2

1   Outline and evaluate *two* explanations of altruism in humans. (30 min)

2   Discuss research relating to the behaviour of bystanders. (30 min)

Test yourself

When you have finished reading these pages, take a blank piece of paper and, in your own words, make a list of the key aspects of each area, and the critical points associated with each.

Checkpoint 3

Why is this referred to as pluralistic 'ignorance'?

Action point

Read about some studies carried out in this area, and make notes about their conclusions.

Action point

Read about this model in your textbook. Draw the five stages on a piece of paper and give your own examples for each stage.

The jargon

Arousal – when we see someone in distress, we become physiologically aroused. This model suggests that we are more likely to label this arousal as personal distress (see earlier in topic spread).

Examiner's secrets

If answering a question on bystander behaviour – try to resist the temptation to spend a lot of time describing examples of 'emergencies' (such as the Kitty Genovese incident).

Media influences on behaviour

Action point

Make your own notes on the words shown in bold in the text.

The jargon

Meta-analysis is a statistical technique that allows a researcher to examine results from a large number of studies in order to detect significant trends.

Checkpoint 1

What, according to this argument, is the main difference between pro-social and antisocial messages in the media?

Checkpoint 2

Why might these programmes be considered 'artificial and lacking real-life application', and why is this a problem?

Much of the research carried out in this area has focused on the potential antisocial effects of the media, particularly its effects on children's aggressive behaviour. Research also shows that the media has the potential to both educate and model a range of pro-social behaviours.

Media effects on pro-social behaviour

In a meta-analysis of research in this area, Hearold (1986) found that despite the relatively fewer studies that have been carried out on the media's pro-social effects compared to its antisocial effects, the effects observed have been larger and consistent for both boys and girls. This is seen as being largely due to the fact that pro-social messages are generally designed to have an influence on viewers where antisocial messages are not. Research has shown that children imitate many forms of pro-social behaviour when exposed to models displaying these behaviours in the media.

Lovelace and Huston (1983) have identified three modelling strategies for the transmission of pro-social messages.

→ Pro-social behaviour modelled only – several studies (e.g. Sprafkin et al 1975) have demonstrated the positive effects of pro-social models on TV, particularly if they model *specific* behaviours.
→ Pro-social conflict resolution – pro-social messages are presented alongside or in contrast to antisocial behaviours. Several studies (e.g. Friedrich and Stein 1973) have shown increased levels of co-operation and helping after viewing such programmes.
→ Conflict without resolution – a character is seen to be struggling with a particular problem (e.g. bullying, divorce etc.) but no decision is made. Some research studies (e.g. Rockman 1980) have found that children are able to understand the programme content and can then generate pro-social solutions to the problems.

Evaluation of research showing pro-social effects

→ Television messages that contain only a pro-social message present these clearly and unambiguously and are generally effective in producing pro-social behaviour in viewers. However, research has often used brief segments of specially produced programmes, and so may be considered artificial and lacking real-life application.
→ Pro-social messages that are presented alongside antisocial messages need to be presented in clear contrast and for the majority of the programme. If this does not happen, children may model the antisocial behaviours as well. Some research studies (e.g. Friedrich-Cofer et al 1979) have shown an *increase* in antisocial behaviour after children viewed programmes that contained both types.
→ Studies show limited support for the beneficial effects of conflict without resolution messages. Children younger than eight may not benefit from this type of **modelling** as effectively as older children.

Media effects on antisocial behaviour ●●●

→ **Correlational studies** (e.g. Robinson and Bachman 1972) suggest a link between watching television violence and engaging in violent behaviour, but this does not demonstrate a *causal* relationship.

→ **Lab experiments** (e.g. Bandura et al 1963) have shown that exposure to televised violence can produce increases in aggression, although these studies may not reflect real-life viewing conditions.

→ **Natural experiments** (e.g. Centrewall 1989) have found *increases* in murder rates following the introduction of television in some countries (e.g. Canada), but *decreases* in others (e.g. South Africa).

→ **Longitudinal studies** (e.g. Belson 1978) have demonstrated long-term effects of early television violence for boys but not for girls. Fictional violence in a familiar and realistic context is seen as having more impact than unfamiliar contexts and fantasy violence.

Explanations for a media/violence relationship include

→ Cognitive priming – children may learn problem-solving **scripts** from their observation of models on television. Frequent viewing of television violence may lead to these scripts being stored in memory and recalled later if any aspect of the original situation is present.

→ Socialization – children may learn aggressive behaviour from the media. Television might inform viewers of the positive and negative consequences of violent behaviour. When this is justified or left unpunished, their concern about consequences is reduced.

→ **Desensitization** – frequent viewing of television violence may cause viewers to be less anxious and sensitive about violence. It is seen as 'normal' and viewers are more likely to engage in it.

Evaluation of research showing antisocial effects

→ Hagell and Newburn (1994) showed that young offenders watched *less* television and video than their non-offending counterparts.

→ Psychological research has underestimated what children understand about the media. Seven-year-olds are able to talk intelligently and cynically about the media (Buckingham 1966).

→ Research studies have consistently produced contradictory findings about the effects of media violence on children. Some have shown effects on boys but not girls, and some the complete opposite.

Exam questions   answers: page 102

1 Discuss research relating to the pro-social effects of the media. (30 min)

2 Discuss research relating to the antisocial effects of the media. (30 min)

Action point

When you have finished reading these pages, take a blank piece of paper and, in your own words, make a list of the key aspects of each area, and the critical points associated with each.

Checkpoint 3

What other reasons might be offered for Centrewall's findings?

"Young media users are portrayed as the inept users of products which can trick them into all kinds of ill-advised behaviour."

Gauntlett (1998)

Checkpoint 4

Why is the Hagell and Newburn finding so important?

Examiner's secrets

It is important to show *why* a particular piece of research is important, and how it contributes to the topic in question.

Answers
Social psychology

Interpersonal relationships

Checkpoints

1 Through argument and negotiation, or perhaps through changing partner. In many cases, individuals may play down the importance of an attitude to minimize any perceived imbalance.

2 Because the selection of mates is seen as a way in which the individual can ensure that their genes stand a 'good chance' in the next generation. Evolutionary explanations of homosexuality might stress the role of inclusive fitness, i.e. helping those with whom we share genes.

3 In many ways – by agreeing with (and thus affirming) our attitudes, by complimenting us (so that we feel good about ourselves), or by providing us with some other experience (e.g. companionship) that we find rewarding.

4 Although the 'West/non-West' divide is a very crude one, it is generally believed that Western relationships are more temporary and voluntary in nature, whereas non-Western relationships are more permanent and involuntary.

Exam question

This question requires an outline description and an evaluation of *two* explanations of interpersonal attraction. It is important, therefore, to plan your response carefully. In a 30-minute answer, you would give 15 minutes to the first explanation, and 15 minutes to the second. This means about four paragraphs, each of about 150 words:

* outline description of interpersonal balance theory – we are attracted to those who share our attitudes; this makes a balanced cognitive world
* evaluation of this theory – people are able to put up with inconsistency; balance can be achieved in a number of other ways, and the theory ignores other important factors
* outline description of the repulsion hypothesis – we are attracted to everyone but then discount those who are dissimilar.
* evaluation of this hypothesis – including the use of the false consensus effect, and the contrary research findings which challenge its claims.

Examiner's secrets

When there are four clear 'parts' to a question, careful use of the time available is vital. Don't waste it including too many examples of such forms of attraction in your answer.

Maintenance and dissolution of relationships

Checkpoints

1 CL involves a comparison between the current rewards offered by a relationship and those offered in the same relationship in the past. CL alt, on the other hand, involves a comparison between current rewards in a relationship and the perceived rewards in another relationship.

2 North American society is an example of an individualist society, where the needs of the individual are perceived as more important than the needs of the group. Individuals are also encouraged to search for the 'perfect partner', therefore are more likely to be demanding in what they expect from their marriage partner.

Exam question

This question focuses you explicitly on research into the *dissolution* (i.e. breakdown) of relationships. As research is such a generous term (see 'Examiner's secrets), there is a lot you might include:

* Duck's stages of relationship breakdown (intra-psychic, dyadic, social, grave-dressing) show the developmental process of dissolution
* social exchange theory uses the concepts of CL and CL alt to explain the processes of comparison that might lead to breakdown
* equity theory sees dissolution as one way of dealing with inequitable relationships
* much of the research on these 'economic' theories has taken place in artificial settings
* only 'exchange' couples show evidence of this 'score-keeping' in their relationships
* the preoccupation with exchange and equity may be a feature of North American relationships rather than more collectivist societies.

Examiner's secrets

The term 'research' allows you to include material that is the product of either actual research studies (empirical research) and/or the construction of theories. Research is a very 'student friendly' term!

Cultural and sub-cultural differences in relationships

Checkpoints

1 Individualist cultures include the USA, Australia and the UK. Collectivist cultures include China, Russia and Guatemala.

2 According to Buss's research, males typically chose females who symbolized youth and health (important for childbearing), whereas females typically chose males who were ambitious and hardworking (important for the provision of resources).

Exam question

Discuss requires both an evaluation and an evaluation of research into differences between relationships in Western and non-Western relationships. It is tempting to fill your answer with examples and anecdotes, but you should keep this answer as psychological as possible. You might include the following:

- differences between individualist (commonly Western) and collectivist (commonly non-Western) cultures and their relevance here
- research relating to voluntary and involuntary relationships (e.g. arranged marriages)
- research relating to permanent and impermanent relationships (e.g. attitudes to divorce in different cultures)
- evaluation of cross-cultural research including the problem of equivalence (i.e. accepting that research questions and responses have the same meaning in different cultures).

Examiner's secrets

This question asks for research into the differences between Western and non-Western relationships. A question that asked for 'cultural differences' without specifying 'Western versus non-Western' might include sub-cultural differences (as defined in this section) in the answer.

The causes of aggression

Checkpoints

1 Children would be most likely to imitate behaviour of models when they see the model being reinforced for their aggressive behaviour.
2 It does not explore aggression in a real-life setting. The Bobo dolls were designed to be hit and, unlike in real-life, the children could strike out without fear of retaliation from the victim of their aggression (i.e. the Bobo doll).
3 People are more likely to be outside on hot days, and more likely to be drinking alcohol (another factor in aggressive behaviour).

Exam questions

1 This a straightforward question, and just requires careful time planning to cover all the different components of the question. There are clearly four parts of the question as follows:
- outline description of social learning theory (nature of SLT and the importance of vicarious learning and imitation)
- evaluation of the SLT theory of aggression (e.g. problems of relevance of original studies, underestimation of biological factors etc.)
- outline of deindividuation theory (social restraints become relaxed when anonymous, demonstrated in the 'baiting crowd')
- evaluation of deindividuation theory (e.g. it may produce increases in pro-social behaviour; individuals may also be 'conforming' to norms).
2 This is also a very straightforward question, requiring 'research' (see earlier comment on page 100) relating to the effects of two environmental stressors. This text has covered heat and noise, but there are others that are also relevant such as pollution and crowding. You should use your textbook to supplement the material covered in this

guide, and organize your answer in the same way as the previous question.

Examiner's secrets

If a question asks for 'two' of something, you would be wasting your time writing about more than two. You should read questions very carefully, and be miserly about what you include and do not include.

Altruism and bystander behaviour

Checkpoints

1 When they were attached in some way to the other person (e.g. related to them or similar to them).
2 Helping because of selfish reasons, e.g. the need to rid oneself of negative feelings such as guilt or depression, rather than acting out of compassion for the person in need.
3 Because this is the wrong interpretation of events. Because no-one reacts as an individual, the consensus comes to be an interpretation of the event as a non-emergency.

Exam questions

1 As in the previous two questions, this question is an invitation to demonstrate your time management skills when constructing your answer. The question asks for two explanations of 'altruism' in humans. You can take a fairly liberal interpretation of the term 'altruism' in the question (Cialdini, for example, argues that 'apparent' altruism is actually selfish – or egoistic – behaviour). It is arguable whether explanations of bystander behaviour constitute explanations of 'altruism', but with the more relevant material available to you, you would not really need to include these.
- The two major theories covered here are Batson's empathy-altruism hypothesis (perspective-taking leads to empathetic concern which leads to altruistic behaviour) and Cialdini's negative-state relief model (we are motivated to reduce our own negative states by helping others).
- You should include research studies to support your description of each of these theories. Research studies also serve the valuable purpose of being able to support or challenge a theoretical assumption.
- It is a good idea to conclude your answer with a statement that offers some resolution to the different claims of the two theories. Batson, for example, suggests that we feel empathy when we feel a close attachment to somebody else, otherwise we feel personal distress – therefore the reasons for helping someone are different in different situations.
2 This question effectively asks you to write everything you know about bystander behaviour. However, there are two important points to remember.

- The question asks for 'research', not stories of bystander apathy or even bystander heroism. Students frequently describe the case of Kitty Genovese in great detail, but this does not count as research so should be avoided.
- Half of your answer should be evaluation, so your answer should be constructed to accommodate that.

Apart from these two points, you are free to include more or less anything you like so long as it is relevant to the question. Try to include a balance of research *studies* and *explanations* of bystander behaviour.

Media influences on behaviour

Checkpoints

1 Pro-social messages are often more subtle and often intended. Antisocial messages are rarely intended but may have high visual impact, and therefore are more memorable.

2 As television is part of our social life, we are more likely to be influenced by events that are an important part of this context. Films and other media that have been specially constructed as educational media do not fit readily into this context and may, therefore, lack the impact of material that we *choose* to watch.

3 There is an assumption here that the *increases* in violent behaviour in Canada were a product of increased exposure to television. The fact that violent behaviour *decreased* in South Africa following the introduction of television suggests that other social changes in the two countries (e.g. the increased urbanization of Canada and the post-Apartheid era in South Africa) might be more responsible for the documented changes in levels of violence.

4 Because it suggests that if young offenders watch *less* television and video than non-offenders, it is unlikely that their behaviour is a direct result of exposure to violent behaviour in the media.

Exam questions

1 Although there hasn't been as much research interest in this area (compared to the antisocial effects of the media), the effects themselves are larger and more consistent. Research has concentrated on three areas:
- pro-social behaviour modelled only
- pro-social conflict resolution
- conflict without resolution.

Evaluation of this area might include the artificiality of some pro-social 'programmes' and the sometimes contradictory research findings.

2 It is easy to get carried away with a question of this sort, there is so much material available (try entering 'television violence' on your internet search). You might try structuring your answer as follows:
- research studies of media violence (e.g. correlational studies and natural experiments)
- theoretical explanations of the media/violence relationship (e.g. cognitive priming, socialization, desensitization)
- evaluation of research showing antisocial effects (e.g. Hagell and Newburn found that young offenders watched *less* television).

Physiological psychology

This section samples one of the more popular areas of physiological psychology: biological rhythms, sleep and dreaming. Many animals show daily rhythms in behaviour and physiological measures, and some show seasonal rhythms. The sleep/waking cycle is an example of such a rhythm. There are a number of explanations of the functions of sleep; some see sleep as a period of brain and body restoration, and others see sleep as an adaptive response to the demands of the environment. The most distinctive feature of REM (rapid eye-movement) sleep is dreaming, although the exact nature and purpose of dreaming is still hotly debated. In this section we review both physiological and psychological explanations of dreaming.

Exam themes

→ Biological rhythms – circadian, infradian and ultradian rhythms

→ Endogenous pacemakers and exogenous zeitgebers

→ Theories of the function of sleep

→ Research into the nature of dreams and the functions of dreaming

Topic checklist

○ AS ● A2	AQA/A	AQA/B	OCR	EDEXCEL
Biological rhythms	●			○
Sleep	●		○	○
Dreaming	●		○	○

Biological rhythms

Many animal and human behaviours are governed by biological rhythms. The cycle for some of these behaviours is less than 24 hours, whereas for others it is seasonal. Whereas some rhythms appear to be endogenous, occurring independently of external changes, most are synchronized with changes in the external environment.

Types of biological rhythm ●●●

Ultradian rhythms

→ These have a frequency of more than one complete cycle every 24 hours (e.g. cycle of sleep stages that occurs during a night's sleep).

→ They are also found in many complex human behaviours – EEG measures of alertness appear to vary with an ultradian rhythm.

→ Ultradian cycles are related to brain and body size – the smaller the animal the more rapid their ultradian cycles.

→ Ultradian rhythms appear to be controlled by different brain mechanisms than circadian rhythms. Destruction of brain mechanisms that control the latter does not seem to affect behaviours that have an ultradian rhythm.

Infradian rhythms

→ These are cycles which occur less than once every 24 hours (e.g. the human menstrual cycle).

→ Some infradian rhythms occur on a seasonal basis and are known as *circannual* rhythms (e.g. migration in birds).

→ Lesions in the SCN tend to disrupt circadian rhythms but do not disrupt circannual rhythms – thus they involve more than simply 'counting' 365 days.

→ Seasonal changes are also evident in human beings (e.g. seasonal affective disorder). People with SAD appear to have a high threshold for *melatonin*, a hormone which has an important regulatory role in sleep and is stimulated by exposure to darkness.

Circadian rhythms

→ These occur every 24 hours (e.g. the human sleep/wake cycle).

→ Other biological functions that display a circadian rhythm include body temperature, hormone secretion and blood pressure.

→ Circadian rhythms have great significance to animals. Nocturnal animals can avoid predators by remaining hidden during daylight hours whereas diurnal animals are adapted to forage during the day.

→ These rhythms are controlled by *endogenous pacemakers* so that animals can anticipate periodic events and engage in appropriate adaptive behaviours (e.g. sleeping when it gets dark).

→ The in-built biological nature of circadian rhythms is such that many will be maintained even when the light/dark cycle is manipulated artificially.

Checkpoint 1

How many complete cycles of sleep stages does someone go through in an average night's sleep?

Checkpoint 2

What other behaviours might occur in a circannual cycle?

Watch out!

A *circannual* rhythm is a type of *infradian* rhythm.

The jargon

Endogenous pacemaker – a physiological structure that regulates the timing of biological rhythms.

Checkpoint 3

What is the most powerful stimulus for resetting the circadian 'clock' in mammals?

Endogenous pacemakers

The pineal gland

In birds and reptiles, the most important endogenous pacemaker (biological clock) is the pineal gland. This contains light receptors, which respond to light penetrating the skull over the pineal. These then influence the activity of neurons in the pineal gland that convert the neurotransmitter serotonin into the hormone melatonin. Melatonin production and release is regulated by the amount of light falling on the pineal, *decreasing* as the level of light *increases*. When released into general circulation, melatonin acts on many organs and glands and is responsible for many of the body's rhythmic behaviours.

The supra-chiasmatic nucleus (SCN)

The SCN is part of the hypothalamus. The neurons of the SCN have an in-built circadian firing pattern. The SCN regulates the manufacture and secretion of melatonin in the pineal gland via an interconnecting pathway. The SCN also connects to the retina of the eye. Through these connections, the amount of light falling on the eye indirectly affects the release of melatonin from the pineal. Although the SCN and the pineal gland operate as endogenous pacemakers, their activity is synchronized with the light/dark rhythm of the external environment. Studies that have removed light as a *zeitgeber* have led to two conclusions:

→ endogenous mechanisms are able to control the sleep/waking cycle even in the absence of light
→ light acts as a zeitgeber to reset the biological clock every day so that circadian rhythms are co-ordinated with the outside world.

Disruption of biological rhythms

The sensitivity of our bodily rhythms to zeitgebers is adaptive so long as external stimuli change only gradually. Sudden changes in zeitgebers (e.g. crossing time zones in air travel) mean we cannot adjust our bodily rhythms quickly enough, and our physiological activities are desynchronized for a while. This desynchronization of the body's physiological rhythms from the external world gives rise to the feelings of tiredness and disorientation known as **jet lag**. After a few days the body and the external world re-synchronize, and we are again in tune with the external world and its zeitgebers. Studies of **shift work** (e.g. Czeisler et al 1982) show that switching shifts disrupts links between zeitgebers and biological rhythms, and that short-rotation shifts cause health problems, sleep difficulties and work-related stress.

> **Don't forget**
>
> Although the pineal gland has a role in sleep regulation in humans, it exerts control over the full daily cycle in other species (e.g. changes in blood pressure, body temperature etc.).

> **Action point**
>
> Human circadian rhythms may also shift when light is applied to the back of the knees.

> **The jargon**
>
> *Zeitgeber* – external cues (such as light) that help animals to maintain their circadian rhythms.

> **Checkpoint 4**
>
> Why does jet lag tend to be greater when flying east to west than when flying west to east?

Exam question   answer: page 110

(a) Describe *two* biological rhythms.

(b) Assess the consequences of disrupting biological rhythms. (30 min)

Sleep

The sleep/waking cycle is an example of a circadian rhythm. Although we spend nearly one third of our lives asleep, psychologists are still unsure of its precise function. Sleep appears to be anything but a passive process, and the universality of sleep suggests that it is vital for all animals.

Restoration theories of sleep

This view of sleep proposes that the purpose of sleep is to restore the body after the exertions of the day. During sleep, growth hormone is released. Growth hormone has an important role in the metabolism of proteins. Proteins are relatively fragile and are constantly renewed during periods of slow-wave sleep (SWS).

Oswald

→ Oswald (1980) claimed that the high levels of brain activity in REM are characteristics of brain recovery during REM sleep, while the increase in hormone activity during SWS reflects the restoration and recovery of the body.

→ REM is seen as essential for brain repair. REM sleep makes up for about half the total sleep time of newborn babies, when there is rapid growth and development of the brain.

Horne

→ Horne (1988) proposes that in humans, only stage 4 sleep and REM sleep are *critical* for normal brain functioning.

→ This is supported by sleep deprivation studies which show that after deprivation, recovery is concentrated in stage 4 and REM sleep.

→ Horne claims that stage 4 and REM sleep make up *core sleep*, with the lighter stages of sleep (stages 1–3) making up *optional sleep*.

→ During core sleep, the brain restores itself after the activities of the day. Horne believes that body restoration is not the main purpose of sleep. This can be achieved during periods of quiet wakefulness.

Evaluation of restoration theories

→ Evidence for the restoration theories only weakly supports these claims. Although intense exercise (increased metabolic expenditure) causes people to fall asleep quicker, they do not sleep for longer.

→ Sleep deprivation does not appear to interfere with the ability to perform physical exercise and there is little evidence of a physiological stress response to the deprivation (Horne 1978).

→ Prolonged sleep deprivation in rats appears to interfere with the immune system which may lead to death. In some species, sleep provides the only opportunity for tissue restoration, whereas in humans, a state of quiet wakefulness can serve the same purpose.

→ Restoration theories claim that a key function of sleep is protein synthesis. But, the main constituents of proteins (amino acids), are only freely available for five hours after eating (i.e. *before* sleep).

Ecological (evolutionary) theories of sleep ●●●

Despite the apparent universality of sleep, there are important differences in the amounts that animals sleep, and the relative proportion of SWS and REM sleep. Many of these differences can be attributed to differences in the ecological niche of these animals.

Meddis (1979) proposed that sleep evolved to keep animals safe from predators at times when their normal activities were impossible. Thus, diurnal and nocturnal animals which have evolved to be active at different parts of the 24-hour cycle are asleep at different parts of this cycle.

→ An animal's ecological niche affects the organization of its sleep. Air breathing aquatic mammals (such as dolphins and porpoises) must continue to come up to the surface to breathe; therefore prolonged sleep is dangerous. The Indus dolphin sleeps for seconds at a time repeatedly throughout the 24-hour day. The bottlenose dolphin 'switches off' one of its cerebral hemispheres at a time.

→ Because animals go to such lengths to sleep, this is a powerful argument for sleep being an essential function (Green 2000).

→ Smaller animals have higher metabolic rates, using up energy resources at a faster rate. Small animals, such as squirrels, sleep for much longer than larger animals, such as cows. Sleep may thus serve the double purpose of conserving resources at the same time as keeping them safe from predators.

→ REM sleep is common in birds and mammals (warm-blooded) but is absent in reptiles (cold-blooded). It has been proposed that REM sleep evolved to maintain the brain's temperature at night when otherwise it might fall to dangerously low levels.

Evaluation of ecological explanations of sleep

→ Research has not tended to support the exclusivity of sleep for preventing the attentions of predators. Although it is plausible that sleep would protect animals in this way, so would a state of behavioural inactivity. It is doubtful that such a complex response would evolve simply to protect animals from predators.

→ Sleep is also found in species which would clearly be better off without it. The Indus river dolphin is blind (the visibility in the river is extremely poor) but it has an excellent sonar system which it uses to navigate and catch prey. Vision has been 'selected out' because it was unnecessary. Despite the dangers of sleeping (e.g. the need to breathe, and the risk of injury from passing debris) the Indus dolphin still goes to great lengths to sleep. If sleep was simply adaptive, it would, as with vision, have been 'selected out'.

Checkpoint 2

When is a nocturnal animal asleep? When is a diurnal animal asleep?

The jargon

Ecological niche is an animal's habitat, to which it is adapted, both physically and behaviourally.

Example

Some animals 'play possum' by freezing when threatened by predators.

Checkpoint 3

Why, according to this argument, would sleep have been 'selected out' in the Indus river dolphin?

Exam question   answer: page 110

Outline and evaluate *two* theories relating to the functions of sleep. (30 min)

Dreaming

Dreams are a form of visual imagery experienced during REM sleep. Dreaming is also found in non-REM sleep, although not as regularly. The exact function of dreams is one of the oldest debates in psychology.

The nature of dreams

→ Although sometimes people woken from non-REM sleep report having been dreaming, they are more likely to do this when woken from REM sleep. That dreams are not *exclusive* to REM sleep means it is inappropriate to describe it as merely 'dreaming sleep'.

→ Dreams may also occur in non-REM sleep, although these are usually less intense, and less emotional in content than REM-based dreams. However, dreaming is clearly an important part of REM sleep, therefore is considered one of the *functions* of REM.

→ Dreams are usually thought of as a series of visual images, but we also experience actions and emotions in dreams. Congenitally blind people have vivid dreams even though they see nothing in them.

→ Nightmares are dreams that contain a series of events that are associated with anxiety. They may become more frequent when the person has experienced considerable anxiety in their waking hours.

Neurobiological theories of dreaming

Crick and Mitchison

Crick and Mitchison (1983) suggest that when we dream, our brains are 'off-line', sifting through the information gathered during the day and discarding any unwanted material. Through this process of 'reverse learning' we are able to rid ourselves of 'parasitic thoughts' which would otherwise disrupt the otherwise efficient organization of memory. These unwanted connections are erased during REM sleep and our dreams thus represent these thoughts as they are being erased.

Support for this theory comes from studies of animals that cannot dream. They must, therefore, have another way to avoid overloading the neural network, for example having bigger brains. The spiny anteater and dolphins are the only mammals so far tested which do not have REM sleep, and *they* have disproportionately large brains. If we follow this line of reasoning, spiny anteaters and dolphins have large brains because they cannot dream. A problem for this theory is the fact that dreams are organized into clear stories which would be unnecessary if the purpose of dreaming was simply to dispose of parasitic thoughts.

The activation-synthesis theory (Hobson 1988)

REM sleep is controlled by mechanisms in the brainstem. When activated, this inhibits activity in the skeletal muscles (the characteristic paralysis of REM sleep) and increases activity in the forebrain. During forebrain activation, sensory and motor information is internally activated and acts as the basis for our dream experience.

Dreams reflect a synthesis of this information, helped by our previous experiences. This theory sees dreaming as an automatic part

Watch out!

Although dreams commonly occur during REM sleep, dreaming and REM sleep are not one and the same thing.

Example

When a person awakes from a nightmare, they may become aware of muscle paralysis (a characteristic of REM sleep). This can contribute to the frightening nature of the nightmare.

Checkpoint 1

What, according to this theory, would be the consequence for our species if we did not dream?

Examiner's secrets

When incorporating information such as this, don't just *describe* it, but draw conclusions from it and show why it is an important piece of information.

of the sleep process, that may have no significance beyond the need to organize material into coherent forms. Neurons in the brainstem are particularly sensitive to the neurotransmitter acetylcholine. Hobson points out that injections of a drug that increases the action of acetylcholine both increases REM sleep *and* dreaming.

A major problem of this theory, and similar theories, is that much of the supporting research takes place in a sleep 'laboratory' which differs significantly from sleep in more natural settings.

Psychological theories of dreams

Freud
Freud believed that dreams were the disguised fulfilment of a repressed desire (which was often sexual or aggressive and therefore would be unacceptable to the person when awake). Dreams thus have two roles:

→ they protect the dreamer from unacceptable impulses when awake
→ they allow expression of these urges during sleep.

Dreams have a *manifest content*, which the person reports and which the analyst must interpret in order to get at the underlying *latent content*. The latent content reflects deep-seated desires and anxieties, which are transformed into the manifest content of dreams through 'dream-work'. The purpose of this dream-work is to prevent the dreamer becoming aware of the real (i.e. latent) desires and anxieties, and the role of the analyst is to reverse this process in order to get at what lies underneath. Recent support for the Freudian explanation of dreaming comes from research with patients with brain damage in the cortical-limbic circuit in the forebrain. Damage to this area is characterized by a reported loss of dreaming. These circuits control our wishes and desires, whereas REM sleep is controlled by mechanisms in the brainstem.

Jung
Jung did not agree with Freud concerning the distinction between manifest and latent content. Dreams were seen as reflecting the mind's current state rather than having some underlying disguised content. The role of the analyst was to interpret the symbolic 'language' of the unconscious mind in dreams. Jung claimed that dreams contained certain universal *archetypal* symbols which are part of our collective unconscious. These include the *persona* (a drive to present oneself in the best light, which may give rise to dreams about anxiety in social situations) and the *anima/animus* (the male aspect of the female and the female aspect of the male – dreams help to balance these aspects for us).

Check the net

http://www.asdreams.org
The home page for the Association for the Study of Dreams.

"The interpretation of dreams is the royal road to a knowledge of the unconscious activities of the unconscious mind."

S. Freud (1909)

The jargon

Dream-work is the process by which underlying desires and anxieties are transformed into dream images.

Checkpoint 2

What is the significance of this finding for Freud's view of dreams and dreaming?

"The brain is so inexorably bent upon the quest for meaning that it attributes and even creates meaning when there is little or none in the data it is asked to process."

Hobson (1988)

Exam question   answer: page 110

Outline and evaluate *one* neurobiological theory and *one* psychological theory of dreaming. (30 min)

Answers
Physiological psychology

Biological rhythms

Checkpoints

1 The average person goes through between four and five complete cycles of sleep stages per night. Each complete cycle lasts about one and a half hours.
2 Another common behaviour that occurs on a circannual cycle is hibernation (e.g. in squirrels and bears).
3 Light, which enters through the eyes, then, via the supra-chiasmatic nucleus, affects the release of melatonin by the pineal gland.
4 The most likely explanation for this is that it is easier for the body to adjust its body clock when it is ahead of local time (known as 'phase delay') than when it is behind (known as 'phase advance').

Exam question

(a) This only asks for a *description* of biological rhythms, so you should restrict your answer to that – don't be tempted to offer any evaluative content. We have covered three different types of rhythms, but you are only asked for two here. It is best not to do both infradian *and* circadian rhythms (as they are both *infradian* rhythms). You would only have 15 minutes to answer this part of the question (that's about 150 words for each rhythm), so you might construct your answer as follows:
   • definition of infradian rhythms and relation with circannual rhythms. SAD in humans and difference in the physiological basis of infradian and circadian rhythms
   • definition of circadian rhythms, examples of circadian rhythm, significance (e.g. for diurnal and nocturnal animals), role of endogenous pacemakers, and the role of the SCN.
(b) This part of the question gives you the chance to assess what would happen if biological rhythms were disrupted. The most common forms of disruption are *jet lag* and *shift work*. As the question asks you to 'assess' the consequences, don't just describe what they might be, but *assess* these (e.g. is there research evidence for this form of disruption, why would it happen, and so on).

Sleep

Checkpoints

1 Stage 4 sleep is characterized by an EEG of only delta waves, metabolic rate at its lowest and the highest arousal threshold (how difficult it is to wake the sleeper) of any of the stages.

2 A nocturnal animal sleeps during the day. A diurnal animal sleeps during the night.
3 Because it served no advantage, but rather because of its disadvantages it would put dolphins in danger.

Exam question

It is appropriate to choose either two *named* theories (such as Oswald and Horne) or two theoretical *perspectives* (such as 'restoration' and 'ecological' explanations). Whichever approach you take, it is vital that equal amounts of coverage are given to each theory, and to the descriptive and evaluative aspects of the question.

Examiner's secrets

Remember that questions such as this require a number of things (two theories, outline *and* evaluate), so effective time management is vital. Practise!

Dreaming

Checkpoints

1 We would need much bigger brains as we would not be able to clear out unwanted connections that had accumulated during the day.
2 Previously, dreams were seen by many as an artefact of REM sleep, or as a simple way of clearing out unwanted information (and therefore of no significance). Although this finding does not directly support Freud's theory, it lends some support to Freud's proposal that dreams are located in that part which deals with our wishes and desires, a fundamental aspect of the Freudian view of dreaming.

Exam question

It is important to read this question carefully. You are not asked for two theories of dreaming, but one *neurobiological* and one *psychological* theory. We have covered Crick and Mitchison's theory which suggests that dreaming is a way of clearing out unwanted information and Hobson's activation-synthesis theory which sees dreams as a synthesis of forebrain activity combined with previous experience. Freud's theory of dreaming believes dreams are the disguised fulfilment of repressed desires or anxieties. Dreams protect the dreamer from unacceptable impulses when awake and allow expression of these urges when asleep. Jung's theory claims that dreams contain universal archetypal symbols which suggest the current state of the dreamer's mind.

Comparative psychology

The study of comparative psychology generally concerns itself with non-human animals, but this section is exclusively about one species, human beings. The study of reproductive behaviour is particularly important as it ties many of the different aspects of human reproductive behaviour (sexual selection, jealousy etc.) to evolutionary factors, particularly male-female differences in parental investment.

The study of mental disorders has tended to see them as purely *maladaptive* behaviours, but evolutionary explanations tend to focus more on the possible adaptive value of different disorders. We will discuss some of these in this section, and show how they originally evolved for a quite different purpose than the one they appear to fulfil now. Although intelligence is largely seen as synonymous with brain size, a simple calculation of absolute brain size appears to tell us very little about the intelligence of the species involved. Why humans have evolved such large (and expensive) brains is now believed to be a product of the social complexity of primate life.

Exam themes

→ Sexual selection and human reproductive behaviour

→ Evolutionary explanations of mental disorders

→ Evolutionary factors in the development of human intelligence

→ The relationship between brain size and intelligence

Topic checklist

O AS ● A2	AQA/A	AQA/B	OCR	EDEXCEL
Human reproductive behaviour	●			
Evolutionary explanations of mental disorders	●			
Evolution of human intelligence	●			

Human reproductive behaviour

Action point

The tendency to see reproductive success in terms of the perpetuation of genes is known as 'selfish-gene' theory. Try to read something about this theory.

Evolutionary psychologists consider that human behaviour is largely part inherited. We seek to increase the distribution of our genes in the next generation. Behaviours that are successful in this respect will become more widespread and there may be significant differences in the way that males and females achieve this.

Sexual selection

The mechanisms of sexual selection

Sexual selection works in two ways, by favouring the development of:

→ characteristics in males that enable them to compete directly against each other in order to gain access to females
→ characteristics in males that enable them to attract females.

To explain male and female differences in reproductive behaviour, Trivers (1972) introduced the idea of *parental investment*. Trivers argued that the degree of disparity in any species, humans included, would be correlated with certain behaviours, such as the extent to which males would be eager to copulate and females eager to select, the proneness of either sex to be faithful or unfaithful and so on. According to Trivers, it would be predicted that human males would be more promiscuous and less discerning, relative to females.

Trivers's theory proposes that the sex investing more in offspring (typically the female) will be selected to exert stronger preferences about mating partners. This greater choosiness by the more heavily investing sex exists because greater reproductive costs are associated with indiscriminate mating and greater benefits are associated with exerting a choice. The costs of less discriminating mating will be lower for the sex investing less and the benefits will be greater.

Checkpoint 1

What are the benefits of careful selection for females?

Checkpoint 2

What are the costs of 'indiscriminate mating' for females?

Insights from anthropology

→ Intrasexual competition is more intense among males than females.
→ Males incline towards polygyny in the majority of cultures, whereas women are more flexible in this respect.
→ Physical characteristics appear to be the most important factors in female sexual attractiveness (signs of health and fecundity).

The jargon

Polygyny is a mating system where a male may mate with (or marry) two or more females.

The jargon

Fecundity is the capacity to produce offspring.

Insights from evolutionary theory

→ Favoured mate characteristics that show some heritability will be represented more frequently in subsequent generations.
→ Current mate preferences may reflect prior selection pressures, in that males and females may show patterns of mate preference that have little relevance today, but may have been very important in our ancestral past.
→ Males are seen as preferring females who are young (i.e. good child-rearing potential), attractive (i.e. healthy), and who have practised chastity (less chance of a male raising another's child).

→ Females are seen as preferring males who have high earning capacity and who display ambition and industriousness (both can be translated into *resources*).

Research evidence

Buss (1989) tested predictions derived from Trivers's parental investment theory in 37 different cultures. Buss discovered that typically females valued the financial capacity of potential mates (i.e. their resources) more than males. Ambition and industriousness were also valued more highly by females across most of the cultures studied. The study also confirmed the importance of relative youth (in females) and physical attractiveness (in females) in all 37 of the cultures. The importance of chastity (in females) was not supported in this study.

Although these results provide powerful support for the evolution-based hypothesis for sex differences in mate preferences, there are important qualifications and limitations to this study.

→ The samples used by Buss cannot be considered representative of the populations of each culture, with rural and less-educated individuals being under-represented.
→ Male and female preferences overlapped considerably, in spite of mean differences.
→ This research offers little information about the social and psychological mechanisms (such as socialization differences between the sexes) that might be responsible for these differences.

Evolutionary explanations of homosexuality ●●●

Evolutionary explanations of homosexuality claim that male homosexuality is an evolutionary by-product of an adaptive advantage, which keeps it balanced in the gene pool despite its diminished reproduction.

One of the major evolutionary explanations is *kin selection theory*. The first variant of this theory argues that a person in some way recognizes that they are going to be poor reproducers and withdraws from the reproductive game, sublimating their heterosexuality into same-sex contacts. The second variant argues that homosexuals have either superior opportunities or superior abilities to gather resources and that this capacity is enhanced if they withdraw from the reproductive stakes. Both variants assume that the homosexual will altruistically help near relatives who are reproductive, and as they share common genes, by that means maintain their own genes within the population.

This view is not without problems. If homosexuals had some superior ability, then why not reproduce themselves. In most cultures, superior abilities equal greater resources and an enhanced ability to reproduce.

Use the net

To find out more about Buss's views and this study in particular, try the following sites: www.abc.net.au/science/descent/trans2.htm
http://cpnss.lse.ac.uk/darwin/evo/buss.htm

Watch out!

Research evidence does not provide conclusive *proof* for an explanation of behaviour.

The jargon

Kin selection – behaviours that may reduce the survival chances or reproductive effectiveness of an individual, but serve to increase the likelihood of their close genetic relatives surviving and reproducing.

Exam question   answer: page 118

Discuss evolutionary explanations of sex differences in parental investment. (30 min)

Evolutionary explanations of mental disorders

Watch out!

Do not assume that all mental disorders are 'abnormal' in their origins.

"He has no hope that never had a fear."

W. Cowper (1782)

The jargon

Environment of evolutionary adaptedness – the kind of environment in which our species is best adapted to live.

"Tell us your phobias and we will tell you what you are afraid of."

R. Benchley (1936)

Checkpoint 1

What do you think is the adaptive origin of *acrophobia* (fear of heights)?

Example

Roads, plastic bags, sharp objects – all are potentially dangerous to young children, yet they seem oblivious to this, despite parental efforts to teach them.

If there is a genetic basis to mental disorders, then why do they still persist in the gene pool and why have they not been weeded out by natural selection? One possibility is that some disorders (such as depression) give rise to behaviours that profit the individual in some direct (e.g. personal survival) or indirect (e.g. increasing the survival of genetic relatives) way. Evolutionary explanations give us an insight into the 'normal' functions of many disorders rather than seeing them as biological or psychological aberrations.

Anxiety disorders

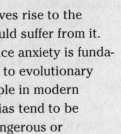

Psychiatric classification of anxiety as an 'illness' gives rise to the (erroneous) belief that no well-adjusted person should suffer from it. This is far from the case as the capacity to experience anxiety is fundamental to survival. Anxiety disorders are of interest to evolutionary psychologists because the phobias suffered by people in modern times do not seem to reflect modern dangers. Phobias tend to be experienced with objects or situations that were dangerous or potentially life-threatening in the environment of evolutionary adaptedness (EEA).

Phobia	Possible adaptive origin
Strangers (*xenophobia*)	Infanticide, particularly from non-kin, is common in primate species
Agoraphobia	Leaving the home range is dangerous for territorial species
Claustrophobia	In small spaces, humans are vulnerable as escape is difficult
Snakes (*ophidiophobia*)	Poisonous snakes have been a threat for millions of years

According to the evolutionary perspective, humans inherit biases to learn certain cues and responses rather than others so as to adapt appropriately to environmental variations (Stevens and Price 1996). As a result of evolution, humans are *prepared* to become active in response to some aspects of their environment in certain specific ways. These biases produce rapid responses with the minimum of experience. Thus, snakes rapidly come to evoke fear, spoiled food to evoke nausea.

Evaluation of evolutionary explanations of anxiety disorders

→ 'Prepared' fears (e.g. fear of the dark or of snakes) are acquired more rapidly than unprepared ones. It is difficult to condition children to fear modern 'unprepared' dangers (e.g. matches etc.).

→ Most people experience enough anxiety to function efficiently. It is clear that anxiety is an *adaptive* response to threats from the environment, particularly those relevant to the ancestral EEA. Rather than seeing anxiety as abnormal, a *lack* of anxiety in these circumstances would be considered abnormal and maladaptive.

Depression ●●●

The rank theory of depression

This proposes that *depression* is an adaptive response to losing rank in a status conflict and seeing oneself as a loser. According to this theory, such a response is adaptive because it helps the individual adjust to the fact that they have lost and must now occupy a subordinate position in the dominance hierarchy. The purpose of the depression is to prevent the loser from risking further injury by continuing the conflict, and to preserve the relative stability of the social group. In defeat, an involuntary process comes into operation which both prevents the individual from continuing to compete, but also reduces his level of aspiration. This involuntary process results in the loss of energy, depressed mood and loss of confidence, which are typical characteristics of depression.

When humans interact together the question of dominance may not arise initially. However, after working or living in close proximity for some time, conflict may arise, perhaps over leadership of a group or over access to resources (such as promotion). Over the course of time, the depressive response may also become triggered by other situations that do not necessarily involve the loss of rank, but involve a loss of some other sort (perhaps the ending of a close relationship).

Evaluation of rank theory

An important contribution of rank theory is that it offers an explanation of how depression might have evolved – it emerged as the yielding component of a status conflict between two individual animals. This yielding following defeat is important for two reasons:

→ it ensures that the loser really does yield and does not make any attempt at a comeback
→ it shows the winner that they really have won so that they break off with no further damage to the loser, thus restoring social harmony.

In such circumstances a response that has been selected by natural selection because it *is* adaptive is activated in such situations that make it psychologically maladaptive. Allen (1995) states:

> It is the depressed mood state that has been selected by evolution, whereas the clinically depressed state is a pathological aberration based on this adaptive emotional mechanism.

Nesse and Williams criticize contemporary psychiatric explanations of depression for 'trying to find the flaws that cause the disease without understanding normal functions of the mechanisms'.

Links

This material can also be used in exam answers on the origins of depression (pages 152–3).

The jargon

Social group – a set of relationships among animals in frequent contact such that an established social order is formed.

Watch out!

This process is not a voluntary one, but an automatic reaction to defeat in a status conflict.

Checkpoint 2

What are the adaptive advantages of this depressive response to the losing individual?

The jargon

The *evolutionary psychiatry* approach (Nesse and Williams 1995) argues that mental illness might be more accepted, and treated more effectively, if we understood its function.

Exam question   answer: page 118

Outline and evaluate evolutionary explanations of *two* types of mental disorder. (30 min)

Evolution of human intelligence

Evolutionary factors in the development of intelligence

One suggestion is the relationship between brain size and intelligence and the increasing evidence of encephalization among the higher primates. However, larger brains are also very expensive in terms of the increased need for energy to run them efficiently, so clearly they must equip us with significant advantages that outweigh the costs of maintaining such an extravagant organ. The two most popular theories concerning the evolution of large human brains and the corresponding increase in intelligence are:

→ foraging demands – the ability to find food would have presented early man with significant challenges that would demand sophistic-ated cognitive skills.

→ group living – the increasing social complexity of social living and the need to maintain group cohesion and minimize group conflict is thought to correlate positively with the increased development of the neocortex in particular.

Exploring the origins of human intelligence

Recent explanations of the origins of human intelligence have stressed the role played by demands of the social world as experienced by primates. Primate intelligence allows an individual to serve their own interests by 'interacting with others, either cooperatively or manipulatively without disturbing the overall social cohesion of the group' (Cartwright 2000). This explanation has become known as the 'Machiavellian intelligence hypothesis'. It proposes that brain enlargement in humans (particularly enlargement of the *neocortex*) was a result of the cognitive demands of the social world.

Dunbar (1993) tested whether the proportional volume of the neocortex against the overall volume of the brain was related more to the amount of environmental complexity (i.e. an indication of potential foraging difficulties) or to average group size in humans and other primates. He found that as group size increased, so did the ratio of neocortex volume to the overall volume of the brain. There appears to be little or no relationship between neocortex volume and environmental complexity.

Brain size and intelligence

The idea that brain size is related to *intelligence* was widespread among neuroanatomists around the turn of the century. The advent of more reliable measures of 'intelligence' coupled with the development of sophisticated brain-scanning methods (such as the MRI) has suggested that such a relationship, albeit a fairly moderate one, may actually exist. It is important to remember that this moderate relationship between absolute brain size and intelligence still allows for the role of many additional factors in the determination of intelligence.

Does bigger mean better?

Using these improved methods, scientists have been able to compare brain size and intelligence with far greater accuracy. Willerman et al (1991) selected college students with no history of neurological problems, and measured their brain size using MRI techniques. Any influence of body size on brain size was removed statistically, as was any possible effect due to the high IQs of the participants. The resulting correlation between brain size and intelligence was 0.35. This finding was supported in a study by Andreasen et al (1993) who advertised in a newspaper for participants. After screening for any neurological disorders, these volunteers were given an IQ test and an MRI scan. The resulting correlation between brain size and intelligence was 0.38.

There is an important ethical problem with research of this type. Historically, scientists have misused information about racially prejudicial ways, yet all racial groups show overlapping and widely varying brain size (Rosensweig 1999).

Humans and other species

It is widely believed that cetaceans (whales, dolphins and porpoises) are also highly 'intelligent'. The major historical basis for this belief is the size and complex surface appearance of cetacean brains.

The brain of a sperm whale is nearly 8 kg, the brain of an African elephant 7.5 kg, and the brain of a human being a miserly 1.5 kg.

But as the species with the biggest brains also tend to be the ones with the biggest bodies, it might be that large animals just need larger brains to control and maintain their larger bodies.

A simple way to make allowance for different body weights is to express brain weight as a percentage of body weight. In this way of determining 'intelligence' humans are seen to have a great advantage over other mammals, including the large whales.

However, research suggests that relative brain size is not necessarily related to intelligence either, as there are too many anomalies. A particular example is the spiny anteater with a neocortex (greatly developed in primates and humans) relatively much larger than that of a human. Despite this endowment, nobody has so far put forward any claims for superior 'intelligence' in spiny anteaters.

Another school of thought (e.g. Holloway, 1979), finds the consideration of brain and body sizes alone insufficient, indeed 'trivial', and emphasizes the importance of the evolutionary changes in brain organization. Holloway claims that brain weight is a poor predictor of the internal structural complexity which he believes to be the most important factor in the evolution of 'intelligence'.

Checkpoint 2

Why was it necessary to 'screen for neurological disorders'?

Links

This would be an example of 'socially sensitive research' (see page 168).

"To think the way we do, he [the whale] would need to use about one-sixth of his total brain."

Lilly (1991)

Action point

Try to find out the average body weight of a fully-grown male sperm whale, African elephant and human. What proportion of the total body weight is the brain for that species?

Checkpoint 3

What other explanation might account for the large brains of dolphins (see page 107)?

Exam question   answer: page 118

Discuss the role of evolutionary factors in the development of human intelligence. (30 min)

Answers
Comparative psychology

Human reproductive behaviour

Checkpoints

1 The female can select males that have good resources or other characteristics that would ensure the best advantage for her offspring.
2 Since the female invests so heavily in so few offspring (particularly in mammals) if she chooses a poor quality male her offspring stand less chance of competing against others or even surviving. The male, particularly in polygynous groups, can invest more widely in many females, a process provocatively known as 'diversifying his portfolio'.

Exam question

Your answer should begin with an explanation of parental investment theory (disparity between the sexes with regard to parental investment) which will be correlated with certain behaviours.

You might then say what these predictions would be when applied to humans (men would be more promiscuous and less discerning).

Examine the evidence from anthropology and evolutionary theory – does this *support* these claims?

Buss's research directly tests these evolutionary hypotheses but should be treated *critically*.

Evolutionary explanations of mental disorders

Checkpoints

1 Heights pose obvious dangers to humans, and fear of heights produces a 'freezing' response that makes it less likely that the person will fall.
2 In group-living primates there are clear advantages to being *inside* the group than being an outsider (e.g. defence against predators, mating opportunities etc.). It is better to retain these advantages as a subordinate than it is to risk further injury or exclusion by continuing the conflict with the victor.

Exam question

The two types of mental disorders specifically included on the AQA specification are anxiety disorders and depression, so we have chosen to cover those here. In 30 minutes you must give a good description of evolutionary explanations of *two* mental disorders, then offer the same level of evaluation.

You might begin with anxiety disorders, and explain that anxiety is fundamental to survival. Phobias are associated with objects or situations that were dangerous in the EEA. Give examples of specific phobias and their adaptive origins.

It is important to offer some evaluation – you might mention the 'logic' of being 'prepared' to learn some things more rapidly than others, and how sensitivity to danger is adaptive rather than abnormal.

Depression should be treated in the same way, description of the adaptive nature of the depressive response (rank theory) followed by evaluation (i.e. the adaptive significance of the depressive response).

Evolution of human intelligence

Checkpoints

1 It is named after Nicolo Machiavelli, the 16th-century Italian politician. It is generally used to signify a pattern of behaviour (such as deviousness, deception and opportunism) whose sole aim is the manipulation of others for one's own ends.
2 Because brain volume may, in some way, have been influenced by a neurological disorder, and this would bias the results of any calculations.
3 Crick and Mitchison (1983) proposed that REM sleep acts to remove undesirable interactions in networks of cells in the cerebral cortex. Animals that cannot use this system need another way to avoid overloading the neural network, for example by having bigger brains. Dolphins do not have REM sleep, and they also have disproportionally large brains. So, following this line of reasoning, dolphins would have to have big brains because they cannot dream.

Exam question

This question allows you to use any of the information on pages 116–7. There could be two parts to your essay:
• a critical examination of the *reasons* for the evolution of human intelligence and highly developed brains (foraging vs group demands)
• a critical examination of the relationship between brain size and intelligence, through correlational studies (e.g. Andreasen et al) and through comparison with other species.

This section is concerned with the following aspects of cognitive psychology: perception, attention and pattern recognition. Perception refers to the processes by which we interpret information provided by the senses. Explanations of perception tend to differ in the degree to which they attribute analysis to information contained within the sensory stimuli (Bottom-up theories) or to models and expectations, which are generated cognitively and are used to process the information accordingly (Top-down theories). In the former, perception may be seen as an accurate representation of external stimuli, in the latter as an active process of inference and hypothesis testing. The other topics of this section consider the cognitive processes involved in focused and divided (or selective) attention, and in pattern recognition.

Exam themes

→ The visual system

→ Theories of perception

→ Perception as a developmental process

→ Perceptual organization

→ Theories and evidence relating to focused and divided attention

→ Pattern recognition

Topic checklist

O AS ● A2

	AQA/A	AQA/B	OCR	EDEXCEL
The visual system	●	O	O	●
Perceptual organization	●			
Perceptual development	●			
Focused attention	●			
Divided attention	●			
Pattern recognition	●			

The visual system

This topic considers the structure and functions of the visual system and theories concerning the nature of visual information processing.

Structure and functions of the visual system

→ Light enters the eye by passing through the transparent protective cornea and through the pupil, the opening just behind the cornea. The iris adjusts the amount of light by constricting or relaxing the size of the pupil. Behind the pupil is the curved lens, which bends light waves, focusing them on the back of the eye – the retina.

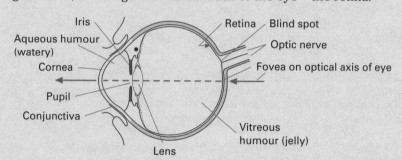

→ The retina has two types of *photoreceptors*: rods and cones. Although rods greatly outnumber cones they are distributed so that cones are densely packed in the fovea, the area of highest activity, while rods are situated in the rest of the retina (the periphery). Rods operate at low intensities of light. Cones respond to high intensity, which results in the sensation of colour.

→ Light adaptation: when it becomes dark, vision shifts from cones to rods. If lighting conditions change quickly, rods and cones adapt to the new condition. It takes longer to adapt to sudden darkness (e.g. entering a cinema) than sudden lightness (leaving the dark of a cinema for daylight).

→ Once photoreceptors (rods and cones) absorb light, responses are transmitted to neurones called bipolar cells and on to other neurones known as ganglion cells. The axons of the ganglion cells extend out of the eye to form the optic nerve. Ganglion cells send action potentials to the brain. Their axons travel through the optic chiasma to the lateral geniculate nucleus (LGN). The LGN can be likened to a relay station, nerves from the retina connecting with nerves to the visual cortex.

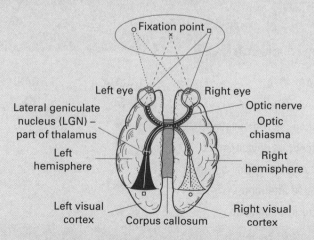

Take note

As we get older, the lens is no longer spherical enough to focus on near objects. Note that many people after their mid-forties try to focus by squinting, and, for example, hold newspapers further away.

Test yourself

Try covering the labelling words in the two diagrams on this page, then check that you know the correct terms.

Checkpoint 1

Something happens in the eye's visual pathway to the brain at the optic chiasma. What is this and what effect does it cause?

Theories of colour vision

Trichromatic theory

This theory (Young-Helmholtz) is based on three types of cones that are sensitive to short, medium and long wavelengths. These cones are, respectively, blue, green and red. Light waves stimulate the cones to fire at certain levels. This combination of different degrees of firing in effect mixes the light waves to produce all the variations of colour we perceive. For example, purple may be achieved by the red cones firing quickly and the blue cones firing slowly, while the green cones do not fire. This theory has no explanation for colour blindness or negative afterimages.

Opponent-process theory

Hering based this theory on the idea of colour-sensitive units within the visual system which are in opposition to each other. DeValois and Jacobs (1984) discovered colour-opponent cells in the LGN, lending greater weight to this theory.

Some researchers (e.g. Jameson and Hurvich 1981) have argued for a combination of the above competing theories. In this model the three types of receptors in the trichomatic theory travel into and are processed by the colour-opponent units at a higher level in the visual cortex.

The visual cortex: feature detection theories

In a series of neurological experiments on anaesthetized cats and monkeys, Hubel and Wiesel (1963) placed microelectrodes in different parts of the visual cortex. They found evidence for what they called **simple cells** (which fired when the animal was shown a stimulus such as a line), **complex cells** and **hypercomplex cells** (which responded to angles and simple shapes). Desimone et al (1984) found that a face-shaped stimulus elicited responses from certain cells of the visual cortex in monkeys.

Research in this field is ongoing, and aspects of Hubel and Wiesel's theories have been modified by other researchers. For example, Bruce, Green and Georgeson (1996) have questioned the existence of hypercomplex cells.

Watch out!

Don't confuse the mixing of light waves with mixing paints. The mixing of lights takes place in the eye; the mixing of paints occurs outside the eye. The rules of colour mixture of the two processes are different.

Take note

An ethological/evolutionary explanation as to why colour vision evolved comes from Katherine Milton (1993). She argues that it was the consumption of edible plants which led to aspects of future primate evolution. Examples of such aspects are visual acuity (including colour vision), grasping hands and larger brains.

Examiner's secrets

Make sure you can write a brief explanatory paragraph on Hubel and Wiesel's research, citing their work and its implications.

Exam question　　　　　　　　　　　　　　answer: page 132

'Many accidents occur at dusk.' How does knowledge of the visual system help to explain this phenomenon? (30 min)

Perceptual organization

An important aspect of perception is that we organize and make sense of the information conveyed to us through our senses. This topic considers the major theories of visual perception, and the explanations of perceptual organization that they offer.

Direct theories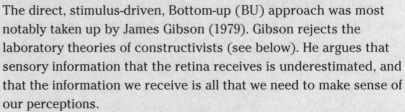

The direct, stimulus-driven, Bottom-up (BU) approach was most notably taken up by James Gibson (1979). Gibson rejects the laboratory theories of constructivists (see below). He argues that sensory information that the retina receives is underestimated, and that the information we receive is all that we need to make sense of our perceptions.

While making pilot training films during the Second World War, Gibson described optic flow patterns: a flow of data past the viewer (pilot) which provides unambiguous information about direction, speed and altitude. Also important are **texture gradients** (systematic changes in the pattern of light), **affordance** (the potentiality of objects) and **resonance** (we receive visual data, just as a radio receiver picks up sound waves). Another element in Gibson's theory is **motion parallax** (movement): as we move around our environment, the patterns of light we receive will change, so changing the patterns in the optic array, giving direct and unambiguous perceptual information. Contrary to constructivist theorists Gibson rejects the need for processes to transform incoming information into internal representation or to enrich it with memory.

Constructivist theories

Constructivist or Top-down (TD) theorists regard perception as an active, constructive process, not entirely determined by stimulus information arriving at the sense organs. For Richard Gregory (1972), visual material received by the retina are ambiguous 'floating scraps of data'. He believes we go beyond simply decoding information, that we form a hypothesis (make inferences), which is then tested by sensory data. Gregory has made use of visual illusions to demonstrate his theories of constructive perception. He argues that previous knowledge which we acquire for the perception of three-dimensional objects is sometimes inappropriately applied to the perception of a two-dimensional figure.

The **Ponzo illusion** occurs because the lines at the side give an impression of depth. The upper line is the same length as the lower, but the false depth cues make it appear further away. Direct theorists have no answer to visual illusions. Gibson argues that they are an unfair test of perception.

Organizational cues in perception

The visual system gathers and processes sensory information into meaningful patterns. The ability to perceive depth depends on cues provided by incoming stimulation. Some examples of monocular cues:

→ linear perspective – parallel lines converge into distance (see Ponzo illusion)
→ relative size – distant objects produce a smaller image on the retina
→ motion parallax – objects closer to the eye move quickly, further objects appear to move more slowly.

Movement cues include motion parallax (see page 122) and retinal image movement – induced by an object moving across the retina. However, when we move our eyes and heads we do not perceive everything around us as moving, because the brain also receives information about the movement of the eye and head and compensates. Sensations of head and eye movements also compensate for external motion. Gibson (1966) proposed that the information we need to perceive movement occurs in the visual stimulus itself.

Constancies

Constancies refer to the ability to see objects as being the same, regardless of orientation (shape constancy), lighting conditions (colour and brightness constancy) and distance (size constancy).

The size of the image of an object on the retina depends on the distance of the object from the eye: the further away, the smaller the image. However, known objects do not appear to 'shrink' or 'grow' as they move away or towards us.

Holway and Boring (1941) demonstrated the importance of *distance* and *background* in size constancy. They found that size constancy decreases as distance and background information decreased. Participants perceived an ambiguous object in accordance with the retinal image when they lacked information about distance and background. This experiment can be interpreted in different ways by constructivists and direct theorists. Gregory (1970) argues that constancy scaling is important. We use information about distance and background to correct the size of the retinal image, keeping perception relatively constant. Gibson (1976) maintains that size constancy occurs because both objects and background change together, e.g. the retinal size and textural change of the background change with the retinal size and textural change of the object.

Checkpoint 2

What other monocular cues are there?

Watch out!

Ensure that you are also aware of Bower's work on size constancy, which is relevant to perceptual development.

Examiner's secrets

Remember to consider the similarities as well as the differences between the two approaches.

Exam question   answer: page 132

Compare and contrast the constructionist and the direct approaches to perceptual organization. (30 min)

Perceptual development

Nativist (or direct) theorists argue that perceptual abilities are inborn. They believe that these abilities are immature and develop through maturation. Empiricists (or constructivists) argue that perceptual abilities are learned through experience. Some key studies of the development of perceptual abilities are outlined below.

The development of perceptual abilities in neonate animals ●●●

→ Riesen (1947) studied chimpanzees reared in the dark until the age of sixteen months. When their perceptual abilities were tested they could not distinguish patterns and were extremely visually impaired.
→ Wieskrantz (1956) argued that the visual impairment was due to retinal damage, caused by lack of exposure to light stimulation.
→ Riesen (1965) used translucent goggles on animals during their first three months. He found light is essential for the normal physical development of the visual system. Furthermore, patterned light is necessary for the development of the more complex visual abilities (perceiving depth, tracking a moving object etc.).

Early visual experience

→ Blakemore and Cooper (1973) tested kittens which were exposed to environments in which there were only vertical or horizontal lines. When tested, kittens raised in the vertical condition could only respond to vertical lines, with corresponding results for kittens raised in the horizontal environment.
→ Held and Hein's kitten carousel research exposed kittens to the same visual experience but one kitten was active (could walk in a carousel) and one passive (only very restricted movement). When tested, the active kitten had better co-ordination and depth perception. When the passive kitten could move it quickly developed better perceptual coordination.
→ Miller and Walk (1975), in a modification of the above experiment, found that depth perception is innate but improves with experience.

Cataract patients

These studies involve adults who have regained their sight. Von Senden (1932) examined 65 case studies from 1700 until 1928. Hebb (1949) re-examined this study. He found patients had *figure unity* – they could detect a figure against a background – but they had no *figure identity*: they could not identify objects without learning. They also lacked perceptual constancy. Gregory and Wallace (1963) studied SB, blind until the age of 52. He was never fully able to use his sight.

Checkpoint 1

These are examples of deprivation studies. Why are such studies carried out on young animals?

Action point

Banks et al (1983) found that delaying eye operation on children until after the age of three years can result in permanent visual impairment.

Distortion-readjustment studies

The phenomenon studied here is the ability of adults to adjust to an altered perceptual world. Stratton (1896) and Synder and Pronko (1952) used goggles which turned their perception upside down. They found that after initial difficulties they were able to cope with inverted vision. In both of these studies, participants bumped into objects but gradually learned to adjust and adapt their behaviour. In a comparison with Held and Hein's kitten carousel experiment, Held (1965) showed that self-produced movement is necessary for humans to adjust to the wearing of inverting goggles. Wheelchair-bound participants who wore the goggles could not adapt to an altered environment.

Cross-cultural studies

These involve the perceptual testing of different cultural communities. It has been found that people living in a non-carpentered environment are generally less likely to be fooled by the Muller-Lyer illusion (Segal et al 1963). Turnbull (1961) described how a pygmy tracker perceived a distant buffalo herd as ants because he was unused to open countryside.

> **Action point**
>
> Make a list of the advantages and disadvantages of cross-cultural studies.

Human neonate studies

A major problem with studying babies and young children is that they cannot tell us what they can actually see. As with animals, researchers have to infer their visual perceptions from observed behaviour. Sensory abilities are not fully mature at birth. Babies are extremely shortsighted and because the lens cannot change shape, visual acuity is limited. Acuity increases rapidly during the first three to six months.

→ Fantz (1961) showed that babies between the ages of four days and six months preferred a complex pattern and a pattern of a human face to non-complex patterns.

→ Bower (1966) found that babies defended themselves against a perceived moving object coming towards them and concluded that depth perception was innate.

→ In Gibson and Walk's visual cliff study (1960) the majority of babies refused to cross over to the deep side. They concluded that depth perception was innate.

→ Although Bower found evidence for size and shape constancy in very young babies, it is generally agreed that perceptual constancies take much longer to develop. Gollins (1965) argued that experience with shapes is needed for children to develop shape constancy.

→ Gibson (1969) proposed that perceptual learning consists of young children learning to make finer and finer discriminations between the distinct features of stimulus objects.

> **Action point**
>
> Various methods to assess perception in infants have been developed. Make sure you can identify these.

> **Checkpoint 2**
>
> Does the visual cliff experiment necessarily prove that depth perception is innate? Can you think of other reasons why babies might refuse to cross to the 'deep' side?

> **Checkpoint 3**
>
> How does Piaget's approach differ from that of Gibson?

> **Exam question**   answer: page 132
>
> Critically consider two studies of perceptual development. What contribution do they make to the nature versus nurture debate? (30 min)

Focused attention

That it is often necessary to pay attention to something to perceive it has prompted research into focused or selective attention. In particular, much work was stimulated by realizing how important vigilance was for the technological workers such as radar operators in the Second World War.

Cherry: dichotic listening task

Cherry (1953) developed the **dichotic listening task** in which participants simultaneously receive two different messages via headphones. They are asked to *shadow* (repeat aloud) one message and then are asked about the unattended message. Cherry found that very little information was extracted from the unattended message (e.g. participants did not notice if it was a foreign language). However, they noticed physical changes and characteristics, such as an insertion of a pure tone, and whether it was a male or female voice.

The various information processing theories of attention differ about the stage at which *filtering* (attenuation) is carried out. They can be broadly divided into early selection and late selection models.

Early selection models

Broadbent (1958), using his own research and the work of Cherry, proposed that it was physical characteristics which determined if something was attended to or not. In his single channel filter model, attention is described as being a filter or bottleneck. Stimuli are selected from the sensory buffer because of their physical characteristics. In Broadbent's split-span task, participants were given digits via headphones. He found they recalled numbers that were presented by individual ear rather than by pair. In other words, if 435 were presented to one ear and 892 to the other, recall would be 435 892 rather than 483 952.

Evidence against this approach comes from Gray and Wedderburn (1960). They found recall by meaning. 'Dear Aunt Jane' was recalled, not 'Dear 5 Jane 3 Aunt 4'. Moray (1959) found that more information from the unattended ear was noticed if the stimulus was important to them, e.g. their own name (the cocktail party phenomenon).

In Treisman's **attenuation model** (1964), the unattended information is attenuated (weakened). This model argues for a hierarchical, two-stage theory of processing. The first stage selects information on physical characteristics, while the second selects on the basis of meaning. In an experiment (Treisman 1960), participants shadowed a meaningful story while a different story was played in the other ear. The stories were switched over to opposite ears during the experiment, but all participants continue to shadow the original story. In another

Watch out!

Ensure that you have a good understanding of the various models of attention.

Checkpoint 1

How was Broadbent's split-span task different from Cherry's dichotic listening task?

Action point

It might help your understanding of this topic to relate it to everyday activities such as having a telephone conversation at the same time as someone else in the room is speaking to you.

experiment (Treisman and Geffen 1967), participants shadowed an attended message but tapped when they heard a target word in either message. Detection was very high for the attended message (87% against 8% for the unattended), supporting Treisman's model, which would predict attenuated (weakened) analysis for the unattended message and therefore fewer responses. Treisman's model accounts for the processing (albeit weakened) of unattended material (e.g. the cocktail party phenomenon).

Late selection models

The **pertinence model** was developed by Deutsch and Deutsch (1963) and revised by Norman (1968). According to this model the filtering occurs later in the process, and all stimuli are analyzed. Deutsch and Deutsch (1967) argued that in the Treisman and Geffen experiment (1967) the shadowed targets were more important than the non-shadowed and that determined the greater response.

Treisman and Riley (1969) in a variation of the **tapping experiment** asked participants to stop shadowing and to tap when they detected a target in either message (giving importance to both messages). A larger proportion of targets were still detected in the shadowed message.

Flexible model

Johnston and Heinz (1978) see focused attention as being more flexible than in the early or late selection models referred to above. In the flexible model, selection is possible at different stages of processing. Johnston and Heinz found that the amount of processing of a non-shadowed message varies as a function of task demands and circumstances.

Eysenck and Keane (1995) propose Treisman's model with the addition of some elements of the flexible model.

Checkpoint 2

What does 'pertinence' mean in this context?

Links

The work of Johnston and Heinz is also relevant to divided attention (pages 128–9).

Exam question   answer: page 132

Critically consider two theories or models of focused attention. (30 min)

Divided attention

Allport and other researchers came to reject filter theories of attention and the assumption of a single capacity central processor. They argued that earlier researchers had failed to account for variables which can markedly influence performance. Research into divided attention typically involves giving participants two tasks, each to be given equal attention. Allport et al (1972) have identified factors affecting performance, including similarity, difficulty and practice.

Similarity

There is evidence that similarity between two tasks interferes with performance levels. In a case study by Shaffer (1975) the participant was an experienced audio-typist. Tasks which were similar such as audio-typing while simultaneously shadowing an audio message proved difficult. However, when asked to copy-type a passage in a language she did not know, she was able simultaneously to shadow successfully a prose passage presented through headphones. Allport et al (1972) found that participants were unable to learn words presented through headphones while simultaneously shadowing a spoken message. In a variation of this experiment, participants were given pictures to learn and performance improved dramatically (90% of stimuli recalled successfully).

Difficulty

Sullivan (1976) found that in a dichotic task participants recalled fewer target words when the shadowing task was made more difficult. Duncan (1979) increased difficulty in a response to stimuli task by altering the co-ordination required of the respondents. He found that confusion, as indicated by the number of errors, increased.

Practice

In an experiment by Spelke et al (1976) two students were given extensive training in reading stories while simultaneously writing down a list of words. Initially their reading speed and handwriting were very poor. After six weeks, improvement in both skills was shown. Allport (1972) found that experienced musicians could shadow read a speech message while at the same time sight reading a piece of music (this was also evidence of dissimilar task competence).

Eysenck and Keane (1995) conclude that two tasks are performed well when dissimilar, when relatively easy and when they are well practised. In contrast, worse levels of performance occur when tasks are highly similar, difficult and little practised.

Automatic processing

Shiffrin and Schneider (1997) disagreed with the concept of attention being equally divided. They argued that practice causes the process of

Watch out!

Difficulty and practice to an extent overlap. Practice almost always causes a task to become less difficult.

Checkpoint 1

Why should a novice driver experience problems when attempting to hold a conversation while driving?

dividing attention to become automatic. Norman and Shallice (1986) identified three levels of **attentional functioning**:

→ fully automatic processing, with little conscious awareness
→ partially automatic processing, entailing more conscious awareness
→ control by a supervisory attentional system, which is important in decision-making.

This theory proposes two separate control systems. Eysenck and Keane (1995) argue that Norman and Shallice's theory is preferable as it accounts for both fully automatic and partially automatic processes.

Kahneman's capacity model of attention

Kahneman (1973) maintained that attention could be understood as a set of cognitive processes for categorizing and recognizing stimuli. Finite attentional resources are organized by a central processor. The capacity of attention can be increased or decreased by factors such as arousal and is influenced by enduring dispositions. According to this model, problems faced in attending to two things at once occur not because of one task interfering with another, but because the task requires more resources than we have available. Johnston and Heinz (1978) point out that the allocation of cognitive resources is flexible; we are in control because we are not slaves to incoming stimuli and are able to redirect limited resources onto important stimuli.

Action slips

When attention is divided and not attended to, action slips or absent-mindedness can easily occur. Reason (1992) identified the oak-yolk effect. Participants responded rapidly to a series of questions. Answers to the questions rhymed and included 'oak', 'joke' etc. The last question was 'What do you call the white of an egg?' 85% answered (incorrectly) 'yolk'. Of participants who were only given the last question, only 5% answered 'yolk'. Sellen and Norman (1992) argue that laboratory conditions are opposite to those that typically exist when we experience action slips in our everyday lives. Diaries are often used for collecting action slips in everyday situations. Reason's diary study (1979) found that 40% of slips were accounted for by storage failures (e.g. people forgetting they had already done something). However, as Eysenck and Keane (1995) point out, more information is needed on why/how action slips occur than the diary method provides. Moreover, with this method one cannot be sure how many action slips have been missed.

Action point

Study of the diagrammatic representation of Kahneman's model should help your understanding of the theory.

Checkpoint 2

Why do you think Sellen and Norman believe that tests under laboratory conditions are not good tests of action slips?

Exam question   answer: page 132

Critically consider how research into divided attention might enable us to understand the difficulties experienced when performing two different tasks at the same time. (30 min)

Pattern recognition

Pattern recognition theorists investigate how people recognize objects. Much of the research is based on how alphabetic and numeric symbols (alphanumeric patterns) are recognized.

Template matching (TM) theories ●●●

These suggest that **internalized templates** (miniature copies) are stored in the memory. A pattern is recognized by means of **template matching**. However, TM fails to explain how we can recognize slight differences in patterns: we would need an infinite number of templates, which is unrealistic (Eysenck 1984).

Feature theories ●●●

These are based on the notion that distinctive features recur in objects even though other features may vary. It is by comparing features with those in the memory that pattern recognition occurs. A triangle's distinctive features include three angles. If we see a smaller or larger version we are able to retrieve the distinctive features from memory and recognize the object as a triangle. Eysenck and Keane (1995) argue that pattern recognition does not only depend on 'listing the features of a stimulus'; there is also a need to 'consider the relationships' between the features. For the letter A, the crucial features and relationships are two angular lines and one connecting horizontal line.

Neisser (1964) found in a visual scanning study that it took longer to pick out the target letter Z from a group of letters with similar features (LWV) than from a group of contrasting letters (OCG).

Gibson et al (1968) found it took longer to decide that P and R are different than G and W.

Hubel and Weisel (1962) provided neurological evidence from work with cats and monkeys that specific brain cells respond to specific features of stimuli.

Prototype theories ●●●

These again suggest that we compare stimuli with internalized mental representations; however, the representation may only be 'something like' (a prototype of) that stimulus, so this approach is less rigid. A visual stimulus is assigned to a category of visual stimuli (e.g. cars) because it shares the general attributes (e.g. four wheels) of other objects in that category. An advantage of Prototype theories over TM and Feature theories is that the number of prototypes the memory needs to store is greatly reduced. A disadvantage of this approach, which is shared with the other two approaches, is that it fails to explain how pattern recognition is affected by context and expectation (Eysenck 1984).

Links

Hubel and Weisel are also discussed in the topic on the visual system (pages 120–1).

Bottom-up and Top-down processing ●●●

All the preceding theories are based on Bottom-up (BU) processing. BU theorists propose that recognition is based on the information about the stimulus that comes 'up' to the brain from the senses. Eysenck (1984) sees these theories as limiting. He argues that in the everyday example of proofreading, errors are common, because the reader 'sees' what she/he expects to see, an example of Top-down processing.

Top-down processing (TD) theorists promote those aspects of recognition that are guided by cognitive processes and by psychological factors such as motivation and expectation. A small round red tomato may be mistakenly perceived as a ball if seen on a snooker table. Leeper (1935) showed how past experience and perceptual set is important in the perception of an ambiguous figure (old woman/young woman). Similarly, Bruner and Minturn (1955) showed that context was important in whether participants saw an ambiguous alphanumeric as B or 13. Gilchrist and Nesburg (1952) showed the effect of motivation when hungry participants perceived pictures of food as brighter.

Face recognition

Face recognition is an area of research in which both BU and TD theorists are actively engaged. That face-processing is in many ways different from the processing of objects comes from the study of patients with **prosopagnosia**, who cannot recognize familiar faces but can recognize familiar objects. The patient studied by DeRenzie (1986) could discriminate between many types of object, but could not recognize his family and friends by sight (though he could by their names and voices).

Sergent et al (1992) discovered that several regions in the right hemisphere of the brain (in non-brain-damaged people) were more active in face identification than object identification.

Bruce and Young's model on face recognition (1986) proposed that familiar and unfamiliar faces are processed in different ways. Malone et al (1982) provided evidence for this theory with their study of brain damaged patients: one had good recognition of familiar faces and poor recognition of unfamiliar faces, while another was the opposite, indicating that the processes involved in recognizing unfamiliar and familiar faces are different. Some of the perceptual processes may be BU (recognizing that what you are looking at is a face), while others are TD (drawing on knowledge and past experience).

Examiner's secrets

Make sure you understand these experiments and can describe them *briefly*. Candidates often spend too long describing experiments of this kind.

Checkpoint 1

In the example of proofreading referred to here, what kind of error might be likely to occur?

Checkpoint 2

In Bruner and Minturn's experiment, what were the different contexts that caused participants to see the ambiguous alphanumeric as B or 13?

The jargon

Prosopagnostic patients have damage to the right hemisphere of their brain.

Links

There is a link here with the work of Fantz, referred to in the topic on perceptual development (pages 124–5).

Exam question answer: page 132

Discuss the different ways in which Bottom-up and Top-down theorists explain pattern recognition. (30 min)

Answers
Cognitive psychology

The visual system

Checkpoint

The pathways from the half of each retina closest to the nose cross over at the optic chiasma, so each side of the brain receives information from both eyes.

Exam question

In answering this question, reference should be made to light adaptation and related physiological factors.

Perceptual organization

Checkpoints

1 According to Gregory, the arrow with ingoing fins provides linear perspective cues which suggest the figure could be an outside corner of a building; the arrow with outgoing fins suggests an inside corner, so that the shaft appears further away and thus longer.
2 Other monocular cues include interposition; texture gradient; height in the visual plane; shading.

Exam question

Gibson's is an ecological approach, emphasizing the direct perceptual information received from senses. Gregory is a constructivist or Top-down theorist, his approach emphasizes role of cognition in perception.

Perceptual development

Checkpoints

1 Research needs to be carried out before learning has taken place. It is considered unethical to carry out such experiments on human babies. Cataract studies on humans can be viewed as somewhat similar; they are deprived because of visual impairment.
2 By the time babies are able to crawl, depth perception may have been learned.
3 Piaget's approach (1954) suggests children enrich sensory input using cognitive schemas.

Exam question

Relevant studies include neonate animal studies, human neonate studies, case studies involving human cataract patients, distortion-readjustment studies and cross-cultural studies. Consider both strengths and weaknesses. In the case of human neonate studies, one general disadvantage is that abilities must be inferred, as babies have limited powers of communication. An advantage is that such studies attempt to investigate children before learning has occurred. In addition, individual studies have their own specific strengths and weaknesses.

Focused attention

Checkpoints

1 In Broadbent's, research participants were not asked to concentrate their attention on one ear or the other – they were simply asked what they had heard.
2 'Pertinence' means relevance or importance.

Exam question

'Critically consider' means demonstrate your knowledge of the models and theories you select, show strengths and limitations. Consider one early selection model, e.g. Broadbent (focusing on physical characteristics) and Treisman (mainly concerned with meaning), and one late selection model e.g. Deutsch and Deutsch's pertinence model.

Divided attention

Checkpoints

1 Difficulties would arise if a novice driver has less practice of driving, and anything that interferes with the concentrated effort required creates problems.
2 Laboratory conditions are artificial and participants' levels of concentration may be unnaturally high.

Exam question

Again show knowledge of relevant theories, consider their strengths and weaknesses. Appropriate theories include resource allocation theories (e.g. Kahneman) and automatic processing theories (e.g. Shriffin and Schneider). To illustrate the difficulties experienced performing different tasks, reference might be made to the vigilance required of car drivers using a mobile phone. Such references should be concise.

Pattern recognition

Checkpoints

1 Spelling mistakes might occur, because we see what we expect to see (i.e. spellings of words).
2 The alphanumeric symbol would be seen as the letter B if it formed part of the sequence ABC, and as number 13 if it was part of the sequence 12 13 14.

Exam question

The difference between Bottom-up and Top-down approaches is that Bottom-up theorists suggest pattern recognition is based on information that comes 'up' to the brain from the senses, while Top-down theorists argue that pattern recognition is dependent on cognitive processes and psychological factors. Bottom-up theories are template matching theories, feature theories and prototype theories. In addition, reference might be made to the work of Hubel and Weisel. In outlining Top-down theories, it would be relevant to refer to Eysenck's approach and to his criticisms of Bottom-up theories. The work of researchers such as Leeper, Bruner and Minturn and Gilchrist and Nesburg is also relevant.

Developmental psychology

Developmental psychology is concerned with the lifelong process of change, although the focus in this section is very much on the developmental changes of childhood and adolescence rather than adulthood and old age (which are not covered here). Each of the areas of development chosen for inclusion reflect the demands of the AQA (A) specification, and cover the central themes of cognitive development, and social and personality development. The former of these stresses the more rational, logical aspects of development, the way in which children think about their world, the influences on the development of early intelligence, and the development of moral understanding. The latter stresses the more diverse areas of personality development, specifically the very different views of Freudian psychology, and the social learning theorists. The influence of biology and socialization is the theme of theories explaining gender role development. To some theorists, gender role is the result of biological differences, while to others such roles are socially constructed and changeable. In the final topic, we examine the particular problems of adolescence, and attempt to find out whether this stage of development really is an inevitable stage of storm and stress.

Exam themes

→ Theories of cognitive development and applications to education

→ Genetics and cultural factors in the development of measured intelligence

→ Theories of moral understanding

→ Explanations of personality development

→ Explanations of the development of gender identity and gender role

→ Social development in adolescence

Topic checklist

O AS ● A2	AQA/A	AQA/B	OCR	EDEXCEL
Development of thinking	●	●	O	O
Development of intelligence	●	●	O	O
Development of moral understanding	●	●		
Personality development	●	●		
Gender development	●	●		
Adolescence	●			

Development of thinking

Understanding the development of thinking is of key importance to psychologists. Three widely influential theories of this aspect of cognitive development are considered in this topic along with some of the ways in which they have been applied in educational settings.

Piaget's theory of cognitive development

Piaget studied children from infancy to adolescence using methods such as naturalistic observation and clinical interviews. Key aspects of his theory are as follows:

→ children's intelligence differs qualitatively from an adult's
→ children actively build up their knowledge about the world
→ the best way to understand children's reasoning was to see things from their point of view.

Piaget viewed the intellect as a structured and organized mental system, which takes in and deals with information about the world. It can change incoming information and be changed by it. The system is made up of schemas and operations that grow and change through assimilation, accommodation and equilibration and the forces of maturation and experience. The intellect grows in invariant stages.

Applying Piagetian ideas in educational settings

Piaget's theory has had a great influence in formal education, particularly in introducing more child-centred approaches in nursery and infant school, in teaching maths at junior level and science at secondary level. The approach is based on the following ideas.

→ Maturational *readiness* is critical. Educational activities and materials should be fitted to the child's stage of development. The teacher's role is to arrange the *curriculum* to fit the child.
→ Children are naturally active and curious. They learn best by *discovering* things for themselves.
→ Piaget emphasized interaction with others less than some theorists but still thought that it was useful if it included argument and discussion and being exposed to more mature ways of thinking.

Vygotsky's theory of cognitive development

Vygotsky died at the age of 34 leaving others such as Bruner (1983) and Wood et al (1976) to develop his ideas. His main objection to Piaget's ideas was that they played down the social context of learning. Rogoff (1990) suggested that Piaget saw the child as a scientist whereas Vygotsky saw the child as an apprentice. Other differences include:

→ *language* plays a key role in pushing the child forward
→ teachers can *actively intervene* in learning rather than wait for the child to be ready but they should still work within what the child can realistically achieve. Vygotsky (1967) called this working within the child's '**zone of proximal development**' (ZPD)

Checkpoint 1

What is meant by 'qualitatively' (as opposed to 'quantitatively') different?

Example

We have other organized systems too, such as the digestive system which is structured and organized to take in and deal with food and drink.

Watch out!

Piaget's ideas have been adapted by others and were not directly suggested by Piaget himself.

Checkpoint 2

Suggest suitable materials/activities that might prove educational for children at each of the major stages of intellectual development proposed by Piaget.

→ knowledge develops *spirally* so a child can understand anything at some level providing it is presented in an appropriate way.

Applying Vygotsky's ideas in educational settings ●●●

Applying the theory involves the use of the following.

→ **Scaffolding**   The teacher, working within the child's ZPD, helps them to solve a problem through supporting them to a solution rather than giving the solution. The teacher constantly adjusts the level of guidance given to the needs and abilities of the child until the child's knowledge is ready to stand alone and the scaffolding can be taken away.

→ **Expert tutoring**   Any 'expert' could work with a child to help them learn, e.g. parents. In *peer tutoring* the tutor is another pupil who is a little ahead of the learner so can work naturally in the learner's ZPD. *Co-operative group-work* is based on the same principle. Computer Assisted Learning (CAL) packages called *Intelligent Tutoring Systems*, using branching programmes, are another kind of expert.

Example

A teacher can 'scaffold' by providing the child with the elements of a problem, encouraging and taking an interest, drawing the child's attention to important information, or even demonstrating.

The information processing approach to cognitive development ●●●

Information processing theorists (e.g. Sternberg 1990) view the mind as analogous to a computer. They are interested in cognitive processes such as thinking, attention, memory and perception. Like Piaget, they view the cognitive system as a structure that matures in an orderly way over time. Differences between the processing abilities of individuals at different ages help theorists to map this development (e.g. Case's research into working memory, 1985). They are also concerned with individual differences in processing ability, e.g. Vernon and Mori (1992) linked speed of neural conduction to measured IQ.

Watch out!

Like Piaget, these theorists play down the role of social influences in cognitive development.

Checkpoint 3

Try to explain this correlation between processing speed and measured IQ.

Applying the information processing approach in educational settings ●●●

Information processing is clearly a key factor in formal education. In mainstream schools, understanding the ways in which young children think, perceive, remember and attend can help in developing educational strategies across the curriculum, e.g. in teaching reading or mathematical problem-solving. Studies of children with learning difficulties can also help teachers to take into account particular information processing deficiencies when planning activities.

More recently, there has been interest in **metacognition.** Older children seem more able to consider their own cognitive strategies. Encouraging them in this leads to more active learning and greater flexibility in thinking (Davis 1984).

The jargon

Metacognition is the ability to reflect upon one's own thinking.

Exam question   answer: page 146

Outline and evaluate two theories of cognitive development. (30 min)

135

Development of intelligence

Early debates about intelligence asked how much was inherited and how much learned. These days we tend to ask how heredity and environment interact with each other to affect intelligence. This raises questions about the inherited inferiority of certain groups of people on the grounds of class, race or gender. Beliefs in such inferiority have been used to excuse all kinds of discrimination.

Research into intelligence test performance

Genetic concordance studies

In the 1950s and 1960s Burt studied 53 pairs of separated MZ twins reasoning that, if intelligence is largely inherited, the twins' IQs should be very similar regardless of their experiences. He claimed the correlation between their IQs was +0.86, only a little lower than that for MZ twins reared together (+0.91). He concluded that heredity was more important than environment in determining intelligence. Erlenmeyer-Kimling and Jarvik (1963) compared people who vary in how similar they are genetically. The results are shown in the table.

Degree of resemblance	Correlation between IQs
MZ twins reared together	+0.87
MZ twins reared apart	+0.75
Siblings reared together	+0.55
Siblings reared apart	+0.47
Parent–child pairs	+0.50
Second cousins	+0.16
Unrelated pairs	−0.01

It seems that heredity plays a vital part in determining intelligence but there are ways in which the data were distorted that makes them very unreliable. Although discredited long ago, they are still quoted in books!

Adoption studies

If intelligence has more to do with heredity than environment, children's IQs should correlate more highly with their natural parents' IQs than with their adoptive parents' IQs. Burks (1928) found correlations between adopted children and their adoptive parents of only +0.13. Skodak and Skeels (1949) found a higher correlation of +0.44 between the IQs of adopted children and their natural parents, suggesting a genetic basis to intelligence. Kamin (1974) argued that, in the 1920s, children were generally placed with better-off families. In the 1940s, children were placed in homes similar to the natural parent's home.

Studies of social class differences

Statistics repeatedly show that children from lower social classes score lower on IQ tests than children from higher social classes. Broman et al (1975) plotted 50 000 four-year-old's IQs against social class. IQ rose with social class and with the mother's level of education.

Watch out!

The definition of intelligence is very problematic. Information in this topic is consequently about studies into the development of performance on tests that purport to measure intelligence.

The jargon

MZ (monozygotic) twins are identical. DZ (dizygotic) twins are non-identical and therefore no more genetically alike than a pair of siblings born at different times.

Checkpoint 1

Separated MZ twins often experienced very similar environments making it difficult to separate the effects of nature and nurture. In what ways might their environments have been similar?

Watch out!

Kamin (1974) claims that Burt invented some of his data. Kimling and Jarvik included it in their calculations.

Checkpoint 2

What do correlation coefficients show? What is the main limitation of correlation?

Watch out!

It is virtually impossible to separate out the effects of environment and heredity in such studies. Children from poorer homes may miss out on all sorts of stimulation, dietary needs and health care which could affect their IQs.

Enrichment studies

If intelligence is largely inherited, attempts to improve it should not work. However, interventions such as **Project Headstart,** which began in the USA in 1965, were designed to give children a boost before they start school. Most programmes resulted in IQ gains of up to 10 points in the short term but the gains did not last long. Follow-up studies, however, have shown lasting gains in things other than IQ, e.g. in behaviour in school, in academic achievement and in later employment. This 'sleeper effect' may occur because enrichment improves children's self-esteem and confidence or because the child's family becomes more supportive and positive about schooling.

Race and intelligence

Jensen (1969) and Eysenck (1971) have argued that differences in IQ scores between black and white Americans, and between British whites and West Indians are due to genetic differences between races. This unpopular conclusion has been widely criticized. For example, there is very little genetic difference between members of different races. Also the role of environment is largely ignored. Studies of children who are black, white or of mixed race and raised in similar environments show that the children's IQs are very similar.

Concluding comments ●●●

Studies in this area are fraught with difficulty.

→ It is impossible to separate the effects of environment and heredity. We cannot have one without the other.
→ For ethical reasons, we cannot do controlled breeding experiments with humans or bring them up in controlled environments.
→ Some aspects of intelligence may emerge through maturation or in a sensitive period. It then appears that environment was responsible when, in fact, it was not at all responsible or only partly so.
→ Genetically determined characteristics may be more open to environmental influence than we realize, some more than others.
→ We will probably never be able to measure so-called 'genetic potential' so we will never know whether it has been reached.
→ There is debate about the worth of IQ tests as a measure of intelligence. Performance on tests is open to many other influences. There are many intellectual qualities that IQ tests do not tap.

A useful way to visualize intelligence development is to view genetic potential as a 'rubber band' which is stretched by experience but can only be stretched so far. Differences between individuals can be explained by both differences between stretchiness of rubber bands and different amounts of stretching.

Example

There were many different types of enrichment on this programme. Some children had home visits from teachers. Other children attended different kinds of pre-school, some of which were quite formal, while others were freer and more discovery learning based.

Watch out!

It is important to consider a whole range of factors that might affect the child.

Checkpoint 3

What factors can influence people's performance on IQ tests.

Example

Two individuals could achieve the same IQ test score but we will never know the exact combination of influences that brought it about.

Exam question   answer: page 146

Describe and evaluate research into the role of genetic factors in the development of intelligence test performance. (30 min)

Development of moral understanding

This topic concerns some of the origins of morality and concentrates on theories arising from the cognitive developmental tradition. These focus on how understanding of moral issues develops. Other approaches have a different emphasis, e.g. psychodynamic theory can explain the origin of the conscience and moral feelings, while behaviourist theory can explain moral or immoral behaviour.

Checkpoint 1

When asked where rules originate, how might the answers of younger and older children differ?

Piaget's theory of moral development ●●●

Piaget (1932) proposed that moral reasoning of children reflects their level of intellectual development (e.g. ability to decentre or reason at the formal operational level). Younger children's reasoning is based on adult constraint; older children's on an understanding of the importance of cooperation, mutuality and rationality.

Piaget's theory has largely been superseded by that of Lawrence Kohlberg who claimed that moral reasoning is dependent on intellectual development *and* social experience.

Example

The Heinz dilemma: Heinz's wife was dying of cancer. Heinz tried to obtain a drug to help her by legal means but eventually stole it. Participants were asked to judge Heinz's actions.

Kohlberg's theory of moral development ●●●

Kohlberg (1969) presented moral dilemmas to participants and explored their moral reasoning through semi-structured interviews. The stage of moral development reached by an individual is determined by the complexity of their reasoning, not by their age or by the actual judgement they reach. Some never reach the higher levels.

Stages of moral development

The jargon

Hedonism involves pleasure seeking and pain avoidance.

Level I Pre-conventional morality

→ The child is seen as responsive to the moral rules of others, either in terms of the power of other people to reward or punish, or the hedonistic consequences of their actions.

Level II Conventional morality

→ Moral reasoning is determined by an attitude of loyalty to interpersonal expectations and the social order (i.e. you do things because you're expected to by others).

Watch out!

Each of these levels has two sub-stages.

Level III Post-conventional morality

→ Morality is based on universal ethical principles. These might include unconditional respect for individuals, the value of human life and an appreciation of justice based on the moral equality of individuals (i.e. doing things because they are *right*).

Evaluation of Kohlberg's theory

→ The theory has a limited database (approximately 50 American males) yet Kohlberg claimed cultural universality.

→ Cross-cultural studies (e.g. Vasudev and Hummel 1987) question the universality assumption. Indian participants were more likely to favour collective decisions.

- → People may reason at higher levels than they behave.
- → There is some evidence that debating moral issues, as Kohlberg suggested, helps children's reasoning to advance.

Gilligan's ethic of caring

Gilligan (1982) interviewed women facing real-life dilemmas and found that their moral reasoning centres more on *care* and men's centres more on *justice*. Kohlberg's scoring places judgements based on care lower than judgements based on justice thus favouring males. Gilligan suggested women go through three stages of moral reasoning:

- → caring for self
- → caring for others, perhaps sacrificing own needs to achieve this
- → balancing caring for self and others.

Evaluation of Gilligan's theory

- → Studies of sex differences in moral reasoning in children generally show no differences in care vs. justice judgements but women seem to centre their judgements more on care than men do (Bee 1992).
- → Walker (1984) found no evidence that girls score lower on Kohlberg's scoring system.
- → Gilligan has alerted us to a possible bias in the way we think of moral issue. In other words, it is determined by males.

Eisenberg's model of pro-social reasoning

Eisenberg (1986) presented children with moral dilemmas in which they had to decide between self-interest and helping someone else. Five levels of pro-social reasoning were proposed. Lower levels concern consequences for self. More mature levels show increasing evidence of ideas about duty, empathy and personal responsibility.

Evaluation of Eisenberg's theory

- → Although the proposed levels resemble Kohlberg's stages of moral reasoning, researchers have found that scores on Eisenberg's and Kohlberg's scales are not strongly related. If anything, pro-social reasoning is ahead of moral reasoning.
- → Eisenberg's proposed that pro-social behaviour can be encouraged by example. Freidrich and Stein (1975) showed a pro-social children's programme to five- and six-year-olds. Children showed better understanding of pro-social behaviour and were more pro-social than children shown a neutral programme.
- → Rheingold (1982) found cross-cultural differences in pro-social development. Children who are encouraged to do domestic chores and care for other children develop pro-social reasoning faster than in cultures where this is all done for them.

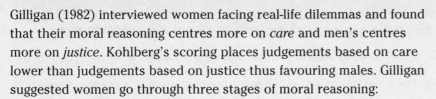

Checkpoint 2

Why might people reason at higher levels than they behave?

Checkpoint 3

Give an example of a real-life moral dilemma.

Watch out!

Much of the work on moral development concentrates on wrongdoing. Eisenberg focused on helpful and altruistic behaviour.

Checkpoint 4

What sources of bias might have been present in Eisenberg's research data?

Exam question   answer: page 147

Describe and evaluate *one* theory of moral understanding. (30 min)

Personality development

Personality could be something that you are born with, or it could develop in childhood and remain difficult to change thereafter, or it could be entirely learned and therefore flexible. Theorists differ in the extent to which they accept these ideas.

Freud's theory of psychosexual development ●●●

Freud's theory is based on clinical case studies of his neurotic clients.

→ The most important influence on behaviour is the unconscious mind.
→ The adult personality has three parts – id, ego and superego. One way in which people's personalities differ is in how powerful these three parts of the personality are in relation to each other.

Psychosexual stages of personality development

→ Personality develops in age-related, invariant stages (**oral**, **anal**, **phallic** and **genital**).
→ Experiences during a stage have lasting effects on our personality.

Unique individual experiences account for different personalities. At each stage, the id seeks a zone of the body (an erogenous zone) from which it can gain feelings of pleasure. Our personalities are affected by how successful the id is at gaining enough pleasure at each stage. If there is too little or too much, **fixation** may result. This means that energy becomes tied up in the stage and unbalances the personality.

Evaluation of Freud's theory of personality development

→ The theory has been very influential in our thinking and in inspiring other psychodynamic theorists.
→ The theory acknowledges the importance of biological and environmental forces in shaping personality.
→ The idea that personality is decided so early on in life is a rather pessimistic one. The only way to change an unbalanced personality would be to undergo lengthy psychoanalysis.
→ Many of the key elements of Freud's theory (e.g. unconscious mind, fixation) have wide appeal but cannot be observed directly. They are, therefore, difficult to test. For example, a study by Yarrow (1973) linked short time periods spent feeding in infancy with later thumb-sucking but these children may have had a stronger urge to suck all along leading them to feed quickly and thumb-suck.
→ There is some evidence for the existence of the personality types predicted by Freud. For example, Kline (1972) describes support for the anal personality type but there is little evidence that this is connected to the type of toilet training experienced in childhood.
→ Some critics question whether the theory is universal although Freud himself drew widely on cross-cultural evidence.

Watch out!

Latency occurs between the phallic and genital stages and is not, strictly speaking, a stage.

Checkpoint 1

When do the outcomes of early stages become evident?

Links

See Alternative therapies (pages 160–1).

Social learning theory (SLT)   ●●●

Social learning theorists accept that much of our behaviour results from *conditioning* by social agents but they also think we learn from *observing* and *imitating* certain important models around us. Personality, therefore, is no more than consistent behaviour patterns.

Examples of supporting research

→ 'Baby X' studies (e.g. Seavey et al 1975) show that adults behave differently towards babies depending on whether they believe them to be boys or girls, being gentler with girls.
→ SLT predicts that what a model does is more important to the observer than what it says. Grusec et al (1978) found that asking or telling children to be generous was less likely to encourage generosity than actually showing them how to be generous.
→ SLT takes into account a learner's thought processes when they are deciding how to behave. It is not merely a matter of reinforcing the desired behaviour. Bandura (1982) found that he could help people overcome anxiety and nervousness by getting them to think of themselves as more capable.

Evaluation of SLT

→ SLT gives us a straightforward and parsimonious explanation of how personality develops and changes.
→ SLT can explain why our personalities may not be consistent. For example, Hartshorne and May (1928) showed that boys' honesty was variable. They had apparently learned different responses in different situations (e.g. home and school) and behaved in ways that had been reinforced or modelled in each place.
→ Mischel's **situationism** (1968) has developed from such ideas. He agreed that there is very little consistency in personality so we should not see it as fixed. An illusion of consistency exists because we tend repeatedly to see people, and ourselves, in similar situations.
→ SLT is optimistic. It should be possible to change people's personalities so that they show fewer negative traits and more positive ones.
→ Some critics think SLT over-emphasizes the power of learning processes. For example, temperament theorists argue that we are born with a fundamental, inbuilt way of responding to the world and other people, and that experience can only build on this.

Checkpoint 2

List as many different kinds of 'model' as you can.

Don't forget

Practise what you preach.

Example

People we think we know well can sometimes surprise us by their behaviour when we encounter them in new situations.

Exam question   answer: page 147

Outline and evaluate the psychodynamic *and* social learning approaches to personality development. (30 min)

Gender development

All the major approaches to psychology explain the development of gender in their own way. Many of them seem not to acknowledge undeniable biological differences between the sexes. A selection of approaches are summarized here – but first, some definitions.

Definitions

The jargon

Androgyny is scoring high on both masculine and feminine characteristics.

→ **Sex** – biological type, i.e. male or female.
→ **Gender** – psychological type, i.e. masculine, feminine or androgynous (Bem 1964).
→ **Sex or gender-role** – the attitudes and behaviour expected of males and females by society.
→ **Sex/gender identity** – being able to label yourself accurately as male or female/masculine or feminine.

Social learning theory (SLT)

SL theorists explain much of our learning, including gender role as the result of:

→ conditioning provided by social agents
→ observational learning of particular role-models.

Example

Social agents might be parents, siblings, peers, and teachers. These, and characters on TV, might also be role models.

Examples of supportive research

→ Lamb et al (1980) found that three- to five-year-old boys and girls tended to play with sex-appropriate toys and were critical of each other for playing with toys seen as appropriate for the opposite sex.
→ Morgan (1982) studied adolescents and found the more TV girls watched, the more stereotyped their attitudes were. Boys' attitudes were highly sex-typed to start with so viewing habits had no effect.
→ Cross-cultural research (e.g. Mead 1935 and Schlegel and Barry 1986) suggests that social context is vital in shaping gender.

Watch out!

Different cultures may provide different role models.

Evaluation of SLT

→ SLT is a parsimonious explanation of gender development.
→ SLT may underplay the role of biological influences.
→ SLT is backed by a wealth of research evidence.
→ The current popularity of SLT may have much to do with its political correctness.

Checkpoint 1

Why might SLT be politically correct at the moment?

Cognitive-developmental theory

Kohlberg (1966) suggested that children need to develop an understanding of gender before they can take on a gender role. He suggested this happens in three stages.

Stage 1: Gender identity (two to five years) Correct identification of self as boy or girl.

Stage 2: Gender stability (four to six years) Child realizes they always have been and always will be a particular sex.

Checkpoint 2

How can this be linked to Lamb's research? (See SLT above.)

Stage 3: Gender constancy (six to seven years) Child understands that changes in appearance do not change a person's sex.

Evaluation of cognitive developmental theory

→ It does seem to be the case that children with gender constancy watch same sex models more *but*

→ children seem to show sex-typed behaviour long before this. Kohlberg cannot explain the finding that children have serious problems adjusting to being assigned to the opposite sex if this is done after three years of age.

Gender schema theory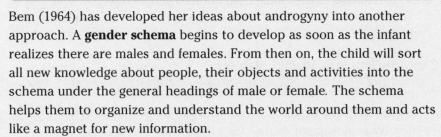

Bem (1964) has developed her ideas about androgyny into another approach. A **gender schema** begins to develop as soon as the infant realizes there are males and females. From then on, the child will sort all new knowledge about people, their objects and activities into the schema under the general headings of male or female. The schema helps them to organize and understand the world around them and acts like a magnet for new information.

Martin and Halverson (1983) suggest the development of the gender schema goes like this:

→ children realize there is a male-female distinction
→ they label themselves accurately as male or female
→ at about four to six years of age they focus on their own gender, learning how their gender play and talk and who they make friends with
→ at about eight to ten years old they will begin to pay more attention to the opposite gender so the schema expands to include more detailed information about both genders
→ after this, the gender concept becomes more flexible, e.g. girls know most boys don't play with dolls but could if they wanted to.

Evaluation of gender schema theory

→ Gender schema theory can explain how children start to show sex-typed behaviour and attitudes even before they have gender constancy. It is all part of the growth of their schema.
→ The theory sees the strong sex-role stereotypes that children hold as a natural stage in their developing understanding of gender. Children's attitudes are not fixed forever and will change depending on their experiences and the role models they encounter.
→ The theory neatly combines SLT and cognitive developmental approaches into one.

The jargon

A *schema* is a mental structure which we use to take in knowledge about the world.

Checkpoint 3

Who else in developmental psychology has used the term schema?

Watch out!

Young children can appear to be very sexist but Bem claims that this can change.

Exam question   answer: page 147

'Biology is destiny.'
Discuss this statement in the light of psychological explanations of gender role development. (30 min)

Adolescence

In Western culture, adolescence is often viewed as a distinct phase of development characterized by 'storm and stress' and identity crisis. The stereotypical teenager is rebellious, at odds with mainstream society in general and parents in particular. Is this view typical of all adolescents?

Identity crisis

Following from Erikson's (1968) psychosocial stage theory of lifespan personality development, Marcia (1980) argues that adolescent identity formation involves:

→ crisis – having to re-evaluate old choices and values
→ commitment – after 'crisis' the individual takes on a set of roles and ideologies.

There are four main identity statuses:

→ moratorium – crisis ongoing; no commitment made
→ foreclosure – crisis not gone through but commitment made
→ identity achievement – crisis fully dealt with
→ identity diffusion – neither in crisis nor committed.

Waterman (1985) found a decrease in diffusion status and an increase in identity achievement with age. Moratorium was uncommon but one-third at all ages were in foreclosure. Identity achievement was later than Erikson predicted but this may have been because most of the participants were college students postponing adult status. Munro and Adams (1977) found that 45% of non-college individuals in work had achieved identity status compared to 38% of college students. This is more in line with Erikson's prediction.

Smith and Cowie (1993) query the theoretical validity of Erikson and Marcia's work, especially regarding the idea of 'crisis'. They say:

→ moratorium could operate in different areas of life at any one time
→ identity achievement is not confined to adolescence.

Coleman suggests that Erikson's view of disturbance in adolescence was affected by the use of atypical and disturbed individuals.

Storm and stress

Rutter et al (1976) looked for evidence of conflict in 2303 14–15-year-olds living on the Isle of Wight. Parents and teachers answered questionnaires about the teenagers' behaviour and teenagers were selected for interviews and psychiatric assessment. A randomly selected and a high deviancy group were compared in terms of conflict between themselves and their parents. The teenagers perceived a higher frequency of conflict than parents did but rarely reported serious disagreements or criticized their parents. For the 'deviant' group conflict in communications with, and in behaviour towards, their parents was generally three times more common. Evidence for inner turmoil (expressed as behaviour psychiatric problems) was also

"A child becomes an adult when he realizes that he has a right not only to be right but also to be wrong."

Thomas Szasz

examined but little support was found for it. The general picture was one of good relationships between parents and their teenage children.

Coleman's focal theory of adolescence

Coleman (1974) suggests that, during adolescence, individuals focus on different aspects of change (e.g. biological, cognitive and social) at different times. Coleman and Hendry (1990) tested this by examining issues important to 800 boys and girls aged 11, 13, 15 or 17 years.

→ Each issue seemed to have a different distribution curve, peaking in importance over a particular age.

→ The coincidence of a number of important issues could cause problems but, generally, adolescents choose when to engage with particular issues mixing stability with adjustment.

Adolescence across cultures

Coleman's recent research has been borne out in New Zealand and North America. Is the pattern universal in other cultures?

→ Margaret Mead (1928) studied Samoan adolescents and suggested that, compared to North American culture, adolescence was tranquil and sexually permissive. She implicated Samoan extended family life and a less repressive child-rearing style than in North American families. Mead's work seemed to suggest that adolescent turmoil was a cultural, rather than universal, phenomenon.

Freeman (1983) questioned whether Mead had established sufficient trust with the Samoan people especially when asking young women to be frank about their sexual experiences. More recently, studies have indicated more repressive parenting practices and a value being placed on virginity at marriage especially in the higher status families.

→ Bronfenbrenner (1974) found that Russian adolescents showed more pro-social behaviour and less of the antisocial behaviour common in the USA adolescents. Russian lifestyle appears to integrate adolescents more with adult society whereas American youths tend to be segregated and discouraged from entering adulthood. The behaviour of the USA adolescents could have resulted from the development of a youth sub-culture distinguishing itself from adults by adopting a different set of values and norms.

Some cultures have closely prescribed rituals designed to confer adult status and demarcate males and females. Others have more nebulous criteria and confuse matters by conferring different kinds of responsibility at different ages. Adolescent experiences are likely to reflect the many ways in which cultures differ, e.g. in how gender is regarded and in how much choice of lifestyle individuals have.

Example

For a school leaver entering work, occupational choice would be a point of focus but for another person contemplating six years of Higher Education it may not be so important.

Watch out!

Studies such as these occupy a niche in history and may not hold true today. Samoans have since been influenced by American air-base staff and Christian missionaries.

Checkpoint 2

In what ways are adolescents in Western culture segregated and discouraged from entering adulthood?

Exam question   answer: page 148

Discuss research relating to social development in adolescence. (30 min)

Answers
Developmental psychology

Development of thinking

Checkpoints

1 Qualitatively different means dissimilar in kind or nature. Quantitatively different means dissimilar in amount. Piaget thought that children think in different ways from adults and that this mattered more than obvious differences in the quantity of knowledge that children and adults have.

2 The **sensori-motor** child needs toys and activities to help them to stimulate the senses and to help them practice and master movements, e.g. shape-sorters and 'activity centres'. **Pre-operational** children need toys which help with physical, manipulative, social and imaginative play such as climbing frames, bead threading and dressing-up clothes. **Concrete operational** children's play can involve more complicated rules, e.g. board games and team games. The **formal operational** child (and adult!) can play games involving complex, abstract reasoning and will often enjoy those requiring strategy to outwit an opponent. Hands-on maths and science teaching at any level encourages learning by discovery.

3 To score highly on many IQ tests it is necessary to solve problems or answer questions quickly. (The Western world has a preoccupation with speed that may not be shared with other cultures.)

Exam question

One of the problems that students have when answering questions such as this is that they frequently know *too* much about one theory, so the second theory gets only the briefest of treatments. It is well worth practising writing a précis of Piaget's theory in just 300 words (you will only be able to write about 600 words in total for this answer). Of that 300 words, half must be evaluative. Dividing your answer in this way ensures that you cover all required aspects of the question and in the right depth, rather than making the mistake outlined earlier.

* Précis (outline description) of Piaget's theory (qualitative differences between children and adults, invariant stages of development, assimilation, accommodation, equilibration etc.).
* Evaluation of Piaget's theory (is it supported by research evidence, does it have worthwhile applications etc.?).
* Précis (outline description) of Vygotsky's theory (e.g. the role of language in development, the nature of the ZPD, and the role of adults – such as teachers – in the development of the child).

Examiner's secrets

Essays such as this might be better viewed as a series of smaller 'units', each with its own requirement. If this question was divided into four paragraphs of about 150 words each, and the same amount of time was given to each (about seven and a half minutes per paragraph), planning becomes straightforward, and time management is so much easier. Questions frequently have multiple requirements (describe *and* evaluate *two* theories of . . .) so this strategy will pay off.

Development of intelligence

Checkpoints

1 In some of the cases studied by Burt, separated twins went to the same school, were brought up in a relative's home very similar to their co-twin's home and had time to play together. We should not forget that their pre-natal environment was also shared.

2 Correlation coefficients show whether there is a linear relationship between samples of paired data. Correlations, such as the ones used in studies of intelligence, do not indicate the cause of the observed pattern, i.e. they do not allow us to say that intelligence is *caused* by genetic factors.

3 People taking IQ tests might differ in their motivation or mood. They may also differ in how much experience they have of taking such tests. It is possible to become test-wise with practice and improve on one's score.

Exam question

In a 30-minute answer, you have to be fairly selective about what you include, so you should only use material around which you feel you can construct an effective answer to the question. You could construct your answer so that it included four parts (each about 150 words):

* research evidence from concordance studies
* research evidence from adoption studies
* contrasting evidence from enrichment and compensatory studies (see note below)
* problems with research in this area (see 'concluding comments' on page 137).

Examiner's secrets

Be careful not to write a 'general' answer to this question. The question asks specifically for the *genetic* influences on intelligence test performance, although evidence for *environmental* influences can be used as part of the evaluative component of the answer. It is vital, however, that any such inclusions are *used* as part of an evaluative argument rather than just being presented in the vain hope that they are somehow relevant to the question.

Development of moral understanding

Checkpoints

1 Younger children usually believe that rules come from outside authorities such as parents or teachers. Older children realize that rules are invented by people and can be changed by negotiation and agreement.

2 People may reason at higher levels than they behave because of social desirability bias (wanting to make a favourable impression). Also when faced with real-life situations they may not have the resources or courage to act as they believe they should.

3 Participants in Gilligan's research dealt with problems such as whether to continue with an unwanted

pregnancy. Another dilemma might be whether to tell a friend that their partner is being unfaithful.

4 There may be a social desirability bias in Eisenberg's study in that older children are more able to work out what they should say and have more options available to them.

Exam question

Although this might appear to be a very 'lightweight' question, it gives you the chance to discuss your chosen theory in detail. You may compare it with other theories, and you have the luxury of being able to elaborate your discussion in greater detail than if you were writing about *two* theories.

If you choose Kohlberg's theory, you might construct your answer in the following way:

- an introduction to the major claim of the theory – that people's moral development proceeds in stages, and these reflect the complexity of their reasoning about moral issues
- a description of the three *levels* of moral development (it is not required to go into detail about the individual stages)
- an evaluation of Kohlberg's theory (e.g. the limited database during the formulation of the theory, the mismatch between a person's level of moral reasoning and their behaviour)
- a contrast with Gilligan's ethic of caring which looks more at the way that people solve everyday dilemmas, involving care for others, than at abstract dilemmas involving universal ethical principles.

Personality development

Checkpoints

1 The outcome of early stages of personality development become evident during the genital stage when the adult personality, which results from all that has gone before, is expressed.

2 Models can be our peers, parents, teachers and other role-models such as those we see on TV, in films, on videos and in books and magazines.

Exam question

In the AQA specification, the theories of personality development specified in the question are preceded by the word 'including'. This indicates that they can appear as a *requirement* in a question. Freud's theory is an example of a *psychodynamic* theory.

Questions like this require careful time management, as there are four distinct parts to the question (see below) and only 30 minutes of writing time!

- Outline description of Freud's theory (e.g. id, ego and superego; stages of development).

- Evaluation of Freud's theory (e.g. its *good* points, such as its influence on other theorists, and its *bad* points, such as problems of observing directly the key elements of the theory).
- Outline description of social learning theory (e.g. personality is no more than consistent *behaviour* patterns; predictions of SLT model).
- Evaluation of SLT (e.g. its *good* points, such as the optimism of the theory, and the *bad* points, such as criticisms that SLT over-emphasizes the power of learning processes).

Gender development

Checkpoints

1 SLT can be seen as politically correct because it emphasizes the role of environment in shaping gender. Equal opportunities would be a nonsense if differences between males and females were entirely genetically determined.

2 At around five years of age children will be reliably identifying themselves as boys or girls. This fits with Lamb's finding that they then start to be critical of each other for playing with toys seen as inappropriate for their sex. They could not do this if they had not developed gender identity.

3 Piaget also used the term 'schema' in his theory of cognitive development.

Exam question

Although this quotation suggests that our development is shaped exclusively by biological factors, it is not a requirement to write about what these might be. Instead, it gives you the chance to take issue with that sentiment by discussing the more psychological explanations of the development of gender role. We have covered the following psychological explanations:

- social learning theory which explains gender role development in terms of conditioning and observational learning
- cognitive-developmental theory which sees gender role developing as a result of a child's increasing understanding of the nature of their gender and the behaviour of others
- gender schema theory which proposes that children develop schemas about maleness and femaleness which help them to organize and understand the world around them.

Remember that you must include an equal amount of evaluative content as descriptive content. Higher marks are awarded for material that is *developed* and for evaluation that is used *effectively*. It is important to remember this, rather than trying to cram as many different perspectives (e.g. all three given above) into a 30-minute answer.

The question starts with a quotation, so it is wise to at least finish with a conclusion that considers whether the psychological explanations discussed (in the light of your critical evaluation) sufficiently challenge the sentiment expressed in the quotation.

Adolescence

Checkpoints

1 Individuals who marry very young or who become parents when young may have had insufficient time to develop a clear identity. They experience foreclosure if their identity is subsumed under another's or under new responsibilities.

2 Western adolescents are discouraged from entering adulthood by being required to remain at school until 16 years of age and being encouraged to remain in education thereafter. Certain behaviours such as voting, being able to buy cigarettes or alcohol, and marrying without parental consent are also prescribed by age.

Exam question

This is a nice general question that lets you use any of the material on pages 144–5. In constructing an answer to this question, try to include the following:

• Marcia's focus on 'crisis' and 'commitment' and the four identity statuses of adolescence (moratorium, foreclosure etc.)
• evidence for and against this view of adolescence (e.g. Waterman 1985; Smith and Cowie 1993)
• storm and stress in adolescence – research (e.g. Rutter et al 1976) tends not to support the view of adolescence as emotional turmoil
• adolescent social development across cultures (e.g. the work of Mead in Samoa and Bronfenbrenner in Russia and USA).

Examiner's secrets

Remember that research studies can be used as critical evaluation because they either *support* or *challenge* theoretical views. To reinforce this point in your answer, make use of these terms (i.e. 'support' and 'challenge') when introducing research studies into your answer.

Individual differences

There are many ways to describe 'individual differences' but this section focuses on the development of psychopathology and its treatment. The first three topics are concerned with psychopathology, a term generally used to refer to the study of mental disorders (such as their characteristic symptoms and causes). The latter three topics are concerned with therapies; processes which help people to overcome their psychological difficulties. A broad distinction may be drawn between psychotherapies (that involve discussion or action) and somatic therapies (medical or biological intervention). Biological therapies such as chemotherapy (drug based treatment) are somatic therapies, while behavioural and psychodynamic therapies are examples of psychotherapies.

Exam themes

→ Characteristics and explanations of schizophrenia

→ Characteristics and explanations of depression (unipolar depression)

→ Characteristics and explanations of anxiety disorders (e.g. post-traumatic stress disorder)

→ Biological therapies (e.g. chemotherapy and ECT)

→ Behavioural therapies (including those based on classical and operant conditioning)

→ Alternatives to biological and behavioural therapies (e.g. psychodynamic therapy)

Topic checklist

○ AS ● A2

	AQA/A	AQA/B	OCR	EDEXCEL
Schizophrenia	●	●		●
Depression	●	●		●
Anxiety disorders	●	●		●
Biological therapies	●	●		●
Behavioural therapies	●	●		○●
Alternative therapies	●	●		○●

Schizophrenia

Schizophrenia is a serious mental disorder that is characterized by severe disruptions in psychological functioning. Schizophrenics may experience a variety of disturbing and frightening symptoms. Although the evidence in favour of the physical origins of the disorder is very strong, psychological factors are also important.

The characteristics of schizophrenia

Symptoms

→ Thought disturbances – a kind of reasoning that appears obscure and incoherent to others. Schizophrenics may suffer from delusions; interpretations of events that have no basis in reality.

→ Perceptual disturbances – a tendency to perceive the world around them differently to others, including hallucinations and an inability to recognize the emotional states of others.

→ Emotional disturbances – some schizophrenics display no emotions; others may display inappropriate emotional reactions.

→ Motor disturbances – schizophrenics may display unusual physical actions such as giggling, or standing immobile for long periods.

→ Disturbances in social functioning – an inability to maintain social relationships with others, together with poor social skills, means that schizophrenics tend to lead a poor-quality life.

Diagnosis of schizophrenia

DSM-IV diagnoses a disorder as schizophrenia when the following criteria are met:

→ the person has shown continuous signs of schizophrenia for more than six months, including an active phase when at least two of the symptoms detailed above are present

→ the person has deteriorated from a previous level of functioning in such areas as work, social life and self-care

→ any manic or depressive episode, if present, occurred either before or after the psychotic symptoms or was brief in comparison

→ the symptoms are not due to substance abuse or any other medical condition.

Categorizations of schizophrenia

DSM-IV has classified schizophrenia into five *types* (disorganized, catatonic, paranoid, undifferentiated, residual) although more recently clinicians have used a distinction between *Type 1* schizophrenia and *Type 2* schizophrenia:

→ **Type 1** is characterized by *positive* symptoms, i.e. the presence of something that is normally absent (such as hallucinations)

→ **Type 2** is characterized by *negative* symptoms, i.e. the absence of something that is normally present (such as the absence of emotion, apathy etc.)

Watch out!

Most of the written explanations stress the biological origins of schizophrenia, but social and family factors are also influential.

The jargon

Hallucinations is the experience of imagined sights, sounds or other sensory experiences as if they were real.

The jargon

DSM-IV – the Diagnostic and Statistical Manual, edition IV is an American system for classifying psychological problems and disorders.

Watch out!

If thought disturbances or hallucinations alone are sufficiently bizarre, this will lead to a diagnosis of schizophrenia without the presence of a second symptom.

Check the net

Read about these five types – if you have access to the internet, you will find an excellent site at:
www.schizophrenia.com

Explanations of schizophrenia ●●●

Biological explanations

→ Schizophrenia appears to be **heritable** which is good evidence for it being a biological disorder. Both adoption studies and twin studies support a genetic link. However, schizophrenia does not appear to be caused by a single gene, as less than 50% of the children whose parents are both schizophrenic have the disorder.

→ Genetic explanations emphasize the inheritance of a genetic vulnerability towards schizophrenia for some individuals. Whether this develops into the disorder depends on the environment being either supportive or stressful (the **diathesis-stress** model).

→ Traditional neuroleptic drugs (e.g. *chlorpromazine*) reduce positive symptoms. They block transmission of the neurotransmitter **dopamine** at the D_2 dopamine receptors and shut down dopamine activity in the mesolimbic region of the brain. 'Atypical' drugs such as *clozapine* help those who do not respond to traditional drugs. *Clozapine* appears to have a beneficial effect on negative symptoms in some patients. It acts only weakly at the D_2 receptors, but also acts at (among others) receptors for serotonin.

→ Most schizophrenics show symptoms which suggest that they are suffering from **brain damage**. Evidence from CT scans shows that there can be damage to the frontal lobes, temporal lobes and hypothalamus. Frontal lobe damage may account for some of the negative symptoms.

Psychological explanations

Cognitive explanations of schizophrenia suggest that biological problems arise first, causing strange sensory experiences. Further features emerge as the individual tries to understand these experiences. As other people fail to confirm the truth of these experiences, so the schizophrenic believes that they are hiding the truth. They reject other people's feedback and develop delusional beliefs that they are being manipulated and persecuted. Direct evidence for this view is not yet developed, but it has parallels in people who begin to lose their hearing and develop delusions that people are whispering about them.

Family explanations of schizophrenia suggest that the family environment contains such confusing elements as a *schizophrenogenic mother* and *double-bind communications*. Laing's *existential theory* claims that schizophrenia is a constructive process where people try to 'cure' themselves of the confusion and unhappiness that are a feature of their social and family environment.

Watch out!

If schizophrenia was entirely inherited, we would expect 100% of children whose parents were schizophrenic to develop the disorder.

The jargon

Diathesis-stress is a belief that individuals may have a predisposition (the diathesis) towards developing a particular disorder which then makes them more vulnerable to later environmental events (the stress).

Checkpoint 1

If *clozapine* acts 'weakly' at dopamine receptors but also acts at serotonin receptors, what does this tell you about the biochemical basis of schizophrenia?

The jargon

CT scan – computed tomography: this involves building up a composite picture of the brain through an amalgamation of horizontal X-ray sections.

> *"The experience and behaviour that gets labelled schizophrenic is a special strategy that a person invents in order to live in an unliveable situation."*
>
> R. D. Laing (1967)

Checkpoint 2

Find out what is meant by the terms 'schizophrenogenic mother' and 'double-bind communications'.

Exam question answer: page 162

Critically consider *two* explanations of schizophrenia. (40 min)

Depression

Depression is a type of mood disorder in which the person experiences feelings of great sadness, worthlessness and guilt, and finds the challenges of life overwhelming. Within DSM-IV, there are two categories of depression, major depression (or unipolar disorder) and bipolar disorder.

The characteristics of depression

Symptoms of depression (unipolar disorder)

→ The mood in a major depressive episode is often described by the person as depressed, sad, hopeless, or 'down in the dumps'.
→ Loss of interest or pleasure is nearly always present.
→ Appetite is usually reduced.
→ The most common sleep disturbance associated with a major depressive episode is insomnia and, less frequently, oversleeping.
→ Psychomotor changes include agitation or retardation.
→ Decreased energy, tiredness and fatigue are common.
→ The sense of worthlessness/guilt may include unrealistic negative self-evaluations or guilty preoccupations with minor past failings.
→ Many people report impaired ability to concentrate or make decisions, being easily distracted or having memory difficulties.
→ Frequently, there may be thoughts of death or even suicide.

Diagnosis of depression (unipolar disorder)

Requirements for a formal diagnosis for a major depressive episode can be met by two conditions. One relates to the severity and duration of the depressed state, though these might be inferred simply by reason of the patient going to the doctor. In addition to depressed mood, the patient should also have evidence of at least four of the remaining eight criteria.

Classification of depressive disorders

The type of depression that we all suffer from time to time in response to events in our lives is referred to as *reactive* depression. However, the form of depression seen in mood disorders is different and is referred to as *endogenous* depression. Bipolar disorder involves both mania and depression but unipolar disorder involves only depression. This depression may be continuous but more often comes in episodes.

Explanations of depression

Biological explanations

Like schizophrenia, there is some evidence that mood disorders are heritable (e.g. Rosenthal 1971). As about twice as many women as men suffer from depression, most studies of the disorder's inheritance have focused on women. Bierut et al (1999) studied depression in a sample of 2 662 pairs of same-gender and mixed-gender twins. They found that stressful events such as the death of a spouse or loss of a job were the major causes of depression in both the men and the women. However,

---

Watch out!

Major depressive disorder is also known as unipolar depression. Bipolar depression is not covered in this section.

Example

A former keen golfer no longer plays golf; a child who used to enjoy football finds excuses not to play.

Watch out!

Thoughts of death and suicide are not always part of a depressive diagnosis, and are frequently absent.

Checkpoint 1

If a patient sought medical help after the death of their spouse, and described themselves as 'prone to tears, disinterested in their work or self-appearance, having difficulty sleeping and eating, and feeling guilty that they didn't do more for their partner when alive', how would you classify their condition?

Action point

There are many other explanations for the greater incidence of depression in women. Try to find out about some of these, they will be very useful in your evaluation of this topic area.

genetic factors were more likely to have contributed to depression in the women than in the men. This appeared to be true for mild as well as severe depression.

Research also suggests a possible link between the neurotransmitters *serotonin* and *noradrenaline* and the development of depression.

→ Depression is thought to stem from a deficiency of noradrenaline in certain brain circuits. Indirect markers of noradrenaline levels in the brain (in the urine and cerebrospinal fluid) are often low in depressed individuals. Post-mortem studies have revealed increased densities of noradrenaline receptors in the cortex of depressed suicide victims.

→ Serotonin depletion might also contribute to depression – serotonin-producing cells extend into many brain regions thought to participate in depressive symptoms. Cerebrospinal fluid in depressed, and especially in suicidal, patients contains reduced amounts of a major serotonin by-product (showing reduced levels of serotonin in the brain itself). Evidence comes from the effectiveness of drugs that inhibit the re-uptake of serotonin from the synaptic cleft. Prozac and other SSRIs are able to block serotonin re-uptake without affecting other neurotransmitters.

Psychological explanations

Cognitive theories emphasize the role of irrational thoughts and beliefs influencing the emotional state of the individual. Beck (1967) sees depression in adulthood as being caused by a bias towards negative interpretations of events. These are a legacy of childhood experiences such as the loss of a parent, social rejection by peers or the depressive attitude of a parent. These biases are activated whenever the individual encounters situations that are in some way similar. Studies have shown that cognitive therapies are better for preventing the recurrence of depression, although the combined advantages of cognitive therapy and drug therapies appear more helpful than either type of therapy alone.

According to the *learned helplessness* view of depression, people become depressed when they perceive a loss of control of the reinforcing aspects of their life. If this is attributed to internal, global and stable factors, they will feel helpless about preventing future negative outcomes and may experience unipolar depression. There is a great deal of research support for this explanation of depression (e.g. Peterson et al 1992), but a number of other studies have failed to find any consistent connection between depression and these negative attributions (see above).

Watch out!

'Noradrenaline' is known as 'norepinephrine' in the USA.

Checkpoint 2

Why do you think there are *increased* densities of noradrenaline receptors if there is a *deficiency* of this neurotransmitter?

The jargon

SSRIs – selective serotonin re-uptake inhibitors: this is a class of anti-depressant drugs that stop serotonin being taken back into the presynaptic cell, thus prolonging its action at that synapse.

Example

'Its my fault (internal), everything I do goes wrong (global), it's always going to be the same (stable).'

Exam question   answer: page 162

(a) Outline the clinical characteristics of depression.

(b) Outline and evaluate *one* explanation of depression. (40 min)

Anxiety disorders

Anxiety disorders are those disorders in which severe anxiety plays a major part. The most common of adult mental disorders, these include post-traumatic stress disorder (PTSD) and phobic anxiety disorders. Only PTSD is covered here, in line with the AQA (A) specification requirement to study one type of anxiety disorder.

Post-traumatic stress disorder (PTSD)

Clinical characteristics of PTSD

PTSD refers to a distinct pattern of symptoms that develop as a result of some traumatic event (war, plane crash, rape). PTSD may be diagnosed if the person has experienced an event that involved actual or threatened death or serious injury and their response involved intense fear, helplessness, or horror (DSM-IV). The symptoms of PTSD begin shortly after the event and may last for months or even years (although in some cases there is a delay of several months before onset of the disorder). PTSD may be classified as *acute* if the symptoms last for less than three months, or *chronic* if they last for more than three months. Symptoms include:

→ re-experiencing the event – recurring recollections, including distressing dreams and flashbacks about the traumatic event
→ avoidance – the person tries to avoid anything that is associated with the traumatic event (including thoughts, activities or memories of the event)
→ reduced responsiveness – the person feels a detachment from others and an inability to have emotional feelings for them
→ increased arousal, anxiety and guilt – people may experience increased arousal and sleep disturbances. In some cases people may experience 'survivor guilt' (a sense of guilt that they survived the event and others did not).

Biological factors associated with PTSD

Because only a proportion of persons exposed to traumatic events develop post-traumatic stress disorder (PTSD), it has become important to discover the factors that increase the risk for the development of PTSD following trauma exposure. Presumed risk factors for PTSD may describe the degree of trauma associated with the event or characteristics of persons who experience those events. Recent data have implicated biological and familial risk factors for PTSD. For example, recent studies (Yehuda 1999) have demonstrated an increased prevalence of PTSD in the adult children of Holocaust survivors, even though these children, as a group, do not report a greater exposure to life-threatening events.

It is difficult to know to what extent the increased vulnerability to PTSD in family members of trauma survivors is related to biological or genetic phenomena, as opposed to experiential ones, because of the large degree of shared environment in families. In particular, at-risk family members, such as children, may be more vulnerable to PTSD as

Watch out!

There are other types of anxiety disorders; only one is covered here. This is sufficient for the AQA (A) specification requirement.

Watch out!

When reading about PTSD, you may also find it referred to as 'shell shock' or 'battle fatigue'.

Checkpoint 1

How might children demonstrate a traumatic experience in their play?

Example

Survivor guilt has been reported in survivors of the Holocaust as well as more recently in survivors of the Hillsborough disaster in1989.

Checkpoint 2

Why is it difficult to disentangle biological influences from experiential influences?

a result of witnessing the extreme suffering of a parent with chronic PTSD rather than because of inherited genes. But even if the diathesis for PTSD were somehow 'biologically transmitted' to children of trauma survivors, the diathesis is still a consequence of the traumatic stress in the parent. Thus, even the most biological of explanations for vulnerability must at some point deal with the fact that a traumatic event *has* occurred (Yehuda 1999).

Psychological factors associated with PTSD

In trying to explain why some people suffer from PTSD and others do not, psychologists have discovered that childhood experiences (such as early abuse) may leave some people vulnerable to later stress. Although reasons for this link are not established, it is thought that children may deal with early trauma by separating themselves from the experience. This becomes a strategy for dealing with trauma in later life.

Breslau et al (1998) studied a representative sample of 2 181 persons in Detroit (USA), 18 to 45 years, to assess the life history of traumatic events and PTSD. PTSD was assessed with respect to a randomly selected trauma from the list of traumas reported by each respondent.

→ The conditional risk of PTSD following exposure to trauma was 9.2%. The highest risk of PTSD was associated with violent assault (20.9%).
→ The trauma most often reported as the precipitating event among persons with PTSD, was the sudden unexpected death of a loved one, an event experienced by 60% of the sample, and with a moderate risk of PTSD (14.3%).
→ Women were at higher risk of PTSD than men, controlling for type of trauma.
→ It was found that the risk of PTSD following a significant trauma was less than previously estimated. The researchers concluded that previous studies had overestimated the risk of PTSD by focusing on the worst events the respondents had ever experienced.

Although recent research has focused on combat, rape, and other violent assaults as causes of PTSD, sudden unexpected death of a loved one is a far more important cause of PTSD in the community, accounting for nearly one third of PTSD cases.

Helzer et al (1987) found that risk of PTSD following a traumatic event was increased among war veterans, particularly those who had been wounded in Vietnam (an example of the *diathesis-stress* explanation).

The jargon

Diathesis is a predisposition towards developing a particular disorder which makes a person more vulnerable to later environmental events.

Use the net

Want to know more? David Baldwin's Trauma Information Pages contain links to many other sites associated with PTSD. You will find this at: www.trauma-pages.com

Action point

Make sure you understand what is meant by 'diathesis-stress' (see page 151).

Exam question   answer: pages 162–3

Discuss research relating to the development of *one* anxiety disorder. (40 min)

Biological therapies

Biological, or biomedical, treatments of mental disorder aim to reduce symptoms by addressing their underlying biological or biochemical cause.

Chemotherapy

This approach involves the use of therapeutic drugs. Their general function is to alter the action of the chemical messengers in the brain known as neurotransmitters. These fall into three major groups:

→ anti-anxiety drugs which relieve tension and nervousness
→ anti-psychotic drugs which are used to reduce psychotic symptoms such as mental confusion and delusions
→ anti-depressant drugs which are used to elevate mood.

Appropriateness and effectiveness of drug therapies

→ Drug therapies may produce clear therapeutic gains for many patients and may be particularly effective with severe disorders that have not responded to other types of treatment.
→ Some critics argue that drug treatments are no more than a chemical straitjacket offering only short-term relief from a problem while doing nothing to attack its root cause.
→ Others argue they are a chemical life-jacket enabling people to make changes in their lives which may prevent a downward spiral.
→ Drug treatments are essentially reductionist. Used on their own they treat the person as merely a malfunctioning biological machine and so fail to treat the whole person.
→ All drugs have side effects and long-term use of them can lead to permanent undesirable changes.

Electroconvulsive therapy (ECT)

ECT is a treatment where a sub-lethal electric shock is passed through the temporal lobes of the brain to produce a cortical seizure and convulsions. Muscle relaxants and a short-acting anaesthetic are given beforehand and other medical procedures followed. Treatment may be given a number of times over several weeks depending on the individual's progress.

The use of ECT has declined since the 1960s and 1970s but is still used today for certain conditions. Its mode of action is uncertain but it seems likely that it produces neurochemical changes in the brain.

Appropriateness and effectiveness of ECT

→ It is said to be highly effective for severe depression, bipolar disorder and in the treatment of secondary (mood) disorders in schizophrenics.
→ Its effects are immediate which make it desirable for use on people who have suicidal feelings. (Drug treatment can take weeks to become effective.)

- ECT may cause death in 1 in 200 patients over 60 at least partly because the associated medical procedures, such as anaesthesia, carry a degree of risk in themselves.
- Irreversible cerebral damage can arise from consistent use (Breggin 1979).
- In a review of the ECT controversy, Small et al (1986) found that ECT produces some short-term intellectual impairment but this is not inevitable and rarely permanent.
- Claims that ECT is merely a placebo have been made but Barton (1977) compared hundreds of studies and found only six that had used a control group to assess the effect of ECT.

Psychosurgery

Psychosurgery involves the use of surgical techniques on the brain. The first treatments of this kind were carried out by Moniz in the 1930s. Examples include:

- Leucotomy or pre-frontal lobotomy – intended to separate the more highly evolved pre-frontal lobes from the more primitive areas of the brain and thus bring extreme expressions of emotions, such as aggression, under control. Such treatments were tried on schizophrenia and certain anxiety disorders.
- Modern day lobotomies – involve insertion of tiny radioactive rods which destroy areas of frontal lobe tissue or other specific areas, e.g. as in tractotomy which is used for severe depression and cingulotomy which is used for obsessive compulsive disorder.

Appropriateness and effectiveness of psychosurgery

Psychosurgery gradually fell from favour and became rare after the 1950s but is still carried out occasionally.

- Lack of careful evaluation studies meant that early practitioners were unsure that what they were doing was appropriate or effective.
- If it goes wrong, or has side effects, it is irreversible.
- It raises serious ethical concerns, e.g. concerning consent.
- Although controversial, psychosurgery can be used as a last resort on certain conditions after other treatments have failed.
- It has been claimed that tractotomy can reduce the risk of suicide in severely depressed people (Verkaik 1995) and that cingulotomy helps in obsessive compulsive disorder.

"[Such techniques are] crimes against humanity."

Heather (1976)

Exam question   answer: page 163

Describe and evaluate the use of *two* biological therapies. (40 min)

Behavioural therapies

Links

See behavioural models of abnormality (page 49).

Watch out!

Walker (1984) distinguished between behaviour therapies based on classical conditioning and behaviour modification based on operant conditioning.

Checkpoint 1

Identify two further examples of flooding/implosion.

Action point

Be sure that you can define all the emboldened terms on this page.

The jargon

An *emetic* is a drug that induces vomiting.

Behaviourists emphasize the role of learning experiences provided by the environment in determining behaviour. Learned behaviour is usually useful or adaptive but sometimes it is not, in which case it may become so problematic that it is seen as a disorder. Abnormal behaviour is open to the same laws of learning as normal behaviour and can be shaped and changed using the same principles.

Therapies based on classical conditioning

These therapies are usually referred to as behaviour therapies and involve the application of classical conditioning principles. They tend to concern behaviours that are difficult to control voluntarily.

Flooding and implosion

Flooding and implosion can be used to treat phobic disorders.

→ **Flooding** involves immediate exposure to a form of the actual feared stimulus, e.g. requiring a lift phobic to travel in a lift.
→ **Implosion** requires the phobic person to imagine their most feared situation, e.g. the lift phobic imagines being trapped in a lift.

Both techniques work on the principle that, if the feared stimulus is repeatedly presented in a supportive setting where the fear can be managed, its association with anxiety will eventually be weakened.

Systematic desensitization (SD)

Wolpe (1958) successfully pioneered SD on phobias. SD has three stages:

→ the client constructs a hierarchy of feared situations ranging from manageable to frightening
→ the client is trained in relaxation techniques
→ the client relaxes and is exposed to the feared situations in their hierarchy beginning with the least frightening. Once they can cope, the next stage is tried until desensitization is achieved.

A variation on this, called graded exposure, dispenses with the relaxation training.

Aversion therapy

Aversion therapy involves training the client to associate sickness or pain with an undesirable aspect of their behaviour in order to discourage them from continuing with it. For example, a problem drinker may take an emetic which makes them vomit only when they drink alcohol.

A variation on this is **covert sensitization** which involves the person being trained to imagine vividly the unpleasant consequences of their behaviour.

Therapies based on operant conditioning

Therapies based on operant conditioning are often called behaviour modification techniques. They work well with behaviour that is more under voluntary control and which is reinforced by its consequences. Consequences can be changed in order to change the frequency of desirable and undesirable behaviour. This involves the use of:

→ extinction – pleasant consequences of undesirable behaviour are removed, e.g. parental attention towards a child's tantrums
→ punishment – children who are mutilating themselves, e.g. head-banging, might be given mild electric shocks to discourage the behaviour
→ reinforcement – rewards can be given to shape desirable behaviour from small beginnings or to increase its frequency. **Token economy** systems, such as reward systems in classrooms, use this principle. **Biofeedback** also uses reinforcement by feeding back to the individual their success in altering their physical state, e.g. heart rate.

Appropriateness and effectiveness

Marks (1981) claimed that behavioural approaches could be brought to bear on about 25% of all non-psychotic conditions including phobias, obsessive compulsions, social skills problems and marital and sexual difficulties. The behavioural approach provides many effective treatments in settings ranging from hospitals, prisons and schools to families in their own homes. In some cases, as with psychotic people on psychiatric wards, it can work as a complement to other forms of treatment.

→ Behaviourists are optimistic about possibility for change.
→ Careful measurements taken before, during and after treatment empirically demonstrate the effectiveness of behaviourist techniques.
→ Some critics question whether symptom removal is thorough enough and say that symptom substitution may occur.
→ Ethical concerns about deprivation and the use of aversive techniques are important.
→ New approaches, e.g. cognitive behavioural therapy, have emerged from this approach.

The jargon

A *token economy* uses a system of tokens such as stars, points or plastic counters which are given for good behaviour and can be saved and exchanged for reinforcers.

Checkpoint 2

How would Freud explain symptom substitution?

Exam question   answer: page 163

Critically consider the use of *two or more* behavioural therapies. (40 min)

Alternative therapies

Well-known alternatives to biological and behavioural therapies include psychodynamic, cognitive-behavioural and humanistic therapies. This topic outlines psychodynamic therapy, taking Freudian psychoanalysis as an example.

Links

See Models of abnormality 1 (pages 48–9).

Psychoanalytic aims

Neurotic symptoms require constant expenditure of psychic energy which is then unavailable for healthy functioning. This may reach a point where the individual is unhappy and/or finding it difficult to function effectively. Psychoanalysis aims to help by:

→ freeing healthy libidinous impulses
→ strengthening the ego and re-educating it so that it approves more of the id and can allow it wider expression
→ altering the superego so that it is more humane and less punitive.

Action point

Make sure you can write a definition of all the terms in bold print in this section.

Psychoanalytic techniques

Traditional psychoanalysis involves '50 minute hours' of analysis six days a week over months, or even years. These days, however, most clients (analysands) spend only three to five hours a week in analysis over a shorter period of time. The analyst endeavours to make the unconscious conscious via:

Links

See 'Freud and dreaming' (page 109).

→ **free association** – the analysand allows the mind to wander and reports everything to the analyst no matter how trivial, disconnected, disagreeable or irrational it may seem.
→ **dream analysis** – examination of the manifest (recalled) content of dreams in order to understand the latent (unconscious) content.
→ **transference** – the analysand transfers conflicts, feelings and attitudes from earlier life, especially the Oedipal stage, onto the analyst. These displaced feelings then become the object of analysis and can eventually be a source of insight for the analysand.
→ **acting out, abreaction or catharsis** – the analysand experiences release of repressed emotions and must engage with them.
→ **interpretation** – the analyst offers the analysand **insight** into his or her ego defences by relating present behaviour to childhood events. The timing of the interpretation is critical – the analysand must be ready. Bad timing could lead to resistance.
→ **resistance** – analysis itself is a threat to the ego's defences so the ego may actively resist progress. Symptoms may have secondary gains, attention from others, which the ego is reluctant to let go.
→ **working through** – the ego is encouraged to take control of repressed libidinal energy by coming to terms with feelings.

Checkpoint 1

How might resistance manifest itself?

Appropriateness and effectiveness

Because psychoanalysis involves strengthening a reality-based ego, it is not suitable for treating psychoses in which a major problem may be lack of contact with reality.

Methodological problems with assessing effectiveness

It is very difficult to demonstrate the effectiveness of any psycho-therapy including psychoanalysis because, to make valid comparisons of therapies, we would need to ensure:

→ client homogeneity, e.g. similarity of symptoms
→ therapist homogeneity, e.g. similarity of experience and skill
→ reliable psychiatric diagnosis
→ agreement on criteria of success/cure
→ that the control groups are adequate.

Does psychoanalysis work?

→ Eysenck (1952) claimed that 70% of people recovered with GP treatment while only 44% of psychoanalytic clients improved. He suggested psychoanalysis was not only worthless but also damaging.
→ Bergin (1971) re-worked the data on different criteria and estimated that only 30% of people recovered without treatment.
→ Further re-working of the data can raise the success rate of psychoanalysis to 66% in line with other psychotherapies.

The debate rests mainly on methodological grounds, particularly on how participants are selected and how assessments of them are made. However, factors in effective psychoanalysis do seem to include:

→ general therapeutic skills of analysts
→ the analysand's:
  → YAVIS factor
  → time, money and motivation
  → insight capabilities
  → tolerance of vulnerability as defences are exposed
  → the analysand's symptoms.

Psychoanalysis now

Psychodynamic therapies do not dominate as they did in the 1950s but they are still an important force. Comer (1995) quotes US statistics:

→ 11% of clinicians practise Freudian psychodynamic therapy
→ 22% practise contemporary psychodynamic therapy
→ 38% are eclectic (so may use some).

Analysis can be shortened, e.g. Malan's (1976), 'brief focal therapy' requires one session a week for 30 weeks to treat a specific problem. Therapeutic techniques that can be used in groups have been developed from psychoanalytic principles. They include psychodrama (Moreno 1946) and transactional analysis (Berne 1964).

Watch out!

Evaluation of any kind of psychotherapy is a methodological minefield.

The jargon

Homogeneity means similarity.

Checkpoint 2

What do you think general therapeutic skills might be?

The jargon

YAVIS stands for young, attractive, verbal, intelligent, successful.

Exam question   answer: page 164

Describe and critically assess the use of *one or more* therapies derived from the psychodynamic approach. (40 min)

Answers
Individual differences

Schizophrenia

Checkpoints

1 This suggests that schizophrenia cannot *just* be a consequence of excessive dopamine activity. Other neurotransmitters and the parts of the brain that they serve also seem to be involved in the disorder.

2 The *schizophrenic mother* (or father) refers to a parent who is cold, rejecting, distant, aloof, but dominating (Reber 1995). This puts the child in a hopeless *double-bind* situation where nothing they do will be satisfactory to the parent. An example might be the adolescent who is criticized by his parents for his independence and rebellion but is also criticized when he shows excessive dependence on the parents.

Exam question

The question asks you to *critically consider*, which in AQA-speak means to show your knowledge and understanding of two explanations of schizophrenia, together with the *strengths* and *limitations* of those explanations. These explanations might be based on two theoretical *perspectives* (such as biological and psychological) or two more specific explanations such as the *dopamine hypothesis* and Laing's *existential theory*. You would probably have more to write about if you chose the former approach, but it is very much up to you. One of the advantages of the internet in preparing for questions of this type is that there is so much material to resource your answer that you may simply find the more global approach (biological versus psychological) too constraining.

Examiner's secrets

This section of the AQA (A) specification is part of the 'synoptic' assessment of your A-level (see pages 182–3), so you will get more marks if you show a wider spread of perspectives and methods. Take care not to spread yourself too thin when doing this, as your answer may become too superficial.

Depression

Checkpoints

1 This person has all the symptoms of depression, but their condition is more likely to be an example of 'reactive depression' through the death of a spouse.

2 When transmitter molecules become unusually scarce in synapses, post-synaptic cells expand receptor numbers in a compensatory attempt to pick up whatever signals are available.

Exam question

This question is in two parts. The first part requires an outline description of the characteristics of depression. You might, therefore:

- outline the symptoms of depression (unipolar disorder)
- outline the main criterion for diagnosis of unipolar depression (i.e. depressed mood plus at least four other criteria)
- classify depressive disorders (e.g. *reactive* depression and *endogenous* depression).

The second part of the question asks for *both* an outline description *and* evaluation of one explanation of depression. (If you are taking the AQA (A) exam, there is an important point about mark distribution – see 'Examiner's secrets' below.)

You might choose to answer this question in terms of the role of neurotransmitters (this is *one* explanation – neurotransmitter imbalance).

- nature of noradrenaline deficiency
- evidence from levels of by-products and post-mortems of suicide victims
- nature of serotonin deficiency
- evidence from by-products and effectiveness of SSRIs.

Examiner's secrets

When questions are parted in this way, you will be given an indication of the marks available for each part of the question. The amount of time you should spend on each part should be proportional to the number of marks awarded, and this should also guide you in deciding how much detail is appropriate when answering that part of the question.

In AQA (A) questions, the number of marks awarded for AO1 (knowledge and understanding) is the same as it is for AO2 (analysis and evaluation). Clearly some of the AO1 marks have been given in part (a), therefore part (b) should be only 25% AO1 (outline description) and 75% AO2 (evaluation).

Anxiety disorders

Checkpoints

1 By engaging in repetitive play where themes or aspects of the trauma are expressed.

2 There are several difficulties. First, it is clear that a traumatic event has occurred and that this is directly responsible for the PTSD reported. However, when researching possible inherited vulnerability in the families of trauma survivors, it is difficult to disentangle what is an inherited factor from what is a reaction to the perceived distress of the parent. Witnessing a parent in distress can itself be a very traumatic event.

Exam question

This is a general question that allows you to use most of the material on pages 154–5. The term 'research' as defined by the AQA in their 'Glossary of Terms', allows for the inclusion of both 'empirical' research and also theoretical insights.

As the question asks for research relating to the *development* of one anxiety disorder (which will be PTSD in this answer), it is not appropriate to dwell too long on the 'characteristics' of the disorder, other than to explain what is meant by PTSD. You can then move on to:

- biological (i.e. inherited) influences in the development of PTSD
- problems of inferring that PTSD is *inherited*
- psychological research into the relationship between trauma and risk of PTSD
- conclusions from research and link to *diathesis-stress* model.

Examiner's secrets

As this question forms part of the AQA *synoptic assessment*, you should aim to include a wide range of perspectives explaining PTSD. In this case, you should include both *biological* and *psychological* explanations.

Biological therapies

Checkpoints

1 The action of certain neurotransmitters can be altered in various ways by therapeutic drugs. Such drugs can work by increasing or reducing the release of excitatory transmitters, by mimicking their effects or by preventing their re-uptake, thus prolonging their life.
2 In Britain, informed consent to ECT is required. This is problematic because sufferers are in a distressed mental state and may find it difficult to reach a decision. In addition, the action of ECT is not fully understood so it is not possible for consent to be fully informed.

Exam question

As this question asks for the 'use' of biological therapies, this would include both the mode of action *and* the appropriateness and effectiveness of your two chosen therapies. The question allows you 45 minutes of writing time, so it is fairly straightforward to divide your response accordingly. A detailed response to this question would be about 800 words, perhaps organized into four 200-word 'sections', for example:

- the nature and mode of action of therapeutic drugs (e.g. anti-anxiety drugs)
- the appropriateness and effectiveness of drug therapies
- the nature and mode of action of electroconvulsive therapy (ECT)
- the appropriateness and effectiveness of ECT.

Examiner's secrets

When a question asks for *two* of something, it means just that. If you only write about *one* therapy, or neglect to evaluate one of them, you will fail to access the marks available for that aspect of the question (no matter how good the rest of your answer). Likewise, if you write about *more than two*, you will only receive credit for two of them. So it makes good sense to only do what the question asks you to do!

Behavioural therapies

Checkpoints

1 People with social phobias may be exposed to busy places where there are plenty of people. People with fear of flying might be encouraged to take a flight.
2 Freud believed that many symptoms were over-determined, by which he meant they had multiple causes, all of which needed to be dealt with to avoid symptoms re-emerging in the future or appearing in another form.

Exam question

If you choose to write about two therapies, you could choose any of the therapies listed on pages 158–9. You would obviously need to supplement these revision notes from your own notes; these are just here to guide you. Alternatively you might choose to include *all* (or any proportion of) the therapies on these pages.

The approach taken on pages 158–9 is to take all the therapies derived from the behavioural approach, describe them independently, then group them together for a general review of the appropriateness and effectiveness of behavioural techniques. This would be a perfectly effective way of answering this question, i.e.

- the nature of behavioural therapies (abnormality is the development of maladaptive behaviour patterns which can be changed through learning new behaviours)
- therapies based on classical conditioning (e.g. flooding, systematic desensitization etc.)
- therapies based on operant conditioning (e.g. token economy, biofeedback)
- strengths and limitations of behavioural techniques (e.g. change can be *demonstrated*, but symptom *removal* is not the same as cure).

Examiner's secrets

This question introduces the offer to write about *two or more* behavioural therapies. Students often worry about whether they would earn more marks by writing about more than two. There is no easy answer to this, as it depends very much on how much you know about each therapy. There are advantages and disadvantages of each approach. If you are taking the AQA (A) exam, then this question appears in the synoptic part of the specification, and a greater variety of techniques would attract more marks. However, more therapies means less detail, so there is a cost. Two therapies (perhaps, as this question allows it, one from each of classical and operant conditioning) are usually the best solution, unless you know little about many therapies.

Alternative therapies

Checkpoints

1 People might resist letting go of their ego's defences by omitting thoughts in FA because of guilt or shame, by

forgetting to attend sessions, by failing to be honest because of fear of rejection or lack of trust, and by rejecting the analyst's interpretation.

2 The humanistic psychologist, Carl Rogers, identified several general characteristics of good therapists. These include warmth, empathy, genuineness and unconditional positive regard towards the client.

Exam question

The spread heading is 'alternative therapies'. This is not to suggest that Freudian psychoanalysis is 'alternative' in the sense that some music is considered 'alternative'. This heading is taken from the AQA (A) topic of 'alternatives to biological and behavioural therapies'. We have chosen Freudian psychoanalysis as an example of a *psychodynamic* therapy.

The question allows for a description and critical assessment (i.e. making an informed judgement of the value of this therapy) of *one or more* psychodynamic therapies. Most students only know about Freudian psychoanalysis, but some also know about other psychodynamic therapies so this question can accommodate more general responses. Your response to this question might take the following form:

- the aims of psychoanalysis (e.g. to free healthy libidinous impulses)
- techniques used in psychoanalysis (e.g. free association, dream analysis)
- methodological problems with assessing effectiveness (e.g. problems of client and therapist homogeneity, criteria of 'cure')
- an assessment of whether psychoanalysis actually works (e.g. Eysenck's claims).

Examiner's secrets

It is easy to be dragged into an exposition of Freudian theory. This is not what is required here. Although the *therapy* is derived from the *theory*, and problems with the theory must reflect on the therapy, they are not one and the same thing. One very important piece of advice is to make sure that you appreciate what *is* and what is *not* a psychodynamic therapy. Do not try and pass off other therapies (such as biological, behavioural, or cognitive-behavioural therapies) as if they were psychodynamic.

Psychology is full of different views about the nature of human behaviour, and the rights of humans (and animals) in our pursuit of knowledge about that behaviour. These 'debates' include different views about the degree to which our behaviour is a product of our own free will, or is determined by forces outside our control. To some scientists, the true cause of our behaviour will always be found by looking underneath to find the most basic biological or mechanical processes responsible (reductionism). This has some links to the study of the biological origins of our behaviour – represented by our genetic inheritance. The debate over the relative contribution of nature and nurture has persisted for many years. Ethical issues in psychology represent concerns with the rights of both humans and non-humans in psychological research, and are based on moral principles that can be justified from a number of different perspectives. Concerns with the pursuit of knowledge have also established that some theories and research methods in psychology offer a view of human behaviour that is biased towards one particular gender and cultural group. Finally, the view of psychology as science is well established, but this may not be justified, and scientific psychology may not be as straightforward as we might imagine.

Exam themes

→ Gender bias in psychological theory and research

→ Cultural bias in psychological theory and research

→ Ethical issues in research with human participants

→ The use of animals in psychological research

→ Free will and determinism

→ Reductionism

→ Psychology as science and the problems of scientific psychology

→ Nature-nurture (heredity versus environment)

Topic checklist

O AS ● A2	AQA/A	AQA/B	OCR	EDEXCEL
Gender and cultural bias	●		O	
Ethical issues and the use of animals	●	●	O	●
Free will and determinism	●	●	O	
Reductionism	●	●	O	
Psychology as science	●	●		●
Nature-nurture	●	●	O	●

Gender and cultural bias

Gender bias is not a new thing. For centuries we have accepted assumptions about the differences between the sexes. Women are frequently 'pathologized' because of their physical differences from men, their pathology being seen as inescapably connected to their femaleness.

Gender bias

Gender bias in psychological theory

Some theories ignore the differences between men and women (*beta bias*), and some exaggerate them (*alpha bias*).

→ Alpha bias theories assume real and enduring differences between men and women. Within sociobiology, for example, differences in male and female behaviour may be attributed to genetic determinism. Thus male social dominance or sexual promiscuity might be seen as a product of their evolutionary history.

→ Beta bias theories have traditionally ignored or minimized sex differences. They have done this either by ignoring questions about women's lives or by assuming that findings from male's studies apply equally well to females. Such theories may be described as *androcentric*.

Androcentric theories tend to offer an interpretation of women based on an understanding of the lives of men. Ideas of 'normal' behaviour may be drawn exclusively from studies of males. An example is Freud's theory, in which the young boy's identification with his father leads to the formation of a superego and of high moral standards. Girls, on the other hand, who do not experience the same Oedipal conflict as boys, cannot, it appears, develop their superego to the same degree as boys. Social psychologists have also typically developed theories from white, male undergraduates. This is then represented as 'human behaviour'.

Gender bias in psychological research

The main source of discontent with psychological research and its bias against women has centred around the use of traditional scientific method, most notably the use of the laboratory experiment.

Nicholson (1995) identifies two main problems with this adherence to an experimental science of psychology.

→ The experiment takes the *behaviour* of an individual research participant as the unit of study rather than the participant herself. This ignores the social, personal and cultural context in which the behaviour is enacted.

→ As a result of such research, women have been labelled as irrational, inappropriately volatile and easily depressed for no reason. They have been pathologized by the labels *pre-menstrual syndrome*, *post-natal depression* and *menopausal symptoms*.

Watch out!

Many of our gender stereotypes have a long history!

Checkpoint 1

Can you find another example of an 'alpha bias' in your textbook?

Example

An example of a beta bias theory is Kohlberg's theory of moral development (see page 138).

Checkpoint 2

Can you find another example of a 'beta bias' in your textbook?

Action point

Read through your textbook – particularly the chapters on adult development. Can you find evidence of an 'androcentric bias'?

Watch out!

The laboratory experiment is seen as the essence of scientific 'proof' about human behaviour. For some reason there is more credibility and prestige associated with the results of laboratory experiments than there is with other methods in psychology.

Cultural bias

Cultural bias in psychological theory

Hofstede (1980) proposed that cultures could be classified on the dimension of *individualism–collectivism*. In making this distinction, Hofstede was careful to avoid what is known as the *ecological fallacy*. This would be the (mistaken) belief that if two cultures differ in terms of their individualist or collectivist bias, then any two individuals taken at random from those cultures would also differ in that way.

The emic-etic distinction (Berry 1969) focuses on the differences in our analysis of human behaviour.

→ *Etic* analyses focus on the universals of human behaviour. For example, Kohlberg's theory (page 138) sees moral development as a universal process. That is, all individuals, regardless of culture, would experience the same developmental processes.

→ An *emic* analysis of behaviour, on the other hand, would focus on the varied ways in which activities and development could be observed in any specific cultural setting.

Attempts to explain human behaviour in different parts of the world often involve using theories and research studies that have been developed within (predominantly) the USA. This *imposed etic* makes the assumption that whatever measures have been used in one cultural context, will have the same meaning when applied in another.

Cultural bias in psychological research

Replicating research studies across cultures presents psychologists with problems. Failure to ensure that participants and procedures are equivalent in different studies means that alternative explanations of the research findings (known as *plausible rival hypotheses*) must be addressed. Some of the problems are as follows:

→ *translation* – instructions and responses must be faithfully translated for the purposes of comparison

→ *participants* – although these may be taken from similar social groups, they may have quite different social backgrounds and experiences in different cultural groups

→ *the research tradition* – in many cultures people are used to scientific research and respond positively to participation. Inherent in this positive attitude is the belief that their responses will remain confidential. Trust in the research process cannot be taken for granted in other cultures where psychological research may be rare.

> *"Culture refers to the collective programming . . . which distinguishes members of one group from another."*
>
> Hofstede (1980)

Action point

Read through your textbooks to find cross-cultural replications of research (e.g. of obedience research). Make a list of any aspects of the research that were different in these studies. Are these factors likely to have affected the outcome of the study?

Example

Milgram's research into obedience has been replicated in a number of other cultures. There has not always been direct equivalence of methods and participants.

Exam question   answer: page 178

With reference to psychological theories and/or research, discuss the view that psychology offers a culturally biased view of behaviour. (40 min)

167

Ethical issues and the use of animals

The ethical issues of psychological research are based on a number of fundamental moral principles. These are rules or standards that can be justified from a variety of theoretical perspectives. These principles underlie the issues that arise in research with human and animal participants.

Ethical issues in research with human participants

Deception

Baumrind (1985) suggests the following as consequences of deception.

→ It may decrease the number of naïve participants available for future research (i.e. those who do not suspect deception is taking place).

→ It may reduce support for psychological research in general (e.g. in the media and within the general population).

→ It may undermine the commitment of researchers to always telling the truth.

→ It removes the ability of research participants to give their fully *informed consent* to take part in an investigation.

Informed consent

The essence of the principle of informed consent is that the human subjects of research should be allowed to agree or refuse to participate in the light of comprehensive information concerning the nature and purpose of the research (Homan 1991).

→ To be *informed* means that all pertinent aspects of what is to happen and what *might* happen are disclosed to the participant. The participants should also be able to understand this information.

→ To give *consent*, the participant must be competent to make a rational and mature judgement. The agreement to participate should be voluntary, free from coercion and undue influence.

The greater the risk, the more meticulous should be the operation of informing potential participants.

Socially sensitive research

Socially sensitive research refers to '... studies in which there are potential social consequences or implications, either directly for the participants in research or the class of individuals represented by the research' (Sieber and Stanley 1988).

Specific issues of socially sensitive research include the following:

→ **Confidentiality** – in some areas of research, questions may reveal information of a sensitive nature. In such situations confidentiality is paramount. Otherwise, participants would be less willing to divulge this information in future research.

→ **Scientific freedom** – it is the role of the researcher to carry out scientific research. This freedom to pursue scientific research is balanced against the obligation to protect those who take part or the sectors of society that they represent.

Watch out!

An ethical *issue* is not the same as an ethical *guideline*. Ethical guidelines are ways of resolving ethical issues.

Action point

Read through your textbook for examples of deception in psychological research. Do you feel these were justified given the aims of the research?

Checkpoint 1

In what ways might we exert pressure on participants to take part (or continue) in a study?

Checkpoint 2

What types of research might be classified as 'socially sensitive' under this definition?

→ **Ownership of data** – a major concern in the interpretation and application of research findings in psychology is that they may be used for reasons other than those for which they were originally intended. It is the responsibility of researchers to consider in advance the ways in which their research might be used.

→ **Ethical guidelines** may protect the immediate needs of research participants, but may not deal with all the possible ways in which research may inflict harm on a group of people or section of society.

The use of non-human animals in research

Arguments *for* animal research

→ Animals may be studied because they are fascinating in their own right (ethology).

→ Animals offer the opportunity for greater control and objectivity in research procedures.

→ Human beings and non-human animals have sufficient of their physiology and evolutionary past in common to justify conclusions drawn from the one being applied to the other.

→ Animal research has produced benefits to humans and to animals.

→ Researchers are sensitive to the suffering experienced by animals and use procedures that ensure animals are humanely treated.

→ Researchers have developed alternative procedures which have led to a reduction in the use of animals. Therefore animals are only used when no other suitable procedure is available (*reduction*, *refinement* and *replacement*).

Arguments *against* animal research

→ Animals have rights by virtue of their 'inherent value'. These rights include the right to be treated with respect and not harmed.

→ The traditional scientific position on animal research treats animals as 'renewable resources' rather than as organisms of value whose rights we must respect.

→ The benefits of animal research have often been accomplished at considerable expense in terms of animal suffering. By calculating the benefits to *humankind*, but not the costs to *animals*, we might be committing speciesism.

→ Critics of animal research often assert that the assumed similarities between human beings and other animals do not exist. Green (1994) argues otherwise: the basic physiology of the brain and nervous systems of all mammals is essentially the same.

Example

The Canadian Psychological Association advises its members to 'analyse likely short-term, ongoing, and long-term risks and benefits of each course of action on the individual(s) or group(s) involved or likely to be affected'.

"Animal liberators need to accept that animal research is beneficial to humans. Animal researchers need to admit that if animals are close enough to humans . . . , then ethical dilemmas surely arise in using them".

B. Orlans (1997)

Checkpoint 3

What is meant by the terms 'reduction, refinement and replacement' in this context?

Watch out!

There are strict laws (e.g. the 1986 Use of Animals Act) and codes of conduct (e.g. BPS and ASAB guidelines) that protect animals that are used in research.

Exam question   answer: page 178

Describe and assess arguments for and against animal research in psychology. (40 min)

Free will and determinism

The idea that we are able to have some choice in how we act is fundamental in most common-sense theories of psychology. The free will versus determinism debate examines the degree to which human behaviour is freed from the causal influences of past events.

Free will

The notion of 'free will' allows us to separate out what is clearly the *intention* of an individual from what has been *caused* by some internal or external event. The idea of free will is inconsistent with the opposite idea of determinism, because under the latter view of human behaviour, individuals act as a result of some prior cause. The term 'free' is taken to mean that a person or their behaviour is independent from the causal determinism of past events. The term 'will' refers to the idea that people make decisions about the goals they are seeking to achieve.

→ Free will enables people to choose a path that is inconsistent with their past. If we do not accept that we are bound to the past, but accept that we have the capacity to formulate plans and goals and act accordingly we are proposing the existence and influence of free will.

→ The concept of free will is therefore not only compatible with a wider view of determinism, but is also very important if we are to view individuals as being morally responsible for their own actions. If our actions are merely the product of some past event or of our biological 'programming', then we cannot be held responsible for our behaviours.

Determinism

When most people talk about determinism, they are, in fact, talking about *efficient causality*, a definition of causality originally put forward by Hume (1951). To say that one event has been determined by another, Hume wrote, meant that:

→ two events must be highly correlated (i.e. when one occurs, so does the other)
→ they must appear in chronological order (i.e. one after the other)
→ they must be located near to one another.

Although the presence of these three criteria does not *necessarily* imply a cause-effect relationship, this belief in the importance of efficient causality has been enough to convince many scientists that the only appropriate way of determining the cause of events is to examine events in the past.

Some approaches tend to see the source of this determinism as being *outside* the individual, a position known as 'environmental determinism'. Others propose the source of this determinism as coming from *inside* the organism, e.g. in the form of unconscious motivation or genetic determinism – a position known as 'biological determinism'.

Checkpoint 1

In what ways might human behaviour be influenced by 'past events'?

Action point

Mostly we act in ways that are consistent with our past (e.g. habits, previously reinforced behaviours etc.). Think of examples of your behaviour that could not be explained in this way.

Checkpoint 2

The notion of free will is particularly important for the issue of moral responsibility. If criminality was genetically determined, what issues would this raise?

Example

Every time John goes into a room, everybody leaves. They always leave just after he enters the room, and only the people in the room he enters leave. Could he be causing this behaviour?

Links

See 'nature-nurture' (pages 176–7) for a more detailed discussion on the degree to which our behaviour is a product of 'biology' or 'experience'.

Major approaches and the free-will debate

The psychodynamic approach

Freud believed that we are controlled by unconscious forces over which we have no control, and of which we are largely unaware. In psychoanalytic theory, events are not seen as occurring by chance; they are purposeful, being related to unconscious processes ('psychic determinism'). This view of human behaviour is in contrast to the belief that we are rational, thinking beings, fully in control of our own actions.

The behavioural approach

Behaviourists believe that our behaviour is a product of the reinforcement provided by the environment. Within our own reinforcement history, we have been conditioned into behaving in specific ways. Most human beings somehow believe that they are both free to choose yet, at the same time, controlled. For behaviourists, however, our actions are solely determined by factors in our environment, which directly or indirectly, mould our behaviour.

The humanistic approach

This approach believes that human beings are free to plan their own actions. People are seen as struggling to grow and to make difficult decisions that will profoundly affect their lives. As a result of these decisions, each of us becomes unique and responsible for our own behaviour. Humanistic therapies such as person-centred therapy are based on the assumption of free will.

The cognitive approach

Cognitive theorists reject biological and environmental determinism. They stress that human beings have a wide range of cognitive schemata that they use in their everyday life. When individuals face new events in their environment, they experience *freedom of decision* as to how they will behave, but are limited (i.e. their behaviour is *determined* to some extent) by the schemata they possess to organize their behaviour.

Conclusion

Scientists who accept a view of humans being guided by their own conscious planning have embraced a less radical view of determinism. This 'soft' determinism view proposes that people act consistently with their character. It is less difficult to reconcile this view of determinism with the idea of free will than it is with the 'hard' determinism view that behaviour is caused by environmental or biological factors.

Example

Because of this control by internal forces, and the belief that any perceived freedom of choice is illusory, this theory is an example of biological determinism.

Example

This approach is an example of environmental determinism.

Examiner's secrets

Make sure you can expand each of these descriptions – exam questions frequently state a certain number of approaches from which to draw your material.

The jargon

Schemata are cognitive 'structures' that act in much the same way as a computer program. They act as a framework for interpreting incoming information and guide our actions.

Watch out!

Cognitive theorists do not see behaviour as a product of free will or determinism alone, but a combination of the two.

Exam question   answer: pages 178–9

With reference to two or more approaches, discuss the free will versus determinism debate in psychology. (40 min)

Reductionism

Psychologists frequently reduce their level of explanation to its simplest level (i.e. biological or mechanical processes). Following a reductionist line of thinking, we might always look for something more basic underneath whatever it is we are trying to explain – that is, the real cause of the event we are experiencing.

Physiological reductionism

As humans are biological organisms, it should be possible to reduce even complex behaviours to their constituent neurophysiological components. There is a clear advantage to this, as it leads to the application of concise and concrete terms, which are then susceptible to scientific methods of research (Wadeley et al 1997).

Scientists interested in the causes of schizophrenia have found evidence that excess activity of the biochemical neurotransmitter dopamine is a characteristic of schizophrenia. Such a 'biochemical' theory of schizophrenia would effectively de-emphasize the importance of environmental factors in the development of the disorder.

Evaluation of physiological reductionism

→ The view that disorders such as schizophrenia can be neatly explained in terms of biochemical deficiencies is changing. Most theorists now agree that schizophrenia is probably 'caused' by a combination of factors. Genetic and biological factors may establish a predisposition to develop the disorder, but psychological factors help to bring the disorder to fruition. Other factors, such as societal labelling, help maintain and, in some cases, worsen the symptoms.

→ Examples such as schizophrenia show us that complex phenomena cannot easily be explained simply by reference to a physiological imbalance. The influence of brain chemicals in disorders such as schizophrenia is indisputable, but to argue that they *cause* schizophrenia is to neglect all other potential influences in the course of this disorder.

Biological reductionism

In Darwinian theory, behaviours that can be shown to arise from genetic factors must have some 'survival value'. It is possible that many human behaviours have also evolved because of their survival value or their ability to increase an individual's opportunities for passing on their genes. The principles of kin selection suggest that in helping biological relatives, with whom we share genes, we are also ensuring the survival of our own genetic code. This, according to Wilson (1975), is the primary motivation behind much of human social behaviour from altruism to xenophobia (fear of strangers). According to sociobiologists, nature 'selects' certain psychological traits and social customs (such as kinship bonds and taboos against female adultery) because they help to ensure the transmission of an individual's genes.

Genetic explanations have also been advanced for behaviours that contribute to some of society's most pressing problems, such as drug abuse, mental illness, and mental retardation. For example, twin and adoption studies suggest that familial resemblance for schizophrenia is due to heredity rather than to shared family environment. Although these data suggest that inheritance plays a major role in schizophrenia, it is also evident that non-genetic factors are of critical importance. A risk of 30% or 50% for an identical co-twin of a schizophrenic far exceeds the population risk of 1%, but is not the 100% concordance expected if schizophrenia was entirely a genetic disorder (Plomin 1990).

Evaluation of biological reductionism

→ Unlike physical characteristics, most behaviours and behavioural problems are not distributed in 'either/or' dichotomies.
→ The role of inheritance in behaviour has become widely accepted, even for sensitive topics such as IQ. Acceptance of genetic influence has even begun to outstrip the data in some cases.
→ For most behaviours, too few studies have been conducted to answer the question of whether genetic influence is significant.
→ Genetic variance rarely accounts for as much as half of the variance of behavioural traits. Evidence for significant genetic influence is often implicitly interpreted as if heritability were 100%, whereas heritabilities for behaviour seldom exceed 50% (Plomin 1990).

Environmental reductionism ●●●

Behaviourists believe that we are controlled by forces outside our control. The complex behaviour of humans is seen as learned 'performances' in response to signals which are present in the environment. The principles for learning behavioural sequences are seen as being the same for all species. The application of these principles in behaviour modification programmes has had considerable success, e.g. the effective control of aggressive behaviour requires a change in the pattern of rewards that aggression brings (Medcof and Roth 1979).

Evaluation of environmental reductionism

→ Restricting ourselves to the study of only one influence at a time may make sense within the context of a laboratory, but we may miss the complexity of influences on a behaviour at any one time.
→ In a world dominated by either reinforcement or punishment, it might appear that the only way to motivate people is with the 'carrot and the stick'. This distracts us from asking whether the behaviour being reinforced is worthwhile in the first place.

Check the net

Use the internet to find out more about some of the genetic explanations for psychopathology. A good starting point is: www.mentalhealth.com

The jargon

Concordance is the degree to which genetically related people share similar traits or characteristics.

Watch out!

High levels of concordance are often interpreted as if the trait was *completely* inherited. This is rarely the case.

Checkpoint 2

Behaviourists believe that learning principles are the same for all species. Why is this particularly significant for their view of behaviour and the methods they use to explore it?

Exam question   answer: page 179

Discuss the nature and value of reductionist explanations of human behaviour. (40 min)

173

Psychology as science

Science is concerned with what we know to be true, rather than what we believe to be true, thus we attach considerable importance to science as a way of distinguishing what is true and real from what is not. Science is seen as both a body of knowledge that we accept as being trustworthy, as well as the method for attaining that knowledge.

The nature of science

What is science?
Science is often seen as both a body of knowledge that we accept as being trustworthy, and also the method for attaining that knowledge (i.e. the *scientific method*).

The characteristics of science
The most fundamental characteristic of science is its reliance on *empirical methods* of observation and investigation, i.e. observation through sensory experience rather than a reliance on thoughts and ideas. All scientific ideas must, at some point, be subjected to empirical investigation through careful observation of perceivable events. For science to 'make sense', it is necessary to explain the results of empirical observation. That means constructing theories, which can then be tested and refined through further empirical observation. Slife and Williams (1995) identify further attributes of science.

→ Scientific observation is made under *objective* conditions.
→ Scientific observation takes place under *controlled* conditions.
→ Science involves making *predictions* about what is expected to happen under specified conditions. We can then *validate* or *falsify* whatever theory or hypothesis led to the observations being made.
→ Scientific investigations are open to public scrutiny. Confidence in results is increased when investigations can be *replicated*.

Psychology as science

Science as knowledge
Science is a body of knowledge that explains the nature of the world.

→ Scientific explanations reject, and are preferred to, other explanations of naturally occurring phenomena (such as magic).
→ Scientific explanations are often stated as laws or general principles about the relationship between different events. Because of the regularity of the way in which these events occur together, it then becomes possible to control and predict them.

Despite significant advances in scientific psychology, it has yet to lead to the development of universal laws of human behaviour. Although most psychologists accept the idea that behaviour tends to be determined, the inability to control all the variables that underlie human behaviour means that accurate control and prediction is impossible.

"Science is built up of facts, as a house is built of stones; but an accumulation of facts is no more a science than a heap of stones is a house."

Henri Poincaré (1905)

"Man is the interpreter of nature, science the right interpretation."

William Whewell (1840)

Science as method

Scientific investigation involves empirical observation and the development of theories that are constantly tested and refined. In psychology, scientific methods are the preferred method of investigation for most psychologists, particularly the laboratory experiment, which offers the psychologist opportunities for control and prediction that are absent in less 'scientific' methods. However, the use of scientific methods is insufficient cause for labelling psychology a 'science'. Parapsychology has been subjected to rigorous scientific study, yet few psychologists would accept it as 'scientific'.

Problems with scientific psychology

Maintaining objectivity

Kuhn (1970) believed that total objectivity was never possible in science. The view that any particular scientific psychologist holds about the world (in Kuhn's terms, their 'paradigm') makes them think about the world in a specific way. This influences what they investigate, the methods they use to investigate it, and the sorts of explanations that are seen as acceptable for the results obtained. As all scientific knowledge emerges from within this specific set of influences, it is questionable whether it is possible to establish universal laws of behaviour.

Operationalization

To carry out a scientific test, we must be able to observe whatever it is we are investigating. This is not always straightforward. For example, there are many events (such as emotion) that we cannot observe directly. Instead, we observe something else that we think represents the thing we are really interested in. Thus psychologists often explore the relationship between two things (e.g. love and happiness) without ever being able to measure either of these directly. As is the case with many investigations in psychology, our observations are always one step removed from the phenomenon that we are really interested in.

Establishing causality

It is generally accepted in scientific psychology that the only way to establish causality is to carry out an experiment. To be confident that any change in a dependent variable has been caused by manipulation of an independent variable, the researcher would need to control everything else that could possibly have a causal effect on the dependent variable. This is impossible when we are dealing with human beings. We cannot know all the possible ways in which any one individual might be influenced to behave at any given time.

Links

See Experimental design 1 and 2 on pages 76–9.

The jargon

Parapsychology is the study of paranormal phenomena (such as ESP and clairvoyance).

Checkpoint 1

In what ways might scientific psychology be influenced by the 'paradigm' of the researcher?

"As soon as questions of will or decision or reason or choice of action arise, human science is at a loss."

Noam Chomsky (1978)

Checkpoint 2

Correlational designs are criticized because they tell us nothing about causal relationships between variables. What important factor exists in experiments that enables us to make causal statements?

Exam question   answer: pages 179–80

Discuss the nature of psychology as science. (40 min)

Nature-nurture

Action point

Use your textbook to find examples of theories that subscribe to each of these perspectives.

Watch out!

Behaviourists believed that differences between species were quantitative rather than qualitative – this was the justification for concentrating their experimental studies on animals.

Links

This view has re-emerged in recent years with the advent of 'evolutionary psychology' (see pages 112–15).

The jargon

Altruistic behaviour is acting in some way to benefit another while incurring some cost to ourselves.

Checkpoint 1

In what ways might the inhibition of aggression or altruistic behaviour benefit the individual?

The jargon

Headstart, originally the name of a programme in the 1960s designed to enrich the academic performance of children from underprivileged backgrounds, the term is now used to cover a range of social and educational programmes with the same broad aim.

Throughout the development of psychology, there has been a tension between those who favour a view of behaviour as a product of heredity (nature) and those who favour the greater influence of environment (nurture). Those who adopted the former viewpoint were called nativists and those who adopted the latter were called empiricists.

Ethology versus behaviourism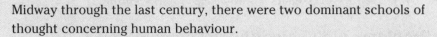

Midway through the last century, there were two dominant schools of thought concerning human behaviour.

→ *Behavourists*, as a result of extensive laboratory work with animals, concluded that all behaviour was the product of learning. This process was considered to be so universal that differences between species were regarded as irrelevant.

→ In contrast, the *ethological* school focused on natural behaviour. According to this position, organisms are born with 'fixed-action patterns' that are little changed by the environment. These fixed-action patterns are the result of evolutionary adaptations.

Although behaviourists accepted that evolution had some relevance in human behaviour, this was merely to acknowledge the continuity between humans and other animals. However, although evolution implies continuity between species, it also implies diversity, each organism being adapted to a specific way of life in a specific environment (De Waal 1999). Behaviourists were forced to adopt some of the ideas of evolutionary biology, especially with the discovery that learning is not the same for all species.

Ethologists also ran into problems explaining some aspects of animal and human behaviour. Behavioural traits such as the inhibition of aggression, or altruistic behaviour, were seen as being 'for the benefit of the species'. These ideas have now been replaced by theories of how an action benefits the individuals concerned and its genetic relatives.

Nature-nurture and intelligence

Until the middle of the 20th century, intelligence was widely regarded as mainly biologically determined (the *nature* view). If intelligence, and therefore potential, was inherited, there seemed little one could do for individuals of low intelligence. A different perspective, which stretches back to the 17th century, proposed that intelligence was largely a product of experience and was, within limits, completely malleable (the *nurture* view). In the 1950s, the predominant view concerning the origins of intelligence shifted from the 'nature' to the 'nurture' side of the argument. Supporters of this view put forward arguments that intelligence was not genetically determined, but was due to the nature of an individual's experience. It was argued that intelligence was particularly malleable in early childhood. This led to the development of a number of compensatory education programmes such as the *Headstart* programme in the USA.

Evaluation of the nature-nurture debate

Piaget and intelligence

Piaget's theory is significant for this debate for two reasons.

→ It bridges the gap between 'nature' and 'nurture' – biologically given structures unfold when placed in a nurturing environment.
→ Piaget proposed four mechanisms of cognitive development (e.g. maturation and equilibrium) through which the environment interacts with the internal structures of the individual.

The individual is the main focus whereas the role of the environment is to facilitate the automatic unfolding of biological, cognitive structures.

Methodological difficulties in the nature-nurture debate

There is no agreement about how we might define or measure the environment in which a person grows up. Research using animals has been much more successful in defining and manipulating environmental variables. It is this kind of research that emphasizes that much of behavioural development is subject to environmental influence in its development. Trying to understand how such environmental variables would affect *human* behavioural development is a more complex issue. It is at the cultural level that this difficulty becomes most pronounced, yet it is probably at the level of cultural influences that the most powerful and subtle environmental variables operate (Horowitz 1993).

Gene-environment interactions

When we say that a behavioural trait such as intelligence or depression is inherited, all we mean is that *part* of its variability is explained by genetic factors. The environment accounts for the rest of the variability. The interaction between genes and environment is complex, e.g. the balance between genetic and environmental influences on a particular behaviour appears to change as a person ages (Plomin 1994).

Research has suggested three types of gene-environment relationships.

→ A *passive* relationship between genes and environment may occur because parents transmit genes that promote a certain trait and also construct the rearing environment.
→ An *evocative* relationship between genes and environment may occur because genetically distinct individuals may evoke different reactions in those around them.
→ An *active* relationship between genes and environment may occur because individuals actively select experiences that fit in with their genetically influenced preferences.

Links

See Development of thinking on pages 134–5.

Checkpoint 2

Why do you think it is so difficult to assess the influence of cultural variables on behaviour?

"Life is like playing a violin solo in public and learning the instrument as one goes on."

Samuel Butler (1895)

Examiner's secrets

This question has a *synoptic* element, so make sure you can resource your answer with a range of different perspectives and topics in psychology.

Exam question   answer: page 180

With reference to *two or more* areas of psychology, discuss the nature-nurture debate as it applies to an understanding of human behaviour. (40 min)

Answers
Perspectives

Gender and cultural bias

Checkpoints

1 Gilligan's theory of moral development (see page 139) is an example of an 'alpha bias' theory. Gilligan claimed that women seem to centre their judgements more on care than do men.

2 Few theories in psychology draw a specific distinction between males and females, therefore most of psychology might be said to show a beta bias.

Exam question

This is a fairly open-ended question as it invites you to draw on psychological theories and/or research. Try to remember, when selecting material for this answer, that this question has a synoptic element. This means that your answer will also be assessed for the range of theories, issues, methods etc. that you include in your answer. A suitable response to this question would be:

- the nature of cultural bias in psychological theory (e.g. the emic-etic distinction) or historical bias (e.g. 'Asch effect' in conformity and the era of McCarthyism in the USA)
- examples of theories that demonstrate a cultural bias (e.g. social exchange theories of relationships and Kohlberg's theory of moral development)
- the nature of cultural bias in psychological research (e.g. problems of translation, research participants and cultural differences in the research tradition)
- discussion of research that has been replicated in other cultures (e.g. Milgram's work on obedience) – relate this to the cultural biases in the previous point.

Examiner's secrets

Questions in the AQA (A) 'Perspectives' section have a synoptic element. This means that, in addition to the material chosen to answer the question, you will be assessed on the breadth of approaches, issues and debates demonstrated in your answer.

Ethical issues and the use of animals

Checkpoints

1 There are a number of ways that participants can be pressurized to take part (or continue) in a study. These include *selection* of participants (e.g. in a school), or through payment of participants (when they may feel pressurized because of their part in a 'contract' with the researcher).

2 Research that might be classified as 'socially sensitive' would include research into racial and gender differences, and research into the nature and origins of sexual diversity.

3 *Reduction* – involves using methods that obtain the same amount of information from fewer animals, or more information from the same number of animals.

Replacement – involves, for example, the increased use of brain imaging and scanning procedures (such as MRI and PET scans) in humans and the use of computer simulations. *Refinement* – this involves using procedures that minimize stress and enhance animal well-being.

Exam question

This question appears to ask for simply a list of arguments for and against animal research in psychology. However, it benefits from a closer second look. You are asked to *describe* and *assess* (i.e. give a considered appraisal of . . .) these arguments. This will require not only a description of arguments for and against animal research, but also a critical appraisal of these arguments. For example, an argument *for* animal research is that it has produced considerable benefits to humans. You might appraise this argument by giving examples of where animal research has proved useful to humans (e.g. in developing a better understanding of stress), but also point out that by judging the value of animal research solely in terms of its benefits to humans, we may be committing speciesism.

Although there is no prescribed order in which material need be presented, the following is a suggested route through the requirements of the question:

- description of the arguments *for* animal research in psychology
- critical appraisal of the arguments *for* animal research in psychology
- description of the arguments *against* animal research in psychology
- critical appraisal of the arguments *against* animal research in psychology.

Examiner's secrets

Remember when answering questions such as this, that arguments *against* animal research can be used as an appraisal of the arguments *for*. This takes practice, and relies on your ability to construct a logical argument rather than simply listing the two sets of arguments without trying to offset one against the other.

Free will and determinism

Checkpoints

1 Biologically, it might be influenced by 'instinct' or inherited characteristics. Alternatively we may be seen as a product of our reinforcement histories.

2 This may be seen to lessen the criminal's personal responsibility for their actions as well as causing anxiety in the genetic relatives of the criminal (who may also carry the same gene or genes). However, behaviour is rarely 'caused' by genes alone, so personal responsibility for behaviour would not be lost.

Exam question

There is a reminder in this question to draw material from at least two approaches in psychology. If you feel you have sufficient relevant material from just *two* approaches (the question gives you the opportunity to include more than two) then don't feel that you have to write about more than this. Trying to cover too many different approaches may produce a superficial answer that would be worth fewer marks than a more detailed one that has a slightly narrower focus.

The material on pages 170–1 would cover all that is required in this answer, but you might like to include your responses to the checkpoints, as these extend the discussion of the topic.

A suggested route through this answer would be:
- the nature of free will in psychological theory
- the nature of determinism in psychological theory
- review of the psychodynamic approach – an example of *biological* determinism
- review of the behavioural approach – an example of *environmental* determinism
- the humanistic and cognitive approaches – alternatives to purely deterministic theories
- conclusion – hard and soft determinism.

Reductionism

Checkpoints

1 Behaviourist explanations of schizophrenia claim that by failing to attend to relevant social cues, schizophrenics develop bizarre responses to the environment. Family explanations stress the role of the family environment in the development of schizophrenia. Sociocultural theorists suggest that many aspects of schizophrenia are caused by the diagnosis itself (e.g. labelling theory).

2 This justifies the use of animals in experimental studies of learning. Findings from animal studies can then be generalized to human beings.

Exam answer

As with the previous question (on free will), this is a fairly open-ended question, but unlike that question, it does not give the 'reminder' that you should draw from more than one approach in psychology. However, you should draw from at least two types of reductionism in order to satisfy the synoptic element of the question.

We have covered three types of reductionism on pages 172–3, and within these different types there are a number of different 'explanations' of human behaviour. Remember that half of the marks available for this question are for the critical part of your answer (the *value* of reductionist explanations), so balance your response accordingly.

A suitable response to this question might be:

- introduction – the nature of reductionism in psychology
- physiological reductionism – e.g. biochemical explanations of schizophrenia
- evaluation of physiological reductionism – e.g. neglect of other possible causes of schizophrenia
- biological reductionism – e.g. genetic explanations of behaviour
- evaluation of biological reductionism – e.g. overestimation of the degree of heritability in behavioural traits
- environmental reductionism – e.g. the universality of learning principles
- evaluation of environmental reductionism – e.g. it ignores the complexity of influences on a specific behaviour at any one time.

Psychology as science

Checkpoints

1 The paradigm of the researcher will influence the predictions made, the methods deemed appropriate to research these predictions, and the interpretation of the results gained. Results will either validate a particular point of view or falsify it. Even when research supports a particular theory, it is possible that other explanations (from outside the paradigm) might better explain the results obtained.

2 Because the independent variable can be systematically varied (i.e. the experimenter can manipulate it), it is possible to study its causal effect on the dependent variable.

Exam question

Your answer to this question can be neatly split into three parts, each part being equivalent to about 13 minutes of writing time (about 200–300 words).

As the question asks you to discuss the *nature* of psychology as science, you should begin by considering what science actually is (including the characteristics of science), and then move on to consider the degree to which psychology satisfies these criteria. As this question also has a critical component, you should follow this with a detailed account of the problems of scientific psychology.

A suitable response to this question might be:

- what is science? – the characteristics of science (e.g. scientific observation takes place under objective and controlled conditions)
- arguments for psychology as science – science as knowledge and science as the preferred method in psychology

- problems with scientific psychology (e.g. maintaining objectivity and establishing causality).

Nature-nurture

Checkpoints

1 By inhibiting aggression, the individual may be able to profit from the co-operation of others. In status conflicts, the loser who inhibits their aggression minimizes the risk of expulsion from the group or further injury.

 Altruistic behaviour has a potential pay-off if it is reciprocated some time in the future (reciprocal altruism) or benefits those with whom the altruist shares genes (kin selection).

2 It is difficult to exactly replicate studies in different cultures, due to problems of translation, the nature of participants etc. Researchers may be unaware of the subtle influences on behaviour within a particular culture.

Exam question

As with the free will versus determinism question earlier, there is a specific requirement to draw your material from more than one area of psychology. Remember that in casting the net wide, you are satisfying the synoptic element of the question.

The question asks you to discuss the nature-nurture debate 'as it applies to psychology', so don't just write about it in the abstract. The material on pages 176–7 splits the relevant content quite neatly into *descriptive* material (e.g. nature-nurture and intelligence) and *evaluative* material (e.g. gene-environment interactions). It is important to point out that few theories in psychology rely on either/or explanations, but most accept the (often subtle) interactions of genes and environment.

A suitable response to this question might be:
- what is meant by 'nature' and 'nurture', and what characterizes these different explanations of behaviour?
- ethology and behaviourism – conflicting views of behaviour
- nature-nurture and intelligence
- Piaget and intelligence – the interactionist perspective on intelligence
- methodological difficulties in exploring the nature-nurture debate
- gene-environment interactions.

Resources

Learning about psychology is only one part of doing well in the AS and A2 exams. It is equally important to know how to apply your knowledge in an exam. Students frequently come unstuck in exams for reasons quite unrelated to the amount of psychology they actually know. Misreading the questions, bad time management or simply not knowing how to write essays are all difficulties that need to be corrected if your exam performance is to match the quality of your psychology. If this worries you, it shouldn't, because good exam preparation can boost good psychology into even better grades, and basic psychology into reasonable grades. In other words, the material in the following pages is designed to help you do well, rather than focus on all the problems you are likely to face in the forthcoming weeks or months.

This last section of the book includes the following:

→ a guide to synoptic assessment in the A2 exam
→ how to make effective revision notes
→ planning and writing effective essays
→ exam words (based largely on the AQA (A) 'Glossary of Terms')
→ glossary of important psychological words and concepts

Synoptic assessment

Synoptic assessment is taken to mean your understanding and critical appreciation of the breadth of theoretical and methodological approaches in psychology. In all specifications in psychology, the synoptic assessment must represent at least 20% of the total A-level marks.

The nature of synoptic assessment

Most examination boards have decided to place the major part of their synoptic assessment in a 'perspectives' section of the exam. The term 'perspective' is used here to refer to the various theoretical approaches in psychology. These may be major orientations such as the *psychodynamic* perspective or *behaviourism*, or they can refer to a particular field of psychology, such as *social psychology* or *abnormal psychology*. There are also a number of important 'issues' and 'debates' (*nature versus nurture*, *ethical issues*, *cultural bias* etc.), and these permeate the perspectives and methods used in psychological inquiry. The idea of synoptic assessment is that it tests your knowledge of psychology as a whole, and your ability to make links between the different things you have learned.

What counts as synoptic assessment?

Synopticity can be demonstrated in many ways, including the following:

→ demonstrating different explanations or perspectives relating to a topic area (e.g. different explanations of schizophrenia, drawn from biology, social learning etc.)
→ demonstrating different methods used to study a topic area (e.g. experiments, clinical studies, epidemiological studies etc.)
→ overarching issues relating to a topic area (e.g. ethical issues, issues relating to free will and determinism, reductionism etc.)
→ links with other areas of the specification (e.g. with evolutionary explanations in comparative psychology, or methods of studying the brain in physiological psychology).

Explaining psychological phenomena from multiple perspectives

To fully appreciate the synoptic nature of psychology, it is necessary to explore the breadth of explanations for different areas of behaviour. The AQA (A) exam will require you to use your knowledge of different 'approaches' in psychology to explain novel areas of behaviour. The list of potential behaviours that could be explained in this 'multi-dimensional' way is almost endless, but might include:

→ moral behaviour
→ altruistic behaviour
→ interpersonal attraction
→ collective behaviour
→ mental disorders.

Watch out!

Synoptic assessment is not necessarily part of every section. Most examination boards restrict this requirement to a 'Perspectives' section.

The jargon

Synoptic is demonstrating a comprehensive mental view of something.

Action point

When revising for those areas of your specification that assess your synoptic understanding, try to develop a spread of explanations and issues.

Test yourself

On a piece of paper, make a note of the different ways that you might explain issues connected with each of these behaviours.

Watch out!

This is not an exhaustive list. These are simply illustrations of typical types of behaviour that might be sampled in AQA (A) 'Approaches' questions.

Approaches

The main approaches to psychology include:

→ **Biological** – assumes that all human behaviour has a biological explanation, and can best be understood by investigating physiological mechanisms such as the nervous system (especially the brain).

→ **Evolutionary** – assumes human behaviour has evolved through adapting to our environment, and emphasizes the importance of heredity.

→ **Psychodynamic** – includes Freud's psychoanalytic approach, and stresses the role of the unconscious mind.

→ **Behavioural** – argues that human behaviour is the result of conditioning, and can be explained in terms of reinforcement and punishment.

→ **Cognitive** – focuses on internal, mental processes such as perception, attention and memory.

→ **Humanistic** – focuses on individual, subjective experience and stresses the importance of self-actualization (fulfilment of individual potential) and freedom of choice.

Developing synoptic skills

There are a number of strategies that will help you develop your synoptic skills. This one involves finding out where each of the major approaches stand on important issues such as *free will*, *reductionism* and so on. This broadens your understanding of each approach, and it fleshes out your appreciation of how each issue is embraced by the major perspectives. Draw out the table underneath (on a larger scale) and enter where each of these major approaches stands on the issues to the right.

Examiner's secrets

Questions in the synoptic module will usually ask you to *apply* your knowledge of these approaches to particular instances of human behaviour. Don't simply give a general explanation of what each approach involves.

The jargon

The humanistic approach is also known as the *phenomenological* approach.

Action point

Do this exercise carefully. It will prove useful later.

	ISSUES			
APPROACHES	Free will versus determinism	Reductionism	Nature versus nurture	Scientific status
Behaviourism				
Humanistic				
Psychodynamic				
Biological				
Cognitive				
Evolutionary				

Effective revision notes

Despite a lot of hard work students still manage to get it all very wrong in the exam. Sometimes this can be put down to poor preparation, at other times poor exam technique. This section of the book aims to put that right.

Effective revision

Many students have real problems when it comes to revising. Some simple pointers may well help.

Make it active

Simply reading something over and over again will do little more than depress you. The more you elaborate a memory at the encoding stage, the more memorable it will become. There are lots of fun ways to do this. You could explain the material to others (even your dog or your teddy bear, far less critical an audience than a younger brother), draw diagrams linking together related points, summarize points in your own words, and so on. The use of 'spider-grams' and 'mind-maps' can be very effective, because they not only make revision active, but they also provide a powerful visual image that you can conjure up in an exam. You will also find that revising with others can be very profitable – your weaknesses may well be your friend's strengths and vice-versa.

Watch out!

Simply reading through something does not make it memorable. *Doing* something with the material will.

Plan it!

There is no greater revision sin than haphazard and unfocused study. If you make some kind of plan (such as filling in the revision icons throughout this book and on the cover flaps), you will be able to dictate exactly what you need to do and when you do it. Nowadays, teachers plan their lessons around a series of specific 'learning outcomes', and this is a good principle to apply in your revision. You can think of everything in your specification as a *skill* that has to be mastered. So, if you think through all the different things you might be asked to *do* with, for example, 'theories of relationships', practise until you can cover them all. This way you can plan your revision around the acquisition of these skills, rather like you might treat your driving lessons or learning the piano.

Action point

Make a list of all the topic areas that you intend to revise. Assign (realistic) time periods for each of these and *stick to them*. Over the next weeks or months, give revision a priority in your life.

Be honest with yourself

It is the greatest temptation to leave out bits that you don't really understand or haven't got time for. Your honesty applies both to *what* you have to do, and *how long* you realistically have to do it. Hopefully nobody should find themselves in a situation where they have more to do than they have time available, but it clearly does happen. That's why effective and *early* revision is so important. If you don't have time to cover everything you should have covered, ask your teacher for advice rather than randomly cutting topics.

Watch out!

Taking risks isn't worth it – listen to your teacher!

Short and frequent is best

Your maximum span of attention is not as great as you might imagine, and the effectiveness of what you are doing will drop off towards the end of this period. Working in 40-minute blocks with rest periods will give you far greater returns than trying to cram as much as you can into a marathon four-hour revision session. Remember at all times that you are a *psychology* student, so put that psychology to good use in your revision.

Memorizing material

Don't forget that the act of retrieval is itself a processing event and increases the ease with which something will be retrieved in the future. Once a memory has been activated, the 'threshold' for recall of that memory is lowered. The more often you retrieve something the stronger the memory for that event becomes. Retrieval does become more difficult with time without any intervening attempts to retrieve the material in question. Memories for information that has been used frequently over a period of time tend to resist this process. This effect declines with time, so constant self-testing of learned material is far better than learning everything sequentially and never checking that you actually remember it. Our memory did not evolve to be crammed with facts about psychology, so you must use it to its best advantage by careful memory-efficient strategies.

→ Memory can be maximized simply by optimizing the physical, emotional and environmental conditions during the encoding stage. Many students like to revise with the radio on or surrounded by an admiring family. Unfortunately, these conditions will not be recreated in the exam, so it is worth setting aside time every day when you can work through your material in silence. Changing the context between learning and retrieval can have devastating effects on the recall of material. Odd as it may seem, getting anxious during revision can only ever be detrimental to future performance as you will recreate that anxiety in the exam. A little bit of anxiety is good for you (it helps you to focus) but too much is counterproductive.

→ The effectiveness of memory is determined by your position in the 24-hour cycle. Working at 2.00 in the morning may well fit in with your hectic social life, but it plays havoc with your cognitive skills. As you may remember from the pages on bodily rhythms, alertness is subject to an ultradian cycle. Working at a time when really you should be sleeping is almost certainly going to be ineffective, unless you shift your body clock. This is not advisable, as the examination boards have set their watches by your original one, not your adjusted one!

Action point

Reward yourself for a good session of revision: a cup of coffee for every 40-minute session and one hour of television after three sessions. Be understanding with yourself!

Watch out!

It is difficult to remember large amounts of information. Use any memory aids that you find useful.

Watch out!

Revising late at night isn't a very efficient use of your time. It is harder to get to grips with the material, and it leaves you drained (and less effective) the next day.

Essay planning and writing

Writing effective essays need not be a daunting prospect if you follow a few simple rules. Essays need to be constructed carefully (both in terms of time and content) and you must always stay focused on the question set.

Time management in essay writing

Managing the time

All examination questions have a specific number of marks attached, and all have an optimum time in which they should be completed. If you know your psychology then all well and good, but can you fit it neatly into the time categories imposed by the question? An example:

Outline and evaluate two theories of aggression (24 marks)

This question makes a number of quite separate demands and as such makes for quite easy division of the 30 or so minutes for its completion. In the AQA (A) exams (other boards have similar skill divisions), AO1 (indicated here by the injunction *outline*) and AO2 (indicated by the injunction *evaluate*) are both worth 12 marks (more in Unit 5), so immediately we have a division into two parts. Notice that this question also has a 'plurality' requirement (i.e. *two* theories) so the content can be divided once again. 24 divided by 4 equals 6; 30 divided by four equals $7^{1}/_{2}$. That's an equation of 6 marks = $7^{1}/_{2}$ minutes.

Managing the length

How much do you write in 30 minutes? Most people find they can write about 500–600 words. If we divide that by 4, we get 125–150 words. If we fit this to our division of the question requirements, we get (for example) 140 words for the AO1 content for the first theory, 140 words for the AO1 content of the second theory and so on. That translates into about 140 words every $7^{1}/_{2}$ minutes. The only thing we have left to do is decide what we would put into each of those 140 word 'chunks'.

The advantages of careful time management

There are several advantages to constructing your answers in this way.

→ The marking criteria that accompany exam questions are highly specific about how and where the marks should be awarded. So, in an AQA (A) exam, failure to offer any evaluation, no matter how good the description, would bring a maximum of two-thirds of the marks available. Not getting around to evaluating the second theory would mean a maximum of 20 marks.

→ It stops you making the mistake of giving too much for too little in return. If the first part of the question is only worth one-quarter of the marks, then that defines the amount of content that is appropriate to answer it. Check the injunctions carefully (see pages 188–9). Sometimes questions invite both AO1 and AO2 but not in the same proportions.

Watch out!

You cannot afford to waste time in an exam. Make sure that you plan your 'response' very carefully to fit the *exact* requirements of the question.

Action point

If you have access to past papers, practise 'deconstructing' exam questions in this way.

Test yourself

This paragraph is just under 100 words. Could you reproduce it in 5 minutes?

Watch out!

Don't spend longer than you should on any one question in the exam. Quite often people write longer responses that simply add more without improving the overall *quality* of the answer – spend the same time on each question.

Writing effective essays

Knowledge and understanding

→ A key piece of advice when planning an essay is to think in the same way as the person who will be marking it. Get hold of the marking criteria for your particular specification. Find out what distinguishes an answer in one mark band from one in another. You will generally find that higher mark band answers are characterized by material being well-detailed, and demonstrating depth *and* breadth of content (rather than *just* depth or *just* breadth).

→ Don't be tempted to include as many different theories, studies, names and dates as possible. The limited time you have available means that you will have to be selective, and use material that is representative of a given area, and which you feel you can do full justice. Studies should be carefully selected to *represent* a particular topic area. Trying to cram too many studies (or points) will produce only a superficial coverage of any one.

→ Sometimes you will be invited to *outline* something. This means to present a summary description, or précis of the topic area. This is a very difficult thing to do if you haven't practised doing these before the exam. As part of your revision programme (see previous pages) you should try to do as many outlines of important studies and topic areas as you can.

→ Although names and dates are not vital when answering questions, they do help to reference material and to show that it is informed psychology. Representing knowledge as personal opinion or subjective assertion does not carry the same weight. Avoid sweeping statements such as 'Everybody knows that . . .' or 'All psychologists agree that . . .'.

Analysis and evaluation

→ If you have managed to inspect the marking criteria, you will see that higher marks are available for critical material that is both *elaborated*, and used *effectively*. For example, '*This study lacked ecological validity*' is not a particularly effective critical point. With elaboration, it becomes much more effective thus: '*This study lacks ecological validity because . . . attempts to replicate the findings in other situations have been largely unsuccessful . . . which means that the results of this study cannot be generalized beyond this situation.*'

→ Not all evaluation has to be negative. To criticize something can also be positive. An invitation to *evaluate* is not an invitation to 'slag off'. Occasionally you will be asked for *both* the strengths and weaknesses (check your injunctions to find out when) of some specified material, so it is a valuable skill to be able to do just that.

Action point

Find out as much as you can about the marking criteria for your specification. Knowing *how* the marks are allocated helps you to tailor your responses accordingly.

Action point

Practise your précis skills as much as possible. Discovering you can't précis when in the middle of an exam may be a disturbing experience!

Watch out!

Make your evaluation *effective* by showing *why* a critical point is so important.

Exam words

"It's not just the amount of psychology you know, it's knowing what to do with it."

P. Humphreys (1999)

Although most of the terms that follow are those explicitly used in the AQA (A) exams, they have more or less the same meaning in all exams. It is important that you understand the precise meaning of these terms, otherwise you may not respond appropriately to a question.

AO1, A02 and AO3

AO1 involves knowledge and understanding. You might think of AO1 as a narrative (i.e. giving information and showing understanding). AO2 involves analysis and evaluation. You might think of this as a commentary (i.e. being able to offer some comments about the narrative, such as evaluating the points made). AO3 tests your ability to design, conduct and report psychological investigations (usually in coursework, but also in some methods questions on the written papers). Exam questions might ask you to offer a slightly different form of AO1 and AO2, depending on the requirements of the question. These are usually 'flagged' by the terms used in the question itself.

→ **AO1** terms require you to demonstrate your knowledge and understanding of psychological *theories*, *terminology*, *concepts*, *studies* and *methods*.

→ **AO2** terms require you to analyse and evaluate psychological *theories*, *concepts*, *studies* and *methods*.

AO1 terms

Consider	show knowledge and understanding of the topic area
Define	explain what is meant by a particular term
Describe	show knowledge of the topic area
Examine	present a detailed descriptive consideration of the topic area
Explain	show understanding of a topic in a coherent and intelligible way
Give	used as an alternative to 'state', e.g. 'give two reasons why ...'
Name	implies that a specific point is required, usually a single word or phrase
Outline	offer a brief description of the topic area
Suggest	implies that there is no unique answer, but you should be able to use your knowledge of the subject area to offer a plausible answer

AO2 terms

Analyse/critically analyse	demonstrate understanding through a consideration of the different components of the topic area
Assess/critically assess	present a considered appraisal of the topic area through a judgement of the strengths and limitations of the information presented

Criticize   evaluate in terms of the strengths and weaknesses of the
                   topic area

Evaluate/critically evaluate   make an informed judgement of the value
                   of a topic area

AO1 + AO2 terms

Compare and contrast   consider both the similarities and differences
                   between the topic areas

Critically consider   show knowledge and understanding of a topic area,
                   plus the strengths and limitations of the material used

Distinguish between   consider the differences between two topic areas

Discuss   describe and evaluate a topic area

Other terms used in psychology examinations

Applications   actual or possible ways of using psychological knowledge
                   in an applied or practical setting

Concept(s)   an idea or group of ideas that are often the basic units of
                   a psychological theory

Evidence   material drawn either from investigations or from
                   theories in order to support or contradict an argument
                   or theory

Findings   the outcome of a research investigation

Insights   perceptions from either investigations or theories that
                   help us to understand or appraise a topic area

Methods   the different ways in which research investigations can be
                   carried out

Model   used synonymously with 'theory' although it may be less
                   elaborate or complex

Research   the process of gaining knowledge and understanding
                   either through theory construction and examination or
                   through empirical data collection

Studies   empirical investigations

Theory   a set of interrelated ideas or principles that can be used
                   to explain observed phenomena

Quality of written communication

As well as being assessed on your AO1, AO2 and AO3 skills, you will
also be assessed on your ability to:

→ select and use a form and style of writing appropriate to the subject
  matter

→ organize relevant information clearly and coherently, using specialist
  vocabulary where appropriate

→ ensure text is legible, and spelling, grammar and punctuation are
  accurate, so that meaning is clear.

Watch out!

Don't assume that the use of these terms
indicates an exact division of AO1 and
AO2 marks. Check the mark divisions in
each question carefully.

Action point

Get hold of some previous papers and
look through the questions. Practise
'unpacking' the questions to see exactly
what is required in each one.

Examiner's secrets

Developing your skills in this area will
pay off handsomely in the final exam.

Index